NINE
COMMENTARIES
ON THE COMMUNIST PARTY

THE EPOCH TIMES

TABLE OF CONTENTS

v

Commentary Three: On the Tyranny of the Chinese Communist Party

Commentary Six: On How the Chinese Communist Party Destroyed
                 Traditional Culture

Commentary Seven: On the Chinese Communist Party's History of Killing

Commentary Eight: On How the Chinese Communist Party Is an Evil Cult

Commentary Nine: On the Unscrupulous Nature of the Chinese Communist Party

FOREWORD

This book is the translation of a remarkable series of nine articles that first appeared as editorials in *Daijiyuan* (www.daijiyuan.com), the Chinese language edition of *The Epoch Times*. For reasons that should be clear upon reading the Commentaries, their authorship needs to remain anonymous.

Daijiyuan published the first of these editorials on November 19, 2004. They have since had an extraordinary effect on the Chinese outside China, and, increasingly, inside China. The Nine Commentaries are beginning a conversation among the Chinese about the character of the Chinese Communist Party.

The editors of *The Epoch Times* (www.theepochtimes.com) believe the English-speaking world needs the chance to join in this conversation, and to this end have published this book.

The Editorial Board
The Epoch Times

INTRODUCTION

More than a decade after the fall of the former Soviet Union and Eastern European communist regimes, the international communist movement has been spurned worldwide. The demise of the Chinese Communist Party (CCP) is only a matter of time.

Nevertheless, before its complete collapse, the CCP is trying to tie its fate to the Chinese nation, with its 5,000 years of civilization. This is a disaster for the Chinese people. The Chinese people must now face the impending questions of how to view the CCP, how to evolve China into a society without the CCP, and how to pass on the Chinese heritage. *The Epoch Times* is now publishing a special editorial series, "Nine Commentaries on the Communist Party." Before the lid is laid on the coffin of the CCP, we wish to pass a final judgment on it and on the international communist movement, which has been a scourge to humanity for over a century.

Throughout its 80-plus years, everything the CCP has touched has been marred with lies, wars, famine, tyranny, massacre and terror. Traditional faiths and principles have been violently destroyed. Original ethical concepts and social structures have been disintegrated by force. Empathy, love and harmony among people have been twisted into struggle and hatred. Veneration and appreciation of the heaven and earth have been replaced by an arrogant desire to "fight with heaven and earth." The result has been a total collapse of social, moral and ecological systems, and a profound crisis for the Chinese people, and indeed for humanity. All these calamities have been brought about through the deliberate planning, organization, and control of the CCP.

As a famous Chinese poem goes, "Deeply I sigh in vain for the falling flowers." The end is near for the communist regime, which is barely struggling to survive. The days before its collapse are numbered. *The Epoch Times* believes the time is now ripe, before the CCP's total demise, for a comprehensive look back, in order to fully expose how this largest cult in history has embodied the wickedness of all times and places. We hope that those who are still deceived by the CCP will now see its nature clearly, purge its poison from their spirits, extricate their minds from its evil control, free themselves from the shackles of terror, and abandon for good all illusions about it.

The CCP's rule is the darkest and the most ridiculous page in Chinese history. Among its unending list of crimes, the vilest must be its persecution of Falun Gong. In persecuting "Truthfulness, Compassion, Tolerance" Jiang Zemin has driven the last nail into the CCP's coffin. *The Epoch Times* believes that by understanding the true history of the CCP, we can help prevent such tragedies from ever recurring. At the same time, we hope each one of us would reflect on our innermost thoughts and examine whether our cowardice and compromise have made us accomplices in many tragedies that could have been avoided.

COMMENTARY ONE

ON WHAT THE COMMUNIST PARTY IS

COMMENTARY ONE

ON WHAT THE COMMUNIST PARTY IS

FOREWORD

For over five thousand years, the Chinese people created a splendid civilization on the land nurtured by the Yellow River and the Yangtze River. During this long period of time, dynasties came and went, and the Chinese culture waxed and waned. Grand and moving stories have played out on the historical stage of China.

The year 1840, the year commonly considered by historians as the beginning of China's contemporary era, marked the start of China's journey from tradition to modernization. Chinese civilization experienced four major episodes of challenge and response. The first three episodes include the invasion of Beijing by the Anglo-French Allied Forces in the early 1860s, the Sino-Japanese War in 1894 (also called "Jiawu War"), and the Russo-Japanese War in China's northeast in 1906. To these three episodes of challenge, China responded with the Westernization Movement, which was marked by the importation of modern goods and weapons, institutional reforms through the Hundred Days' Reform in 1898[1] and the attempt at the end of the late Qing Dynasty (1644-1911) to establish constitutional rule, and later, the Xinhai Revolution (or Hsinhai Revolution)[2] in 1911.

At the end of the First World War, China, though it emerged victorious, was not listed among the stronger powers at that time. Many Chinese believed that the first three episodes of response had failed. The May Fourth Movement[3] would lead to the fourth attempt at responding to previous challenges and culminate in the

3

complete westernization of Chinese culture through the communist movement and its extreme revolution.

This article concerns the outcome of the last episode, which is the communist movement and the Communist Party. Let's take a close look at the result of what China chose, or perhaps one can say, what was imposed on China, after over 160 years, nearly 100 million unnatural deaths, and the destruction of nearly all Chinese traditional culture and civilization.

I. RELYING ON VIOLENCE AND TERROR TO GAIN AND MAINTAIN POWER

"The Communists disdain to conceal their views and aims. They openly declare that their ends can be attained only by the forcible overthrow of all existing social conditions."[4] This quote is taken from the concluding paragraph of the *Communist Manifesto*, the Communist Party's principal document. Violence is the one main means by which the Communist Party gained power. This character trait has been passed on to all subsequent forms of the Party that have arisen since its birth.

In fact, the world's first Communist Party was established many years after Karl Marx's death. The next year after the October Revolution in 1917, the "All Russian Communist Party (Bolshevik)" (later to be known as the "Communist Party of the Soviet Union") was born. This party grew out of the use of violence against "class enemies" and was maintained through violence against party members and ordinary citizens. During Stalin's purges in the 1930s, the Communist Party of the Soviet Union slaughtered over 20 million so-called spies and traitors, and those thought to have different opinions.

The Chinese Communist Party (CCP) first started as a branch of the Communist Party of the Soviet Union in the Third Communist International. Therefore, it naturally inherited the willingness to kill. During China's first Communist-Kuomintang civil war between 1927 and 1936, the population in Jiangxi province dropped from over 20 million to about 10 million. The damage wrought by the CCP's use of violence can be seen from these figures alone.

Using violence may be unavoidable when attempting to gain political power, but there has never been a regime as eager to kill as the CCP, especially during otherwise peaceful periods. Since 1949, the number of deaths caused by CCP's violence has surpassed the total deaths during the wars waged between 1921 and 1949.

An excellent example of the Communist Party's use of violence is its support of the Cambodian Khmer Rouge. Under the Khmer Rouge a quarter of Cambodia's population, including a majority of Chinese immigrants and descents, were murdered. China still blocks the international community from putting the Khmer Rouge on trial, so as to cover up the CCP's notorious role in the genocide.

The CCP has close connections with the world's most brutal revolutionary armed forces and despotic regimes. In addition to the Khmer Rouge, these include the communist parties in Indonesia, the Philippines, Malaysia, Vietnam, Burma, Laos, and Nepal—all of which were established under the support of the CCP. Many leaders in these communist parties are Chinese; some of them are still hiding in China to this day.

Other Maoist-based Communist Parties include South America's Shining Path and the Japanese Red Army, whose atrocities have been condemned by the world community.

One of the theories the communists employ is social Darwinism. The Communist Party applies Darwin's inter-species competition to human relationships and human history, maintaining that class struggle is the only driving force for societal development. Struggle, therefore, became the primary "belief" of the Communist party, a tool in gaining and maintaining political control. Mao's famous words plainly betray this logic of the survival of the fittest: "With 800 million people, how can it work without struggle?"

Another one of Mao's claims that is similarly famous is that the Cultural Revolution should be conducted "every seven or eight years."[5] Repetitive use of force is an important means for the CCP to maintain its ruling in China. The goal of using force is to create terror. Every struggle and movement served as an exercise in terror, so that the Chinese people trembled in their hearts, submitted to the terror and gradually became enslaved under the CCP's control.

Today, terrorism has become the main enemy of the civilized and free world. The CCP's exercise of violent terrorism, thanks to the apparatus of the state, has been larger in scale, much longer lasting, and its results more devastating. Today, in the twenty-first century, we should not forget this inherited character of the Communist Party, since it will definitely play a crucial role to the destiny of the CCP some time in the future.

II. USING LIES TO JUSTIFY VIOLENCE

The level of civilization can be measured by the degree to which violence is used in a regime. By resorting to the use of violence, the Communist regimes clearly represent a huge step backward in human civilization. Unfortunately, the Communist Party has been seen as progressive by those who believe that violence is an essential and inevitable means to societal advancement.

This acceptance of violence has to be viewed as an unrivaled and skillful employment of deception and lies by the Communist Party, which is another inherited trait of the CCP.

"Since a young age, we have thought of the US as a lovable country. We believe this is partly due to the fact that the US has never occupied China, nor has it launched any attacks on China. More fundamentally, the Chinese people hold good impressions of the US based on the democratic and open-minded character of its people."

This excerpt came from an editorial published on July 4, 1947 in the CCP's official newspaper *Xinhua Daily*. A mere three years later, the CCP sent soldiers to fight American troops in North Korea, and painted the Americans as the most evil imperialists in the world. Every Chinese from Mainland China would be astonished to read this editorial written over 50 years ago. The CCP has banned all publications quoting similar early passages and published rewritten versions.

Since coming to power, the CCP has employed similar artifices in every single movement, including its elimination of counter-revolutionaries (1950-1953), the "partnership" of public and private enterprises (1954-1957), the Anti-Rightist Movement (1957), the Cultural Revolution (1966-1976), the Tiananmen Square Massacre (1989), and most recently, the persecution of Falun Gong since 1999. The most infamous instance was the persecution of intellectuals in 1957. The CCP called on the intellectuals to offer their opinions, but then persecuted them as "rightists," using their own speeches as evidence of their "crimes." When some criticized the persecution as a conspiracy, or "plot in the dark," Mao claimed publicly, "That is not a plot in the dark, but a stratagem in the open."

Deception and lies have played a very important role in the CCP's gaining and maintaining control. China enjoys the longest and most complete history in the world, and Chinese intellectuals have had the greatest faith in history since ancient times. The Chinese people have used history to assess current reality and even to achieve personal spiritual improvement. To make history serve the current regime, the CCP has made a practice of altering and concealing historical truth. The CCP in its propaganda and publications has rewritten history for periods from as early as the Spring and Autumn period (770-476 BC) and the Warring States period (475-221 BC) to as recently as the Cultural Revolution. Such historical alterations have continued for more than 50 years since 1949, and all efforts to restore historical truth have been ruthlessly blocked and eliminated by the CCP.

When violence becomes too weak to sustain control, the CCP resorts to deception and lies, which serve to justify and mask the rule by violence.

One must admit that deception and lies were not invented by the Communist Party, but are age-old scoundrel acts that the Communist Party has utilized without shame. The CCP promised land to the peasants, factories to the workers, freedom and democracy to the intellectuals, and peace to all. None of these promises has ever been realized. One generation of Chinese died deceived and another generation continues to be cheated. This is the biggest sorrow of the Chinese people, the most unfortunate aspect of the Chinese nation.

III. EVER-CHANGING PRINCIPLES

In one of the televised 2004 US Presidential Debates, one presidential candidate said that, one could change tactics when one needed to, but one should never change his "beliefs" or "core values," otherwise "he is just not credible."[6] This statement really makes clear a general principle.

The Communist Party is a typical example. For instance, since its establishment 80 years ago, the CCP has held sixteen national representative conventions and modified the Party Constitution 16 times. Over the five decades since it came to power, the CCP has made five major modifications to the Chinese Constitution.

The ideal of the Communist Party is social equality leading to a communist society. Today, however, communist-controlled China has become a nation with the most serious economic inequalities in the world. Many CCP members have become extremely rich, while the country has 800 million living in poverty.

The guiding theories of the CCP started with Marxism-Leninism, to which was added Maoism, and then Deng's thoughts and recently Jiang's "Three Represents." Marxism-Leninism and Maoism are not at all compatible with Deng's theories and Jiang's ideology—they are actually opposite to them. This hodgepodge of communist theories employed by the CCP is indeed a rarity in human history.

The Communist Party's evolving principles have largely contradicted one another. From the idea of a global integration transcending the nation-state to today's extreme nationalism, from eliminating all private ownership and all exploitative classes to today's notion of promoting capitalists to join the party, yesterday's principles have become reversed in today's politics, with further change expected tomorrow. No matter how often the CCP changes its principles, the goal remains clear: gaining and maintaining power, and sustaining absolute control of the society.

In the history of the CCP, there have been more than a dozen movements that are "life and death" struggles. In reality, all of these struggles have coincided with the transfer of power following changes of basic Party principles.

Every change in principles has come from an inevitable crisis faced by the CCP, threatening its legitimacy and survival. Whether it be collaborating with the Kuomintang Party, a pro-US foreign policy, economic reform and market expansion, or promoting nationalism—each of these decisions occurred at a moment of crisis, and all had to do with gaining or solidifying power. Every cycle of a group suffering persecution followed by reversal of that persecution has been connected with changes in the basic principles of the CCP.

A western proverb states that truths are sustainable and lies mutable. There is wisdom in this saying.

IV. HOW THE PARTY NATURE REPLACES AND ELIMINATES HUMAN NATURE

The CCP is a Leninist authoritarian regime. Since the inception of the CCP, three basic lines have been established: the intellectual line, the political line, and the organization line. The intellectual line refers to the Communist Party's philosophical foundation. The political line refers to setting up goals. The organization line refers to how the goals are achieved within the format of strict organization.

The first and foremost requirement of all CCP members and those ruled by the CCP is to obey commands unconditionally. This is what the organization line is all about.

In China, most people know about the double personalities of CCP members. In private settings, CCP members are ordinary human beings with feelings of happiness, anger, sorrow and joy. They possess ordinary human beings' merits and shortcomings. They may be parents, husbands, wives, or friends. But placed above human nature and feelings is the Party nature, which, according to the requirements of the Communist Party, transcends humanity. Thus, humanity becomes relative and changeable, while Party nature becomes absolute, beyond any doubt or challenge.

During the Cultural Revolution, it was all too common that fathers and sons tortured each other, husbands and wives struggled with each other, mothers and daughters reported on each other, and students and teachers treated each other as enemies. Party nature motivated the conflicts and hatred in these cases. During the early period of the CCP rule, many high-ranking CCP officials were helpless as their family members were labeled as class enemies. This, again, was driven by Party nature.

The power of the Party nature over the individual results from the CCP's prolonged course of indoctrination. This training starts in preschools and kindergartens, where party-sanctioned answers to questions are rewarded, answers that do not comply with common sense or a child's human nature. Students receive political education when they attend primary school, middle school and all the way to college, and they learn to follow party-sanctioned standard answers, otherwise, they are not allowed to pass the exam and graduate.

A Party member must remain consistent with the Party line when speaking publicly, no matter how he feels privately. The organizational structure of the CCP is a gigantic pyramid, with the central power on top controlling the entire hierarchy. This unique structure is one of the most important features of the CCP regime, one that helps produce absolute conformity.

Today, the CCP has completely degenerated into a political entity struggling to maintain self-interest. It no longer pursues any of the lofty goals of communism. However, the organizational structure of communism remains, and its demand for unconditional conformity has not changed. This party, situating itself above humanity and human nature, removes any organizations or persons deemed detrimental or potentially detrimental to its own power, be it ordinary citizens or high-ranking CCP officials.

V. AN EVIL SPECTER OPPOSES NATURE AND HUMAN NATURE

Everything under heaven experiences a life cycle of birth, maturity, decay, and death.

Unlike the communist regime, non-communist societies, even those suffering under rigid totalitarian rule and a dictatorship, often allow some degree of self-organization and self-determination. Ancient Chinese society was in fact ruled according to a binary structure. In rural regions clans were the center of an independent social organization, while urban areas were organized around the guild. The top-down government did not extend below the county level.

The Nazi regime, perhaps the cruelest regime under a dictatorship other than the Communist Party, still allowed rights to private property. The communist regimes eradicated any forms of social organization or elements independent of the Party, replacing them with highly centralized power structures from the top-down.

If the bottom-up social structures allow for the self-determination of individuals or groups to occur naturally, then the communist regime is anti-nature in its essence.

The Communist Party does not hold universal standards for human nature. The concepts of good and evil, as well as all laws and rules, are arbitrarily manipulated. Communists do not allow murder, except for those categorized as enemies by the Communist Party. Filial piety is welcomed, except for those parents deemed class enemies. Benevolence, righteousness, propriety, wisdom, and faithfulness are all good, but not applicable when the Party is not willing or doesn't want to consider these traditional virtues. The Communist Party completely overthrows the universal standards for human nature, and builds itself on principles that oppose human nature.

Non-communist societies generally consider humanity's dual nature of good and evil and they rely on fixed social contracts to maintain a balance in society. In communist societies, however, the very concept of human nature is denied, and neither good nor evil is acknowledged. Eliminating the concepts of good and evil, according to Marx, serves to completely overthrow the superstructure[7] of the old society.

The Communist Party does not believe in God, nor does it even respect physical nature. "Battle with heaven, fight with the earth, struggle with humans—therein lies endless joy." This was the motto of the CCP during the Cultural Revolution. Great suffering was inflicted on the Chinese people and the land.

The Chinese traditionally believe in the unity of heaven and human beings. Lao Zi said in *Dao de Jing* (*Tao-Te Ching*), "Man follows the earth, the earth follows heaven, heaven follows the Dao, and the Dao follows what is natural."[8] Human beings and nature exist within a harmonious relationship in the continuous cosmos.

The communist party is a kind of being. However, it opposes nature, heaven, earth and mankind. It is an evil specter against the universe.

VI. SOME FEATURES OF EVIL POSSESSION

The Communist Party's organs themselves never participate in productive or creative activities. Once they grasp power, they attach themselves to the people, controlling and manipulating them. They extend their power down to the most basic unit of society for fear of losing control. They monopolize the resources of production and extract wealth from the society.

In China, the CCP extends everywhere and controls everything, but nobody has ever seen the CCP's accounting records, only accounting records for the state, local governments, and enterprises. From the central government to the village committees in rural areas, the municipal officials are always ranked lower than the communist cadres, so the municipal governments have to follow instructions from the communist party committees of the same level. The expenditures of the Party are supplied by the municipal units and accounted for in the municipal system.

The organization of the CCP, like a giant evil possessing spirit, attaches to every single unit and cell of the Chinese society as tightly as a shadow following an object. It penetrates deeply into every capillary and cell of the society with its finest blood-sucking vessels and thereby controls and manipulates society.

This peculiar structure of evil possession has existed in human history in the past, either partially or temporarily. Never has it operated for so long and controlled a society so completely as under the rule of the Communist Party.

For this reason, Chinese farmers live in such poverty and drudgery. They not only have to support the traditional municipal officials, but also as many or even more communist cadres.

For this reason, Chinese workers lost their employment in vast numbers. The omnipresent blood-sucking vessels of the possessing CCP have been extracting funds from their factories for many years.

For this reason, Chinese intellectuals find it so difficult to gain intellectual freedom. In addition to their administrators, there are CCP shadows lingering everywhere, doing nothing but monitoring people.

A possessing spirit has to control absolutely the mind of the possessed in order to drain energy for its survival.

According to modern political science, power comes from three main sources: force, wealth, and knowledge. The Communist Party has never hesitated to use monopoly control and force to rob people of their property. More importantly, it has deprived people of their freedoms of speech and of the press. It has raped people's spirit and will in order to maintain its absolute control of power. From this aspect, the CCP's evil possession controls society so tightly that it can hardly be compared to any other regime in the world.

15

VII. EXAMINE ONESELF AND GET RID OF THE CCP'S POSSESSION

In the *Communist Manifesto*, the first programmatic document of the communist party, Marx proclaimed that "In 1848, a specter is haunting Europe—the specter of Communism."[9] Over a century later, communism is more than a haunting specter. It has possessed a concrete, material body. It spread around the world like an epidemic, killed tens of millions and took away property and a free mind and spirit from hundreds of millions.

The basic tenet of the Communist Party is to take away all private property so as to eliminate the "exploitative class." Private property is the basis of all social rights, and often carries national culture. People who are robbed of private property also lose a free mind and spirit. They may further lose the freedom to acquire social and political rights.

Facing a crisis of survival, the CCP was forced to reform China's economy in the 1980s. Some of the rights to private property were restored to the people. This created a hole in the massive CCP machine of precise control. This hole has become enlarged as the CCP's members strive to accumulate their private fortunes.

The CCP, an evil possessing specter supported by force, deception and the frequent change of its appearance and images, has now shown signs of decay, nervous at every slight disturbance. It attempts to survive by accumulating more wealth and tightening control, but these actions only serve to intensify the crisis.

Today's China appears prosperous, but social conflicts have been built up to a level never seen before. Using political intrigues from the past, the CCP may attempt some sort of retreat, redressing the Tiananmen Square Massacre or Falun Gong, or making another group its chosen enemy, thereby continuing to exercise the power of terror.

Facing challenges over the past one hundred years, the Chinese nation has responded by importing weapons, reforming its systems, and enacting extreme and violent revolutions. Countless lives have been lost, and most of the Chinese traditional culture has been abandoned. It appears that the responses have failed. When agitation and anxiety occupied the Chinese mind, the CCP took the opportunity to enter the scene, and eventually controlled this last surviving ancient civilization in the world.

In future challenges, the Chinese people will inevitably have to choose again. No matter how the choice is made, every Chinese must understand that any lingering hope in the CCP will only worsen the damage done to the Chinese nation and inject new energy into this evil possessing CCP.

We must abandon all illusions, thoroughly examine ourselves without being influenced by hatred, greed or desires. Only then can we rid ourselves of the nightmarish control by the possessing spirit of the CCP over the last 50 years. In the name of a free nation, we can reestablish the Chinese civilization based on respect for human nature and compassion for all.

COMMENTARY TWO

ON THE BEGINNINGS OF THE
CHINESE COMMUNIST PARTY

COMMENTARY TWO

ON THE BEGINNINGS OF
THE CHINESE COMMUNIST PARTY

FOREWORD

According to the book *Explaining Simple and Analyzing Compound Characters*[1], the traditional Chinese character *Dang*, meaning "party" or "gang," consists of two radicals that correspond to "promote or advocate" and "dark or black" respectively. Putting the two radicals together, the character means "promoting darkness." "Party" or "party member" (which can also be interpreted as "gang" or "gang member") carries a derogatory meaning. Confucius said, "A nobleman is proud but not aggressive, sociable but not partisan." The footnotes of *Analects* (*Lunyu*) explain, "People who help one another conceal their wrongdoings are said to be forming a gang (party)."[2] In Chinese history, political cliques were often called *Peng Dang* (cabal). It is a synonym for "gang of scoundrels" in traditional Chinese culture and the meaning implies ganging up for selfish purposes.

Why did the Communist Party emerge, grow and eventually seize power in contemporary China? The CCP has constantly instilled into the Chinese people's minds that history chose the CCP, that the people chose the CCP, and that "without the CCP there would be no new China."

Did the Chinese people choose the Communist Party? Or, did the Communist Party "gang up" and force Chinese people to accept it? We must find answers from history.

21

From the late Qing Dynasty (1644-1911) to the early years of the Republic period (1911-1949), China experienced tremendous external shocks and extensive attempts at internal reform. Chinese society was in painful turmoil. Many intellectuals and people with lofty ideals wanted to save the country and its people. However, in the midst of national crisis and chaos, their sense of anxiety grew, leading first to disappointment and then complete despair. Like people who turn to any available doctor in times of illness, they looked outside China for a solution. When the British and French styles failed, they switched to the Russian method. They did not hesitate to prescribe the most extreme remedy for the illness, in the hope that China would quickly become strong.

The May Fourth movement in 1919 was a thorough reflection of this despair. Some people advocated anarchism; others proposed to overthrow the doctrines of Confucius, and still others suggested bringing in foreign culture. In short, they rejected Chinese traditional culture and opposed the Confucian doctrine of the middle way. Eager to take a shortcut, they advocated the destruction of everything traditional. On the one hand, the radical members among them did not have a way to serve the country, and on the other hand, they believed firmly in their own ideals and will. They felt the world was hopeless, believing that only they had found the right approach to China's future development. They were passionate for revolution and violence.

Different experiences led to different theories, principles and paths among various groups. Eventually a group of people met Communist Party representatives from the Soviet Union. The idea of "using violent revolution to seize political power," lifted from the theory of Marxism-Leninism, appealed to their anxious minds and conformed to their desire to save the country and its people. They immediately formed an alliance with each other and introduced communism, a completely foreign concept, into China. Altogether thirteen representatives attended the first CCP Congress. Later, some of them died, some ran away, and some, betraying the CCP or becoming opportunistic, worked for the occupying Japanese and became traitors to China, or quit the CCP and joined the Kuomintang (the Nationalist Party, hereafter referred to as KMT). By 1949 when the CCP came to power in China, only Mao Zedong (also spelled Mao Tse-Tung) and Dong Biwu still remained of the original thirteen Party members. It is unclear whether the founders of the CCP were aware at the time that the "deity" they had introduced from the Soviet Union was in reality an evil specter, and the remedy they sought for strengthening the nation was actually a deadly poison.

The All-Russian Communist Party (Bolshevik, later known as the Communist Party of the Soviet Union), having just won its revolution, was obsessed with ambition for China. In 1920, the Soviet Union established the Far Eastern Bureau, a branch of the Third Communist International, or the Comintern. It was responsible for the establishment of a Communist Party in China and other countries. Sumiltsky was the head of the bureau, and Grigori Voitinsky was a deputy manager. They began to prepare for the establishment of the CCP with Chen Duxiao and others. The proposal they submitted to the Far Eastern Bureau in June 1921 to establish a China branch of the Comintern indicated that the CCP was a branch led by the Comintern. On July 23, 1921, under the help of Nikolsky and Maring from the Far East Bureau, the CCP was officially formed.

The Communist movement was then introduced to China as an experiment, and the CCP has set itself above all, conquering all in its path, thereby bringing endless catastrophe to China.

I. THE CCP GREW BY STEADILY ACCUMULATING WICKEDNESS

It is not an easy task to introduce a foreign and evil specter such as the Communist Party, one that is totally incompatible with the Chinese tradition, into China, a country with a history of 5,000 years of civilization. The CCP deceived the populace and the patriotic intellectuals who wanted to serve the country with the promise of the "communist utopia." It further distorted the theory of communism, which had already been seriously distorted by Lenin, to provide a theoretical basis for destroying all traditional morals and principles. In addition, the CCP's distorted theory of communism was used to destroy all that was disadvantageous to the CCP's rule and to eliminate all social classes and people that might pose threats to its control. The CCP adopted the Industrial Revolution's destruction of belief as well as the more complete atheism of communism. The CCP inherited communism's denial of private ownership, and imported Lenin's theory of violent revolution. At the same time, the CCP inherited and further strengthened the worst parts of the Chinese monarchy.

The history of the CCP shows a process of its gradual accumulation of every kind of wickedness, both domestic and foreign. The CCP has perfected its nine inherited traits, giving them "Chinese characteristics": evil, deceit, incitement, unleashing the scum of society, espionage, robbery, fighting, elimination, and control. Responding to continuous crisis, the CCP has consolidated and strengthened the means and extent to which these malignant characteristics have been playing out.

FIRST INHERITED TRAIT: EVIL—PUTTING ON THE EVIL FORM OF MARXISM-LENINISM

Marxism initially attracted the Chinese communists with its declaration to "use violent revolution to destroy the old state apparatus and to establish a dictatorship of the proletariat." This is precisely the root of evil in Marxism and Leninism.

Marxist materialism is predicated on the narrow economic concepts of forces of production, production relations, and surplus value. During the early, underdeveloped stages of capitalism, Marx made a shortsighted prediction that capitalism would die and the proletariat would win, which has been proven wrong by history and reality. Marxist-Leninist violent revolution and dictatorship of the proletariat promote power-politics and proletarian domination. The *Communist Manifesto* related the Communist Party's historical and philosophical basis to class conflict and struggle. The proletariat broke free from traditional morals and social relations for the sake of seizing power. Upon their first appearance, the doctrines of communism were set in opposition to all tradition.

Human nature universally repels violence. Violence makes people ruthless and tyrannical. Thus, in all places and all times, humanity has fundamentally rejected the premises of the Communist Party's theory of violence, a theory that has no antecedent in any earlier systems of thought, philosophy, or tradition. The communist system of terror fell upon the earth as if from nowhere.

The CCP's evil ideology is built on the premise that humans can conquer nature and transform the world. The Communist Party attracted many people with its ideals of "emancipating all mankind" and "world unity."[3] The CCP deceived many people, especially those who were concerned about the human condition and were eager to make their own mark in society. The CCP forgot that there is a heaven above. Inspired by the beautiful yet misguided notion of "building heaven on earth," they despised traditions and looked down upon the lives of others, which in turn degraded themselves. They did all of this in an attempt to provide the CCP with praiseworthy service and gain honor.

The Communist Party presented the fantasy of a "communist paradise" as the truth, and aroused people's enthusiasm to fight for it: "For reason thunders new creation, 'Tis a better world in birth."[4] Employing such an absolutely absurd idea, the CCP severed the connections between humanity and heaven, and cut the lifeline that connected the Chinese people to their ancestors and national traditions. By summoning people to give their lives for communism, the CCP strengthened its ability to do harm.

SECOND INHERITED TRAIT: DECEIT—EVIL MUST CHEAT TO PRETEND TO BE RIGHTEOUS

Evil must lie. To take advantage of the working class, the CCP conferred upon it the titles of "the most advanced class," "selfless class," "leading class," and "pioneers of the proletarian revolution." When the Communist Party needed the peasants, it promised "land to the tiller." Mao applauded the peasants, saying, "Without the poor peasants there would be no revolution; to deny their role is to deny the revolution."[5] When the Communist Party needed help from the capitalist class, it called them "fellow travelers in the proletarian revolution" and promised them "democratic republicanism." When the Communist Party was almost exterminated by the KMT, it appealed loudly, "Chinese do not fight Chinese" and promised to submit itself to the leadership of the KMT. As soon as the Anti-Japanese War (1937-1945) was over, the CCP turned full force against the KMT and overthrew its government. Similarly, the CCP eliminated the capitalist class shortly after taking control of China and in the end transformed the peasants and workers into a truly penniless proletariat.

The notion of a united front is a typical example of the lies the CCP tells. In order to win the civil war against the KMT, the CCP departed from its usual tactic of killing every family member of the landlords and rich peasants and adopted a "temporary policy of unification" with its class enemies such as the landlords and rich peasants. On July 20, 1947, Mao Zedong announced that, "Except for a few reactionary elements, we should adopt a more relaxed attitude towards the landlord class...in order to reduce hostile elements." After the CCP gained power, however, the landlords and rich peasants did not escape genocide.

Saying one thing and doing another is normal for the Communist Party. When the CCP needed to use the democratic parties, it urged all parties to "strive for long-term coexistence, exercise mutual supervision, be sincere with each other, and share honor and disgrace." Anybody who disagreed with or refused to conform to the Party's concepts, words, deeds, or organization was eliminated. Marx, Lenin and the CCP leaders have all said that the Communist Party's political power would not be shared with any other individuals or groups. From the very beginning, communism clearly carried within it the gene of dictatorship. The CCP is despotic and exclusive. It has never coexisted with any other political parties or groups in a sincere manner, neither when it attempted to seize power nor after it gained control. Even during the so-called "relaxed" period, the CCP's coexistence with others was at most a choreographed performance.

History tells us never to believe any promises made by the CCP, nor to trust that any of the CCP's commitments will be fulfilled. To believe the words of the Communist Party in whatever issue, that would be the issue that would cost one's life.

THIRD INHERITED TRAIT: INCITEMENT—SKILLFULLY STIRRING UP HATRED AND INCITING STRUGGLE AMONG THE MASSES

Deceit serves to incite hatred. Struggle relies on hatred. Where hatred does not exist, it can be created.

The deeply-rooted patriarchal clan system in the Chinese countryside served as a fundamental barrier to the Communist Party's establishment of political power. The rural society was initially harmonious, and the relationship between the landowners and tenants was not entirely confrontational. The landowners offered the peasants a means to live, and in return the peasants supported the landowners.

This somewhat mutually dependent relationship was twisted by the CCP into extreme class antagonism and class exploitation. Harmony was turned into hostility, hatred, and struggle. The reasonable was made to be unreasonable, order was made to be chaos, and republicanism made to be despotism. The Communist Party encouraged expropriation, murder for money, and the slaughter of landlords, rich peasants, their families and their clans. Many peasants were not willing to take the property of others. Some returned at night the property they took from the landlords during the day, but they were criticized by CCP work teams in rural regions as having "low class consciousness."

To incite class hatred, the CCP reduced the Chinese theater to a propaganda tool. A well-known story of class oppression, the White-Haired Girl[6], was originally about a female immortal and had nothing to do with class conflicts. Under the pens of the military writers, however, it was transformed into a "modern" drama, opera, and ballet used to incite class hatred. When Japan invaded China during World War II, the CCP did not fight with the Japanese troops.

Instead, it attacked the KMT government with accusations that the KMT betrayed the country by not fighting against Japan. Even at the most critical moment of national calamity, it incited people to oppose the KMT government.

Inciting the masses to struggle against each other is a classic trick of the CCP. The CCP created the 95:5 formula of class assignment: 95 percent of the population would be assigned to various classes that could be won over, while the remaining 5 percent would be designated as class enemies. People within the 95 percent were safe, but those within the 5 percent were "struggled" against. Out of fear and to protect themselves, the people strived to be included in the 95 percent. This resulted in many cases in which people brought harm to others, even adding insult to injury. The CCP has, through the use of incitement in many of its political movements, perfected this technique.

FOURTH INHERITED TRAIT: UNLEASHING THE SCUM OF SOCIETY— HOODLUMS AND SOCIAL SCUM FORM THE RANKS OF THE CCP

Unleashing the scum of society leads to evil, and evil must utilize the scum of society. Communist revolutions have often made use of the rebellion of hoodlums and social scum. The "Paris Commune," actually involved homicide, arson, and violence led by social scum. Even Marx looked down upon the "lumpen proletariat."[7] In the *Communist Manifesto*[8], Marx said, "The 'dangerous class,' the social scum, that passively rotting mass thrown off by the lowest layers of the old society, may, here and there, be swept into the movement by a proletarian revolution; its conditions of life, however, prepare it far more for the part of a bribed tool of reactionary intrigue." Peasants, on the other hand, were considered by Marx and Engels to be unqualified to be any social class because of their so-called fragmentation and ignorance.

The CCP developed further the dark side of Marx's theory. Mao Zedong said, "The social scum and hoodlums have always been spurned by the society, but they are actually the bravest, the most thorough and firmest in the revolution in the rural areas."[9] The lumpen proletariat enhanced the violent nature of the CCP and established the early political power of the Communist Party in rural areas. The word "revolution" in Chinese literally means "taking lives," which sounds horrific and disastrous to all good people. However, the Party managed to imbue "revolution" with positive meaning. Similarly, in a debate over the term "lumpen proletariat" during the Cultural Revolution, the CCP felt that "lumpen" did not sound good, and so the CCP simply replaced it with "proletariat."

Another behavior of the scum of society is to play the rascal. When criticized for being dictators, Party officials would reveal their tendency to bully and shamelessly pronounce something along the lines of, "You are right, that is precisely what we are doing. The Chinese experience accumulated through the past decades requires that we exercise this power of democratic dictatorship. We call it the 'people's democratic autocracy.'"

FIFTH INHERITED TRAIT: ESPIONAGE—INFILTRATE, SOW DISSENSION, DISINTEGRATE AND REPLACE

In addition to cheating, inciting violence, and employing the scum of society, the techniques of espionage and sowing dissension were also used. The CCP is skillful in infiltration. Decades ago, the "Top Three" outstanding undercover agents of the CCP, Qian Zhuangfei, Li Kenong and Hu Beifeng, were in fact working for Chen Geng, the manager of the Second Branch of the Spy Section of the Central Committee of the CCP. When Qian Zhuangfei was working as a confidential secretary and trusted subordinate of Xu Enzeng, the Director of the Investigation Office of the KMT Central Committee, he sent secret information of the KMT's first and second strategic plans to encircle the CCP troops in Jiangxi province to Li Kenong through the internal mail of the Organization Department of the KMT Central Committee, who further hand delivered it to Zhou Enlai[10]. In April 1930, a special double-agent organization funded by the Central Investigation Branch of the KMT was set up in the Northeast region of China. On the surface, it belonged to the KMT and was managed by Qian Zhuangfei, but behind the scenes it was controlled by the CCP and led by Chen Geng.

Li Kenong also joined the KMT's army headquarters as a cryptographer. Li was the one who decoded the urgent message pertaining to the arrest and revolt of Gu Shunzhang[11], a CCP Security Bureau Director. Qian Zhuangfei immediately sent the decoded message to Zhou Enlai, thereby keeping the whole lot of spies from being caught in a dragnet.

Yang Dengying was a pro-Communist special representative for the KMT's Central Investigation Office stationed in Shanghai. The CCP ordered him to arrest and execute those party members whom the CCP considered unreliable. A senior CCP officer from Henan Province once offended a party cadre, and his own people pulled some strings to put him in the KMT's jail for several years.

During the Liberation War[12], the CCP managed to plant a secret agent whom Chiang Kai-shek (also called Jiang Jieshi)[13] kept in close confidence. Liu Pei, a Lieutenant General and the Deputy Minister of the Ministry of Defense, was in charge of dispatching the KMT Army. Liu was in fact an undercover agent for the CCP. Before the KMT Army found out about their next assignment, the information about the planned deployment had already reached Yan'an, headquarters of the CCP. The Communist Party would then come up with a plan of defense accordingly. Xiong Xianghui, a secretary and trusted subordinate of Hu Zongnan[14], revealed Hu's plan to invade Yan'an to Zhou Enlai. So when Hu Zongnan and his forces reached Yan'an, it was already deserted. Zhou Enlai once said, "Chairman Mao knew the military orders issued by Chiang Kai-shek before they even made it to Chiang's Army Commander."

SIXTH INHERITED TRAIT: ROBBERY—PLUNDERING BY TRICKS OR VIOLENCE BECOMES A "NEW ORDER"

Everything the CCP has obtained through robbery. When it pulled the Red Army together to establish its rule through military force, they needed money for arms and ammunition, food and clothes. The CCP raised funds by suppressing the local tyrants and robbing banks, behaving just like bandits. In a mission led by Li Xiannian[15], one of the CCP's senior leaders, the Red Army kidnapped the richest families in county seats in the area of western Hubei Province. They did not just kidnap one single person, but one from every rich family in the clan. Those kidnapped were kept alive to be ransomed back to their families for continued monetary support for the army. It was not until either the Red Army was satisfied or the kidnapped families were completely drained of resources that the hostages were sent home, many at death's door. Some had been terrorized or tortured so badly that they died before they could return.

Through "cracking down on the local tyrants and confiscating their lands," the CCP extended the tricks and violence of their plunder to the whole society, replacing tradition with "the new order." The Communist Party has committed all manner of ill deeds, large and small, while it has done nothing good at all. It offers small favors to everyone in order to incite some to denounce others. As a result, compassion and virtue disappear completely, and are replaced with strife and killing. The "communist utopia" is actually a euphemism for violent plunder.

SEVENTH INHERITED TRAIT: FIGHTING—DESTROYS THE NATIONAL SYSTEM, AND TRADITIONAL RANKS AND ORDERS

Deceit, incitement, unleashing social scum, and espionage are all for the purpose of robbing and fighting. Communist philosophy promotes fighting. The communist revolution was absolutely not just some disorganized beating, smashing and robbing. Mao said, "The main targets of peasants' attacks are local tyrants, the evil gentry and lawless landlords, but in passing they also struck out against all kinds of patriarchal ideas and institutions, against the corrupt officials in the cities and against the bad practices and customs in the rural areas."[16] Mao clearly ordered that the entire traditional system and customs of the countryside should be destroyed.

Communist fighting also includes armed forces and armed struggle. "A revolution is not a dinner party, or writing an essay, or painting a picture, or doing embroidery; it cannot be so refined, so leisurely and gentle, so temperate, kind, courteous, restrained and magnanimous. A revolution is an insurrection, an act of violence by which one class overthrows another."[17] Fighting was used by the CCP when it attempted to seize state power by force. A few decades later, the CCP used the same characteristic of fighting to "educate" the next generation during the Cultural Revolution.

EIGHTH INHERITED TRAIT: ELIMINATION—ESTABLISHES A COMPLETE IDEOLOGY OF GENOCIDE

Communism has done many things with absolute cruelty. The CCP promised the intellectuals a "heaven on earth." Later it labeled them "rightist" and put them into the infamous ninth category[18] of persecuted people, alongside landlords and spies. It deprived landlords and capitalists of their property, exterminated the landlord and rich peasant classes, destroyed rank and order in the countryside, took authority away from local figures, kidnapped and extorted bribes from the richer people, brainwashed war prisoners, "reformed" industrialists and capitalists, infiltrated the KMT and disintegrated it, split from the Communist International and betrayed it, cleaned out all dissidents through successive political movements after it came to power in 1949, and threatened its own members with coercion. Everything it did was to the extreme.

The above-mentioned occurrences were all based on the CCP's theory of genocide. Its every past political movement was a campaign of terror with genocidal intent. The CCP started to build its theoretical system of genocide at its early stage as a composite of its theories on class, revolution, struggle, violence, dictatorship, movements, and political parties. It encompasses all of the experiences it has embraced and accumulated through its various genocidal practices.

The essential expression of CCP genocide is the extermination of conscience and independent thought. In this way a "reign of terror" serves the fundamental interests of the CCP. The CCP will not only eliminate you if you are against it, but it may also destroy you even if you are for it. It will eliminate whomever it deems should be eliminated. Consequently, everyone lives in the shadow of terror and fears the CCP.

Ninth Inherited Trait: Control—The Use of Party Nature to Control the Entire Party, and Subsequently the Rest of Society

All of the inherited characteristics aim to achieve a single goal: to control the populace through the use of terror. Through its evil actions, the CCP has proved itself to be the natural enemy of all existing social forces. Since its inception, the CCP has struggled through one crisis after another, among which the crisis of survival has been the most critical. The CCP exists in a state of perpetual fear for its survival. Its sole purpose has been to maintain its own existence and power—its own highest benefit. To supplement its declining power, the CCP has to turn to even more evil measures on a regular basis. The Party's interest is not the interest of any single Party member, nor is it a collection of any individual interests. Rather, it is the interest of the Party as a collective entity which overrides any sense of the individual.

"Party nature" has been the most vicious characteristic of this evil specter. Party nature overwhelms human nature so completely that the Chinese people have lost their humanity. For instance, Zhou Enlai and Sun Bingwen were once comrades. After Sun Bingwen died, Zhou Enlai took his daughter, Sun Weishi, as his adopted daughter. During the Cultural Revolution, Sun Weishi was reprimanded. She later died in custody from a long nail driven into her head. Her arrest warrant had been signed by her stepfather, Zhou Enlai.

One of the early leaders of the CCP was Ren Bishi, who was in charge of opium sales during the anti-Japanese war. Opium was a symbol of foreign invasion at that time, as the British used opium exported into China to drain the Chinese economy and turn the Chinese people into addicts. Despite the strong national sentiment against opium, Ren dared to plant opium in a large area because of his "sense of Party nature," risking universal condemnation. Due to the sensitive and illegal nature of the opium dealings, the CCP used the word "soap" as a code-word for opium.

The CCP used the revenue from the illicit drug trade with bordering countries to fund its existence. At the Centenary of Ren's birth, one of the new generation of Chinese leaders highly praised Ren's aptitude for the Party or sense of Party nature, claiming that, "Ren possessed superior character and was a model Party member. He also had a firm belief in Communism and unlimited loyalty to the cause of the Party."[19]

An example of good aptitude for the Party was Zhang Side. The Party said that he was killed by the sudden collapse of a kiln, but others claimed that he died while roasting opium. Since he was a quiet person, having served in the Central Guard Division and having never asked for a promotion, it was said, "his death is weightier than Mount Taishan,"[20] meaning that his life held the greatest importance.

Another model of "Party nature," Lei Feng, was well known as the "screw that never rusts, functioning in the revolutionary machine." For a long period of time, both Lei and Zhang were used to educate the Chinese people to be loyal to the Party. Mao Zedong said, "The power of examples is boundless." Many Party heroes were used to model the "iron will and principle of the Party spirit."

Upon gaining power, the CCP launched an aggressive campaign of mind control to mold many new "tools" and "screws" from the successive generations. The Party formed a set of "proper thoughts" and a range of stereotypical behaviors. These protocols were initially used within the Party, but quickly expanded to the entire public. Clothed in the name of the nation, these thoughts and actions worked to brainwash people into complying with the evil mechanism of the CCP.

II. THE CCP'S DISHONORABLE FOUNDATION

The CCP lays claim to a brilliant history, one that has seen victory after victory. This is merely an attempt to prettify itself and glorify the CCP's image in the eyes of the public. As a matter of fact, the CCP has no glory to advertise at all. Only by using the nine inherited evil traits could it establish and maintain power.

ESTABLISHMENT OF THE CCP—RAISED ON THE BREAST OF THE SOVIET UNION

"With the report of the first cannon during the October Revolution, it brought us Marxism and Leninism."[21] That was how the Party portrayed itself to the people. However, when the Party was first founded, it was just the Asian branch of the Soviet Union. From the beginning, it was a traitorous party.

During the founding period of the Party, they had no money, no ideology, nor any experience. They had no foundation upon which to support themselves. The CCP joined the Comintern to link its destiny with the existing violent revolution. The CCP's violent revolution was just a descendent of Marx and Lenin's revolution. The Comintern was the global headquarters to overthrow political powers all over the world, and the CCP was simply an eastern branch of Soviet Communism, carrying out the imperialism of the Russian Red Army. The CCP shared the experience of the Soviet Union's Communist Party of violent political takeover and dictatorship of the proletariat and followed the Soviet Party's instructions on its political line, intellectual line and organizational line. The CCP copied the secret and underground means by which an external illegal organization survived, adopting extreme surveillance and control measures. The Soviet Union was the backbone and patron of the CCP.

The CCP constitution passed by the First Congress of the CCP was formulated by the Comintern, based upon Marxism-Leninism and the theories of class struggle, dictatorship of the proletariat and party establishment. The Soviet party constitution provided its fundamental basis. The soul of the CCP consists of ideology imported from the Soviet Union. Chen Duxiu, one of the foremost officials of the CCP, had different opinions from Maring, the representative from the Comintern. Maring wrote a memo to Chen stating that if Chen were a real member of the Communist Party, he must follow orders from the Comintern. Even though Chen Duxiu was one of the CCP's founding fathers, he could do nothing but listen and obey orders. Truly, he and the Party were simply subordinates of the Soviet Union.

During the Third Congress of the CCP in 1923, Chen Duxiu publicly acknowledged that the Party was funded almost entirely by contributions from the Soviet Comintern. In one year, the Comintern contributed over 200,000 yuan to the CCP, with unsatisfactory results. The Comintern accused the CCP of not being diligent enough in their efforts.

According to incomplete statistics from declassified Party documents, the CCP received 16,655 Chinese yuan from October 1921 to June 1922. In 1924, they received USD $1,500 and 31,927.17 yuan, and in 1927 they received 187,674 yuan. The monthly contribution from the Comintern averaged around 20,000 yuan. Tactics commonly used by the CCP today, such as lobbying, going through the backdoor, offering bribes, and using threats, were already in use back then. The Comintern accused the CCP of continuously lobbying for funds.

They take advantage of the different funding sources (International Communications Office, representatives for the Comintern, and military organizations, etc.) to get their funds, because one organization does not know that the other organization has already dispersed the funds…the funny thing is, they not only understand the psychology of our Soviet comrades. Most importantly, they know how to treat differently the comrades in charge of dispersing funds. Once they know that they won't be able to get it through normal means, they delay meetings. In the end they use the crudest means to blackmail, like spreading rumors that some grass-root officials have conflicts with the Soviets, and that money is being given to warlords instead of the CCP.[22]

THE FIRST KMT AND CCP ALLIANCE—A PARASITE INFILTRATES TO THE CORE AND SABOTAGES THE NORTHERN EXPEDITION[23]

The CCP has always taught its people that Chiang Kai-shek betrayed the National Revolution movement[24], forcing the CCP to rise in armed revolt.

In reality, the CCP is a parasite or possessing specter. It cooperated with the KMT in the first KMT-CCP alliance for the sake of expanding its influence by taking advantage of the National Revolution. Moreover, the CCP was eager to launch the Soviet-supported revolution and seize power, and its desire for power in fact destroyed and betrayed the National Revolution movement.

At the Second National Congress of the CCP in July 1922, those opposing the alliance with the KMT dominated the congress, because the party members were anxious to seize power. However, the Comintern vetoed the resolution reached in the congress and ordered the CCP to join the KMT.

During the first KMT-CCP alliance, the CCP held its Fourth National Congress in Shanghai in January 1925 and raised the question of leadership in China before Sun Yat-sen[25] died on March 12, 1925. Had he not died, he, instead of Chiang Kai-shek would have been the target of the CCP in its quest for power.

With the support of the Soviet Union, the CCP wantonly seized political power inside the KMT during their alliance. Tan Pingshan (1886-1956, one of the early CCP leaders in Guangdong Province) became the Minister of the Central Personnel Department of the KMT. Feng Jupo (1899-1954, one of the early CCP leaders in Guangdong Province), Secretary of the Ministry of Labor, was granted full power to deal with all labor-related affairs. Lin Zuhan (also Lin Boqu, 1886-1960, one of the earliest CCP members) was the Minister of Rural Affairs, while Peng Pai (1896-1929, one of the CCP leaders) was Secretary of this Ministry. Mao Zedong assumed the position of acting Propaganda Minister of the KMT Propaganda Ministry. The military schools and leadership of the military were always the focus of the CCP: Zhou Enlai held the position of Director of the Political Department of the Huangpu (Whampoa) Military Academy, and Zhang Shenfu (also Zhang Songnian, 1893-1986, one of the founders of the CCP who introduced Zhou Enlai to join the CCP) was the Associate Director. Zhou Enlai was also Chief of the Judge Advocates Section, and he planted Russian military advisers here and there. Many communists held positions of political instructors and faculty at KMT military schools. CCP members also served as KMT Party representatives at various levels of the National Revolutionary Army.[26] It was also stipulated that without a CCP representative's signature, no order would be deemed effective. As a result of this parasitic attachment to the National Revolution movement, the number of CCP members increased dramatically from less than 1000 in 1925 to 30,000 by 1928.

The Northern Expedition started in February of 1926. From October 1926 to March 1927, the CCP launched three armed rebellions in Shanghai. Later, it attacked the Northern Expedition military headquarters but failed. The pickets for the general strikes in Guangdong Province engaged in violent conflicts with the police every day. Such uprisings caused the April 12 purge of the CCP by the KMT in 1927.[27]

In August 1927, the CCP members within the KMT Revolutionary Army initiated the Nanchang Rebellion, which was quickly suppressed. In September, the CCP launched the Autumn Harvest Uprising to attack Changsha, but that attack was suppressed as well. The CCP began to implement a network of control in the army whereby "Party branches are established at the level of the company in the army," and it fled to the Jinggangshan Mountain area in Jiangxi Province,[28] establishing rule over the countryside there.

THE HUNAN PEASANT REBELLION—INCITING THE SCUM OF SOCIETY TO REVOLT

During the Northern Expedition, when the National Revolutionary Army was at war with the warlords, the CCP instigated rebellions in the rural areas in an attempt to capture power.

The Hunan Peasant Rebellion in 1927 was a revolt of the riffraff, the scum of society, as was the well-known Paris Commune of 1871—the first communist revolt. French nationals and foreigners in Paris at the time witnessed that the Paris Commune was a group of destructive roving bandits with no vision. Living in exquisite buildings and large mansions and eating extravagant and luxurious meals, they cared only about enjoying their momentary happiness and didn't worry about the future. During the rebellion of the Paris Commune, they censored the press. They took as hostage and later shot the Archbishop of Paris, Georges Darboy, who gave sermons to the King. For their personal enjoyment they cruelly killed 64 clergymen, set fire to palaces, and destroyed government offices, private residences, monuments, and inscription columns. The wealth and beauty of the French capital had been second to none in Europe. However, during the Paris Commune uprising, buildings were reduced to ashes and people to skeletons. Such atrocities and cruelty had rarely been seen throughout history.

As Mao Zedong admitted,

It is true that the peasants are in a sense "unruly" in the countryside. Supreme in authority, the peasant association allows the landlord no say and sweeps away his prestige. This amounts to striking the landlord down to the dust and keeping him there. The peasants threaten, "We will put you in the other register [the register of reactionaries]!" They fine the local tyrants and evil gentry, they demand contributions from them, and they smash their sedan-chairs. People swarm into the houses of local tyrants and evil gentry who are against the peasant association, slaughter their pigs and consume their grain. They even loll for a minute or two on the ivory-inlaid beds belonging to the young ladies in the households of the local tyrants and evil gentry. At the slightest provocation they make arrests, crown the arrested with tall paper hats, and parade them through the village, saying, "You dirty landlords, now you know who we are!" Doing whatever they like and turning everything upside down, they have created a kind of terror in the countryside.[29]

But Mao gave such "unruly" actions full approval, saying,

To put it bluntly, it is necessary to create terror for a while in every rural area, or otherwise it would be impossible to suppress the activities of the counter-revolutionaries in the countryside or overthrow the authority of the gentry. Proper limits have to be exceeded in order to right a wrong, or else the wrong cannot be righted.... Many of their deeds in the period of revolutionary action, which were seen as going too far, were in fact the very things the revolution required.[30]

Communist revolution creates a system of terror.

The "Anti-Japanese" North-Bound Operation—The Flight of the Defeated

The CCP labeled the "Long March" as a northbound anti-Japanese operation. It trumpeted the "Long March" as a Chinese revolutionary fairy tale. It claimed that the "Long March" was a "manifesto," a "propaganda team" and a "seeding machine," which ended with the CCP's victory and their enemies' defeat.

The CCP fabricated such obvious lies about marching north to fight the Japanese to cover its failures. From October 1933 to January 1934, the Communist Party suffered a total defeat. In the fifth operation by the KMT, which aimed to encircle and annihilate the CCP, the CCP lost its rural strongholds one after another. With its base areas continually shrinking, the main Red Army had to flee. This is the true origin of the "Long March."

The "Long March" was in fact aimed at breaking out of the encirclement and fleeing to Outer Mongolia and Soviet Russia along an arc that first went west and then north. Once in place, the CCP could escape into the Soviet Union in case of defeat.

The CCP encountered great difficulties when en route towards Outer Mongolia. They chose to go through Shanxi and Suiyuan. On the one hand by marching through these northern provinces, they could claim to be "anti-Japanese" and win people's hearts. On the other hand, those areas were safe as no Japanese troops were deployed there. The area occupied by the Japanese army was along the Great Wall. A year later, when the CCP finally arrived at Shanbei (northern Shaanxi province), the main force of the Central Red Army had decreased from 80,000 to 6,000 people.

THE XI'AN INCIDENT—THE CCP SUCCESSFULLY SOWED DISSENSION AND LATCHED ONTO THE KMT A SECOND TIME

In December 1936, Zhang Xueliang and Yang Hucheng, two KMT Generals, kidnapped Chiang Kai-shek in Xi'an. This has since been referred to as the Xi'an Incident.

According to CCP textbooks, the Xi'an Incident was a "military coup" initiated by Zhang and Yang, who delivered a life or death ultimatum to Chiang Kai-shek. He was forced to take a stance against the Japanese invaders. Zhou Enlai was reportedly invited to Xi'an as a CCP representative to help negotiate a peaceful resolution. With different groups in China mediating, the incident was resolved peacefully, thereby ending a civil war of ten years and starting a unified national alliance against the Japanese. The CCP history books say that this incident was a crucial turning point for China in her crisis and depict the CCP as the patriotic party that takes the interests of the whole nation into account.

More and more documents have revealed that many CCP spies had already gathered around Yang Hucheng and Zhang Xueliang before the Xi'an Incident. Liu Ding, an underground CCP member was introduced to Zhang Xueliang by Song Qingling, wife of Sun Yat-sen, sister of Madame Chiang and a CCP member. After the Xi'an Incident, Mao Zedong praised Liu Ding saying that, "Liu Ding performed meritorious service in the Xi'an Incident." Among those working at Yang Hucheng's side, his own wife Xie Baozhen was a CCP member and worked in Yang's Political Department of the Army. Xie married Yang Hucheng in January of 1928 with the approval of the CCP. In addition, CCP member Wang Bingnan was an honored guest in Yang's home at the time. Wang later became a Vice Minister for the CCP Ministry of Foreign Affairs. It was these CCP members around Yang and Zhang who directly instigated the coup.

At the beginning of the incident, the leaders of the CCP wanted to kill Chiang Kai-shek, avenging his earlier suppression of the CCP. At that time, the CCP had a very weak base in northern Shaanxi Province, and had been in danger of being completely eliminated in a single battle. The CCP, utilizing all its acquired skills of deception, instigated Zhang and Yang to revolt. In order to pin down the Japanese and prevent them from attacking the Soviet Union, Stalin personally wrote to the Central Committee of the CCP, asking them not to kill Chiang Kai-shek, but to cooperate with him for a second time. Mao Zedong and Zhou Enlai realized that they could not destroy the KMT with the limited strength of the CCP; if they killed Chiang Kai-shek, they would be defeated and even eliminated by the avenging KMT Army. Under these circumstances, the CCP changed its tone. The CCP forced Chiang Kai-shek to accept cooperation a second time in the name of joint resistance against the Japanese.

The CCP first instigated a revolt, pointing the gun at Chiang Kai-shek, but then turned around and, acting like a stage hero, forced him to accept the CCP again. The CCP not only escaped a crisis of disintegration, but also used the opportunity to latch onto the KMT government for the second time. The Red Army was soon turned into the Eighth Route Army and grew bigger and more powerful than before. One must admire the CCP's unmatchable skills of deception.

ANTI-JAPANESE WAR—THE CCP GREW BY KILLING WITH BORROWED WEAPONS

When the Anti-Japanese War broke out in 1937, the KMT had more than 1.7 million armed soldiers, ships with 110,000 tons displacement, and about 600 fighter planes of various kinds. The total size of the CCP Army, including the New Fourth Army, which was newly grouped in November of 1937, did not exceed 70,000 people. Its power was weakened further by internal fractional politics and could be eliminated in a single battle. The CCP realized that if it were to face battle with the Japanese, it would not be able to defeat even a single division of the Japanese troops. In the eyes of the CCP, sustaining its own power rather than ensuring the survival of the nation was the central focus of its emphasis on "national unity." Therefore, during its cooperation with the KMT, the CCP exercised an internal policy of "giving priority to the struggle for political power, which is to be disclosed internally and realized in actual practice."

After the Japanese occupied the city of Shenyang on September 18, 1931, thereby extending their control over large areas in northeastern China, the CCP fought shoulder to shoulder with Japanese invaders to defeat the KMT. In a declaration written in response to the Japanese occupation, the CCP exhorted the people in the KMT-controlled areas to rebel, calling on "workers to strike, peasants to make trouble, students to boycott classes, poor people to quit working, soldiers to revolt" so as to overthrow the Nationalist government.

The CCP held up a banner calling for resistance to the Japanese, but they only had local armies and guerrilla forces in camps away from the frontlines. Except for a few battles, including the one fought at Pingxing Pass, the CCP did not make much of a contribution to the war against the Japanese at all. Instead, they spent their energy expanding their own base. When the Japanese surrendered, the CCP incorporated the surrendering soldiers into its army, claiming to have expanded to more than 900,000 regular soldiers, in addition to two million militia fighters. The KMT Army was essentially alone on the frontlines while fighting the Japanese, losing over 200 marshalls in the war. The commanding officers on the CCP side bore nearly no losses. However, the textbooks of the CCP constantly claimed that the KMT did not resist the Japanese, and that it was the CCP that led the great victory in the Anti-Japanese War.

RECTIFICATION IN YAN'AN—CREATING THE MOST FEARSOME METHODS OF PERSECUTION

The CCP attracted countless patriotic youths to Yan'an in the name of fighting against the Japanese, but persecuted tens of thousands of them during the rectification movement in Yan'an. Since gaining control of China, the CCP has depicted Yan'an as the revolutionary "holy land," but has not made any mention of the crimes it committed during the rectification.

The rectification movement in Yan'an was the largest, darkest and most ferocious power game ever played out in the human world. In the name of cleansing petty bourgeoisie toxins, the Party washed away morality, independence of thought, freedom of action, tolerance, and dignity. The first step of the rectification was to set up individual personnel archives, which included: 1) a personal statement; 2) a chronicle of one's political life; 3) family background and social relationships; 4) autobiography and ideological transformation; 5) evaluation according to Party nature.

In the personnel archive, one had to list all acquaintances since birth, all important events and the time and place of their occurrence. People were asked to write repeatedly for the archive, and any omissions would be seen as signs of impurity. One had to describe all social activities they had ever participated in, especially those related to joining the Party. The emphasis was placed on personal thought processes during these social activities. Evaluation based on Party nature was even more important, and one had to confess any anti-Party thoughts or behavior in one's consciousness, speech, work attitudes, everyday life, or social activities. For example, in evaluating one's consciousness, one was required to scrutinize whether one had been concerned for self-interest, whether one had used work for the Party to reach personal goals, whether one had wavered in trust in the revolutionary future, feared death during battles, or missed family members and spouses after joining the Party or the army. There were no objective standards, so nearly everyone was found to have problems.

Coercion was used to extract "confessions" from cadres who were being inspected in order to eliminate "hidden traitors." Countless frame-ups and false and wrong accusations resulted, and a large number of cadres were persecuted. During the rectification, Yan'an was called "a place for purging human nature." A work team entered the University of Military Affairs and Politics to examine the cadres' personal histories, causing "Red Terror" for two months. Various methods were used to extract confessions, including extemporaneous confessions, demonstrative confessions, "group persuasions," "five-minute persuasions," private advice, conference reports, and identifying the "radishes" (meaning red outside and white inside). There was also "picture taking"—lining up everyone on the stage for examination. Those who appeared nervous were identified as suspects and targeted as subjects to be investigated.

Even representatives from the Comintern recoiled at the methods used during the rectification, saying that the Yan'an situation was depressing. People did not dare interact with one another. Each person had his own axe to grind and everyone was nervous and frightened. No one dared to speak the truth or protect mistreated friends, because each was trying to save his own life. The vicious— those who flattered, lied, and insulted others—were promoted; humiliation became a fact of life in Yan'an— either humiliate other comrades or humiliate oneself. People were pushed to the brink of insanity, having been forced to abandon dignity, a sense of honor or shame, and love for one another in order to save their own lives and their own jobs. They ceased to express their own opinions, but recited Party leaders' articles instead.

This same system of oppression has been employed in all CCP political activities since it seized power in China.

THREE YEARS OF CIVIL WAR—BETRAYING THE COUNTRY TO SEIZE POWER

The Russian Bourgeois Revolution in February 1917 was a relatively mild uprising. The Tsar placed the interests of the country first and surrendered the throne instead of resisting. Lenin hurriedly returned to Russia from Germany, staged another coup, and in the name of communist revolution murdered the revolutionaries of the capitalist class who had overthrown the Tsar, thus strangling Russia's bourgeois revolution. The CCP, like Lenin, picked the fruits of a nationalist revolution. After the anti-Japanese war was over, the CCP launched a so-called "War of Liberation" (1946-1949) to overthrow the KMT government, bringing the disaster of war to China once more.

The CCP is well known for its "huge-crowd strategy," the sacrifice of massive casualties and lives to win a battle. In several battles with the KMT, including those fought in Liaoxi-Shenyang, Beijing-Tianjin, and Huai-Hai[31], the CCP used the most primitive, barbarous, and inhumane tactics that sacrificed huge numbers of its own people. When besieging Changchun City in Jilin Province, Northeast China, in order to exhaust the food supply in the city, the People's Liberation Army (PLA) was ordered to forbid ordinary people from leaving the city. During the two months of siege, nearly 200,000 people died of hunger and cold. But the PLA did not allow people to leave. After the battle was over, the CCP, without a tinge of shame, claimed that they had "liberated Changchun without firing a shot."

From 1947 to 1948, the CCP signed the "Harbin Agreement" and the "Moscow Agreement" with the Soviet Union, surrendering national assets and giving away resources from the northeast in exchange for the Soviet Union's full support in foreign relations and military affairs. According to the agreements, the Soviet Union would supply the CCP with 50 airplanes; it would give the CCP weapons left by the surrendered Japanese in two installments; and it would sell the Soviet-controlled ammunition and military supplies in China's northeast to the CCP at low prices. If the KMT launched an amphibious landing in the northeast, the Soviet Union would secretly support the CCP Army. In addition, the Soviet Union would help the CCP gain control over Xinjiang in Northwest China; the CCP and the Soviet Union would build an allied air force; the Soviets would help equip 11 divisions of the CCP Army, and transport one-third of its US-supplied weapons (worth $13 billion USD) into Northeast China.   •

To gain Soviet support, the CCP promised the Soviet Union special transportation privileges in the northeast both on land and by air; offered information about the actions of both the KMT government and the US military; provided them with products from the northeast (cotton, soybeans) and military supplies in exchange for advanced weapons; granted them preferential mining rights in China; allowed them to station armies in the northeast and Xinjiang; and permitted them to set up the Far East Intelligence Bureau in China. If war broke out in Europe, the CCP would send an expeditionary army of 100,000 plus 2 million laborers to support the Soviet Union. In addition, the CCP promised to merge some special regions in Liaoning Province into North Korea if necessary.

III. DEMONSTRATING EVIL TRAITS

ETERNAL FEAR MARKS THE PARTY'S HISTORY

The most prominent characteristic of the CCP is its eternal fear. Survival has been the CCP's highest interest since its inception. Such interest managed to overcome the fear hidden underneath its ever-changing appearance. The CCP is like a cancer cell that diffuses and infiltrates every part of the body, kills the surrounding normal cells and grows malignantly beyond control. In our cycle of history, society has been unable to dissolve such a mutated factor as the CCP and has no alternative but to let it proliferate at will. This mutated factor is so powerful that nothing within the level and range of its expansion can stop it. Much of society has become polluted, and larger and larger areas have been flooded with communism or communist elements. These elements are further strengthened and taken advantage of by the CCP and have fundamentally degraded the morality and society of humankind.

The CCP doesn't believe in any generally recognized principle of morality and justice. All of its principles are used entirely for its own interest. It is fundamentally selfish, and there are no principles that could restrain and control its desires. Based on its own principles, the Party needs to keep changing its surface appearance by putting on new skins. During the early period when its survival was at stake, the CCP attached to the Communist Party of the Soviet Union, to the KMT, to the KMT's governing body, and to the National Revolution. After capturing power, the CCP attached itself to various forms of opportunism, to the citizens' minds and feelings, to social structures and means—to anything it could put its hands on. It has utilized every crisis as an opportunity to gather more power and to strengthen its means of control.

STEADFAST PURSUIT OF EVIL IS THE CCP'S "MAGIC WEAPON"

The CCP claims that revolutionary victory depends upon three "magic weapons": the Party's construction, armed struggle, and united fronts. The experience with the KMT offered the CCP two more such "weapons": propaganda and espionage. The Party's various "magic weapons" have all been infused with the CCP's nine inherited traits: evil, deceit, incitement, unleashing the scum of society, espionage, robbery, fighting, elimination, and control.

Marxism-Leninism is evil in its nature. Ironically, the Chinese Communists do not really understand Marxism-Leninism. Lin Biao[32] said that there were very few CCP members who had really read the works of Marx or Lenin. The public considered Qu Qiubai[33] an ideologue but he admitted to have only read very little of Marxist-Leninist theory. Mao Zedong's ideology is a rural version of Marxism-Leninism that advocates the rebellion of peasants. Deng Xiaoping's theory of the primary stage of socialism has capitalism as its last name. Jiang Zemin's "Three Represents"[34] was pieced together out of nothing. The CCP has never really understood what Marxism-Leninism is, but has inherited its evil aspects, upon which the CCP has foisted its own even more wicked stuff.

The CCP's united front is a conjunction of deceit and short-term pay-offs. The goal of unity was to strengthen its power, to help it grow from a loner to a huge clan and to change the ratio of its friends to its enemies. Unity required discernment—identifying who were enemies and who were friends; who were on the left, in the middle, on the right; who should be befriended and when, and who should be attacked and when. It easily turned former enemies into friends and then back to enemies again. For example, during the period of the democratic revolution, the party allied with the capitalists; during the socialist revolution it eliminated the capitalists. In another example, leaders of other democratic parties such as Zhang Bojun[35] and Luo Longji,[36] co-founders of the China Democratic League, were made use of as supporters of the CCP during the period of seizing state power, but later were persecuted as "rightists."

THE COMMUNIST PARTY IS A SOPHISTICATED PROFESSIONAL GANG

The Communist Party has used two-sided strategies, one side soft and flexible and the other hard and stern. Its softer strategies include propaganda, united fronts, sowing dissension, espionage, instigating rebellion, double-dealing, getting into people's minds, brainwashing, lies and deception, covering up the truth, psychological abuse, and generating an atmosphere of terror. In doing these things, the CCP creates a syndrome of fear inside the people's hearts that leads them to easily forget the Party's wrongdoings. These myriad methods could stamp out human nature and foster maliciousness in humanity. The CCP's hard tactics include violence, armed struggle, persecution, political movements, murdering witnesses, kidnapping, suppressing different voices, armed attacks, periodic crack-downs, etc. These aggressive methods create and perpetuate terror.

The CCP uses both soft and hard methods concurrently. They would be relaxed in some instances while strict in others, or they would be relaxed on the outside while stiff in their internal affairs. In a relaxed atmosphere, the CCP encouraged the expression of different opinions, but, as if luring the snake out of its hole, those who did speak up would only be persecuted in the following period of strict control. The CCP often used democracy to challenge the KMT, but when intellectuals in the CCP-controlled areas disagreed with the Party, they would be tortured or even beheaded. As an example, we can look at the infamous "Wild Lilies incident," in which the intellectual Wang Shiwei (1906-1947) who wrote an essay *Wild Lilies* to express his ideal of equality, democracy and humanitarianism was purged in the Yan'an rectification movement and hacked to death with axes by the CCP in 1947.

A veteran official who had suffered torments in the Yan'an Rectification movement recalled that when he was under intense pressure, dragged and forced to confess, the only thing he could do was to betray his own conscience and make up lies. At first, he felt bad to be implicating and framing his fellow comrades. He hated himself so much that he wanted to end his life. Coincidentally, a gun had been placed on the table. He grabbed it, pointed it at his head and pulled the trigger. The gun had no bullets! The person who was investigating him walked in and said, "It's good that you admitted what you've done was wrong. The Party's policies are lenient." The Communist Party would know that you had reached your limit, knew that you were "loyal" to the Party, and had therefore passed the test. The CCP always puts one in a deathtrap first and then enjoys one's every pain and humiliation. When one reaches the limit and just wishes for death, the Party would "kindly" come out to show one a way to live. It is said "better a live coward than a dead hero." One becomes grateful to the Party as one's savior. Years later, this official learned about Falun Gong, a Qigong and cultivation practice that started in China. He felt the practice to be good. When the persecution of Falun Gong started in 1999, however, his painful memories of the past revisited him, and he no longer dared to say that Falun Gong was good.

The experience of China's last Emperor Puyi[37] was similar to this officer. Imprisoned in the CCP's cells and seeing people killed one after another, he thought that he would die soon. In order to live, he allowed himself to be brainwashed and cooperated with the prison guards. Later, he wrote an autobiography, *The First Half of My Life,* which was used by the CCP as a successful example of ideological remolding.

According to modern medical studies, many victims of intense pressure and isolation fall prey to an abnormal sense of dependency on their captors known as the Stockholm Syndrome. The victims' moods—happiness or anger, joy or sorrow—would be dictated by those of their captors. The slightest favor for the victims is received with deep gratitude. There are accounts in which the victims develop "love" for their captors. This psychological phenomenon has long been used successfully by the CCP both against its enemies and in controlling and remolding the minds of its citizens.

THE PARTY IS THE MOST WICKED

A majority of the General Secretaries of the CCP have been labeled anti-communist. Clearly, the CCP has a life of its own, with its own independent body. The party runs the officials and not the other way around. In the "Soviet areas" of Jiangxi

Province, while the CCP was encircled by the KMT and could hardly survive, it still conducted internal cleansing operations in the name of cracking down on the "Anti-Bolshevik Corps (AB Corps),[38]" executing its own soldiers at night or stoning them to death to save bullets. In northern Shaanxi Province, while sandwiched between the Japanese and the KMT, the CCP began the Yan'an rectification movement of mass cleansing, killing many people. This type of repetitive massacre on such a massive scale did not prevent the CCP from expanding its power to eventually rule all of China. The CCP expanded this pattern of internal rivalry and killing each other from the small Soviet areas to the whole nation.

The CCP is like a malignant tumor: in its rapid development, the center of the tumor has already died, but it continues to diffuse to the healthy organisms on the outer edges. After the organisms and bodies are infiltrated, new tumors grow. No matter how good or bad a person is to start with, after joining the CCP, he or she would become a part of its destructive force. The more honest the person is, the more destructive he would become. Undoubtedly, this CCP tumor will continue to grow until there is nothing left for it to feed upon. Then, the cancer will surely die.

The founder of the CCP, Chen Duxiu, was an intellectual and a leader of the May Fourth student movement. He showed himself not a fan of violence, and warned the CCP members that if they attempted to convert the KMT to the communist ideologies or had too much interest in power, that would certainly lead to strained relationships. While one of the most active in the May Fourth generation, Chen was also tolerant. However, he was the first to be labeled a "right-wing opportunist."

Another CCP leader, Qu Qiubai, believed that the CCP members should engage in battles and fighting, organize rebellions, overthrow authority, and use extreme means to return Chinese society to its normal functioning. However, he confessed before his death, "I do not want to die as a revolutionary. I left your movement a long time ago. Well, history played a trick, bringing me, an intellectual, onto the political stage of revolution and keeping me there for many years. In the end, I still could not overcome my own gentry notions. I cannot become a warrior of the proletariat class after all."[39]

The CCP leader Wang Ming, at the advice of the Comintern, argued for unity with the KMT in the war against the Japanese, instead of expanding the CCP base. At the CCP meetings, Mao Zedong and Zhang Wentian[40] could not persuade this fellow comrade, nor could they reveal the truth of their situation: according to the limited military strength of the Red Army, they would not be able to hold back even a division of the Japanese by themselves. If, against good sense, the CCP had decided to fight, then the history of China would certainly have been different. Mao Zedong was forced to remain silent at the meetings. Later, Wang Ming was ousted, first for a "left wing" deviation and then branded an opportunist of the right wing ideology.

Hu Yaobang, another Party Secretary who was forced to resign in January of 1987, had won back support for the CCP from the Chinese people by bringing justice to many innocent victims who had been criminalized during the Cultural Revolution. Still, in the end, he was kicked out.

Zhao Ziyang, the CCP's most recently-fallen Secretary,[41] wanted to help the CCP in furthering reform, yet his actions brought him dire consequences.

So what could each new leader of the CCP accomplish? Truly to reform the CCP would imply its death. The reformers would quickly find their power taken away by the CCP itself. There is a certain limit on what the CCP members can do themselves to transform the CCP system. So there is no chance for reformation of the CCP to succeed.

If the Party leaders have all turned into "bad people," how could the CCP have expanded the revolution? In many instances when the CCP was at its best—also the most evil, their highest officials failed in their positions. This was because their degree of evil did not meet the high standard of the Party, which has, over and over, selected only the most evil. Many Party leaders ended their political lives in tragedy, yet the CCP has survived. The CCP leaders who survived their positions were not those who could influence the Party, but those who could comprehend the Party's evil intentions and follow them. They strengthened the CCP's ability to survive while in crisis, and gave themselves entirely to the Party. No wonder Party members were capable of battling with heaven, fighting with the earth, and struggling against other human beings. But never could they oppose the Party. They are tame tools of the Party, or at most, symbiotically related to the Party.

Shamelessness has become a marvelous quality of today's CCP. According to the Party, its mistakes were all made by individual Party leaders, such as Zhang Guotao[42] or the Gang of Four.[43] Mao Zedong was judged by the Party as having three parts mistakes and seven parts achievements, while Deng Xiaoping judged himself to have four parts mistakes and six parts achievements, but the Party itself was never wrong. Even if the Party was wrong, well, it is the Party itself that has corrected the mistakes. Therefore, the Party tells its members to "look forward" and "not to be tangled in past accounts." Many things could change: The communist paradise is turned into a lowly goal of socialist food and shelter; Marxism-Leninism is replaced by the "Three Represents." People should not be surprised to see the CCP promoting democracy, opening up of freedom of belief, abandoning Jiang Zemin overnight, or redressing the persecution of Falun Gong, if it deems doing so necessary to maintain its control. There is one thing that never changes about the CCP: The fundamental pursuit of the Party's goals—survival and maintenance of its power and control.

The CCP has mixed violence, terror and high-pressure indoctrination to form its theoretical basis, which is then turned into the Party nature, the supreme principles of the Party, the spirit of its leaders, the functioning mechanism of the entire Party, and the criteria for the actions of all CCP members. The Communist Party is as hard as steel, and its discipline is as solid as iron. The intentions of all members must be unified, and the actions of all members must be in complete compliance with the Party's political agenda.

CONCLUSION

Why has history chosen the Communist Party over any other political force in China? As we all know, in this world there are two forces, two choices. One is the old and the evil, whose goal is to do evil and choose the negative way. The other is the righteous and the good, which will choose the right and the benevolent way. The CCP was chosen by the old forces. The reason for the choice is precisely because the CCP has gathered together all the evil of the world, Chinese or foreign, past or present. It is a typical representative of the evil forces. The CCP took the greatest advantage of people's inborn innocence and benevolence to cheat them, and, step-by-step, it has prevailed in gaining today's capacity to destroy.

What did the Party mean when it claimed that there would be no new China without the Communist Party? From its founding in 1921 until it took political power in 1949, the evidence clearly shows that without deceit and violence, the CCP would not be in power. The CCP differs from all other types of organizations in that it follows a twisted ideology of Marxism-Leninism, and does as it pleases. It explains all that it does with high theories and cleverly links them to certain portions of the masses, thus "justifying" its actions. It broadcasts propaganda every day, clothing its strategies in various principles and theories and proving itself to be forever correct.

The development of the CCP has been a process of accumulating evil, with nothing glorious at all. The history of the CCP itself precisely shows its illegitimacy. The Chinese people did not choose the CCP; instead, the CCP forced communism, this foreign evil specter, upon the Chinese people by applying the evil traits that it inherited from the Communist Party—evil, deceit, incitement, unleashing the scum of society, espionage, robbery, fighting, elimination, and control.

COMMENTARY THREE

ON THE TYRANNY OF THE
CHINESE COMMUNIST PARTY

COMMENTARY THREE

ON THE TYRANNY OF
THE CHINESE COMMUNIST PARTY

FOREWORD

When speaking about tyranny, most Chinese people are reminded of Qin Shi Huang (259-210 BC), the first Emperor of the Qin Dynasty, whose oppressive court burnt philosophical books and buried Confucian scholars alive. Qin Shi Huang's harsh treatment of his people came from his policy of "supporting his rule with all of the resources under heaven."[1] This policy had four main aspects: excessively heavy taxation; wasting human labor for projects to glorify himself; brutal torture under harsh laws and punishing even the offenders' family members and neighbors; and controlling people's minds by blocking all avenues of free thinking and expression through burning books and even burying scholars alive. Under the rule of Qin Shi Huang, China had a population of about ten million; Qin's court drafted over two million to perform forced labor. Qin Shi Huang brought his harsh laws into the intellectual realm, prohibiting freedom of thought on a massive scale. During his rule, thousands of Confucian scholars and officials who criticized the government were killed.

Today the CCP's violence and abuses are even more severe than those of the tyrannical Qin Dynasty. The CCP's philosophy is one of struggle, and the CCP's rule has been built upon a series of class struggles, path struggles, and ideological struggles, both in China and toward other nations. Mao Zedong, the first CCP leader of the People's Republic of China (PRC), put it bluntly by saying, "What can Emperor Qin Shi Huang brag about? He only killed 460

Confucian scholars, but we killed 46,000 intellectuals. There are people who accuse us of practicing dictatorship like Emperor Qin Shihuang and we admit it all. It fits the reality. It is a pity that they did not give us enough credit, so we need to add to it."⁼

Let's take a look at China's arduous 55 years under the rule of the CCP. As its founding philosophy is one of class struggle, the CCP has spared no efforts since taking power to commit class genocide, and has achieved its reign of terror by means of violent revolution. Killing and brainwashing have been used hand-in-hand to suppress any beliefs other than communist theory. The CCP has launched one movement after another to portray itself as infallible and godlike. Following its theories of class struggle and violent revolution, the CCP has tried to purge dissidents and opposing social classes, using violence and deception to force all Chinese people to become the obedient servants of its tyrannical rule.

I. LAND REFORM—ELIMINATING THE LANDLORD CLASS

Barely three months after the founding of communist China, the CCP called for the elimination of the landlord class as one of the guidelines for its nationwide land reform program. The Party's slogan "land to the tiller" indulged the selfish side of the landless peasants, encouraged them to struggle with the landowners by whatever means and to disregard the moral implications of their actions. The land reform campaign explicitly stipulated eliminating the landlord class, and classified the rural population into different social categories. Twenty million rural inhabitants nationwide were labeled landlords, rich peasants, reactionaries, or bad elements. These new outcasts faced discrimination, humiliation, and loss of all their civil rights. As the land reform campaign extended its reach to remote areas and the villages of ethnic minorities, the CCP's organizations also expanded quickly. Township Party committees and village Party branches spread all over China. The local branches were the mouthpiece for passing instructions from the CCP's central committee and were at the frontline of the class struggle, inciting peasants to rise up against their landlords. Nearly 100,000 landlords died during this movement. In certain areas the CCP and the peasants killed the landlords' entire families, disregarding gender or age, as a way to completely wipe out the landlord class.

In the meantime, the CCP launched its first wave of propaganda, declaring that "Chairman Mao is the great savior of the people" and that "only the CCP can save China." During the land reform, landless farmers got what they wanted through the CCP's policy of reaping without laboring, robbing without concern for the means. Poor peasants credited the CCP for the improvement in their lives and so accepted the CCP's propaganda that the Party worked for the interests of the people.

For the owners of the newly acquired land, the good days of "land to the tiller" were short-lived. Within two years, the CCP imposed a number of practices on the farmers such as mutual-aid groups, primary cooperatives, advanced cooperatives, and people's communes. Using the slogan of criticizing "women with bound feet"—meaning those who are slow paced—the CCP drove and pushed, year after year, urging peasants to dash into socialism. With grain, cotton, and cooking oil placed under a unified procurement system nationwide, the major agricultural products were excluded from market exchange. In addition, the CCP established a residential registration system, barring peasants from going to the cities to find work or dwell. Those who are registered as rural residents were not allowed to buy grain at state-run stores and their children were prohibited from receiving education in cities. Peasants' children could only be peasants, turning 360 million rural residents cf the early 1950s into second-class citizens.

Beginning in 1978, in the first five years after moving from a collective system to a household contract system, some among the 900 million peasants became better off, with their income increasing slightly and their social status improving somewhat. However, such a meager benefit was soon lost due to a price structure that favored industrial commodities over agricultural goods; peasants plunged into poverty once again. The income gap between the urban and rural population has drastically increased, and economic disparity continues to widen. New landlords and rich peasants have re-emerged in the rural areas. Data from Xinhua News Agency, the CCP's mouthpiece, show that since 1997 the revenue of the major grain production areas and the income of most rural households have been at a standstill, or even declined in some cases. In other words, the peasants' gain from agricultural production did not really increase. The ratio of urban to rural incomes has increased from 1.8 to 1 in the mid 1980s to 3.1 to 1 today.

II. REFORMS IN INDUSTRY AND COMMERCE— ELIMINATING THE CAPITALIST CLASS

Another class that the CCP wanted to eliminate was the national bourgeoisie who owned capital in cities and rural towns. While reforming China's industry and commerce, the CCP claimed that the capitalist class and the working class were different in nature: the former was the exploiting class while the latter was the non-exploiting and anti-exploiting class. According to this logic, the capitalist class was born to exploit and wouldn't stop doing so until it perished; it could only be eliminated, not reformed. Under such premises, the CCP used both killing and brainwashing to transform capitalists and merchants. The CCP used its long-tested method of supporting the obedient and destroying those who disagreed. If you surrendered your assets to the state and supported the CCP, you were considered just a minor problem among the people. If, on the other hand, you disagreed with or complained about the CCP's policy, you would be labeled a reactionary and become the target of the CCP's draconian dictatorship.

During the reign of terror that ensued during these reforms, capitalists and business owners all surrendered their assets. Many of them couldn't bear the humiliation they faced and committed suicide. Chen Yi, then mayor of Shanghai, asked every day, "How many paratroopers did we have today?" referring to the number of capitalists who had committed suicide by jumping from the tops of buildings that day. In only a few years, the CCP completely eliminated private ownership in China.

While carrying out its land and industrial reform programs, the CCP launched many massive movements that persecuted the Chinese people. These movements included the suppression of counter-revolutionaries, thought reform campaigns, cleansing the anti-CCP clique headed by Gao Gang and Rao Shushi[3], probing Hu Feng's[4] counter-revolutionary group, the Three Anti Campaign, the Five Anti Campaign, and the further cleansing of counter-revolutionaries. The CCP used these movements to target and brutally persecute countless innocent people. In every political movement, the CCP fully utilized its control of government resources in conjunction with the Party's committees, branches, and sub-branches. Three party members would form a small combat team, infiltrating all villages and neighborhoods. These combat teams were ubiquitous, leaving no stone unturned. This deeply-entrenched Party control network, inherited from the CCP's network of Party branches installed within the army during the war years, has since played a key role in later political movements.

III. CRACKDOWN ON RELIGIONS AND RELIGIOUS GROUPS

The CCP committed another atrocity in the brutal suppression of religion and the complete ban of all grass-roots religious groups following the founding of the People's Republic of China. In 1950, the CCP instructed its local governments to ban all unofficial religious faiths and secret societies. The CCP stated that those feudalistic underground groups were mere tools in the hands of landlords, rich farmers, reactionaries, and the special agents of the KMT. In the nationwide crackdown, the government mobilized the classes they trusted to identify and persecute members of religious groups. Governments at various levels were directly involved in disbanding such superstitious groups as communities of Christians, Catholics, Taoists (especially believers of I-Kuan Tao), and Buddhists. They ordered all members of these churches, temples, and religious societies to register with government agencies and to repent for their involvement. Failure to do so would mean severe punishment. In 1951, the government formally promulgated regulations threatening that those who continued their activities in unofficial religious groups would face a life sentence or the death penalty.

This movement persecuted a large number of kind-hearted and law-abiding believers in God. Incomplete statistics indicate that the CCP in the 1950s persecuted at least three million religious believers and underground group members, some of whom were killed. The CCP searched almost every household across the nation and interrogated its members, even smashing statues of the Kitchen

God that Chinese peasants traditionally worshipped. The executions reinforced the CCP's message that communist ideology was the only legitimate ideology and the only legitimate faith. The concept of patriotic believers soon emerged. The state constitution protected only patriotic believers. The reality was whatever religion one believed in, there was only one criterion: you had to follow the CCP's instructions and you had to acknowledge that the CCP was above all religions. If you were a Christian, the CCP was the God of the Christian God. If you were a Buddhist, the CCP was the Master Buddha of the Master Buddha. Among Muslims, the CCP was the Allah of the Allah. When it came to the Living Buddha in Tibetan Buddhism, the CCP would intervene and itself choose who the Living Buddha would be. The CCP left you no choice but to say and do what the CCP demanded you to say and do. All believers were forced to carry out the CCP's objectives while upholding their respective faiths in name only. Failing to do so would make one the target of the CCP's persecution and dictatorship.

According to a February 22, 2002, report by *Humanity and Human Rights* online magazine, 20,000 Christians conducted a survey among 560,000 Christians in house churches in 207 cities in 22 provinces in China. The survey found that, among house church attendees, 130,000 were under government surveillance. In the book *How the Chinese Communist Party Persecuted Christians*[5], it is stated that by 1957, the CCP had killed over 11,000 religious adherents and had arbitrarily arrested and extorted money from many more.

By eliminating the landlord class and the capitalist class and by persecuting large numbers of God-worshipping and law-abiding people, the CCP cleared the way for communism to become the all-encompassing religion of China.

71

IV. THE ANTI-RIGHTIST MOVEMENT—NATIONWIDE BRAINWASHING

In 1956, a group of Hungarian intellectuals formed the Petofi Circle, which held forums and debates critical of the Hungarian government. The group sparked a nationwide revolution in Hungary, which was crushed by Soviet soldiers. Mao Zedong took this Hungarian Event as a lesson. In 1957, Mao called upon the Chinese intellectuals and other people to "help the CCP rectify itself." This movement, known as the Hundred Flowers Movement for short, followed the slogan of "letting a hundred flowers blossom and a hundred schools of thought contend." Mao's purpose was to lure out the anti-Party elements among the people. In his letter to provincial Party chiefs in 1957, Mao Zedong spoke his intention of "luring the snakes out of their holes" by letting them air their views freely in the name of freedom of thought and rectifying the CCP.

Slogans at the time encouraged people to speak up and promised no reprisals—the Party would not "grab pigtails, strike with sticks, issue hats, or settle accounts after the autumn," meaning the party would not find fault, make attacks, place labels, or seek to retaliate. Yet soon the CCP initiated an Anti-Rightist Movement, declaring 540,000 of the people who dared to speak up as "rightists." Among them, 270,000 lost their jobs and 230,000 were labeled medium rightists or anti-CCP anti-socialist elements. Later some summarized the CCP's political stratagems of persecution into four items: Luring the snakes out of their holes; fabricating crimes, attacking suddenly, and punishing with a single accusation; attacking relentlessly in the name of saving people; and forcing self-criticism and using the most severe labels.

What then were the "reactionary speeches" that had caused so many rightists and anti-communists to be exiled for nearly 30 years in far-flung corners of the nation? The three major reactionary theories, the targets of general and intensive assaults at the time, consisted of a few speeches by Luo Longji, Zhang Bojun, and Chu Anping. A closer look at what they proposed and suggested shows that their wishes were quite benign.

Luo suggested forming a joint commission of the CCP and various "democratic" parties to investigate the deviations in the Three Anti Campaign and Five Anti Campaign, and the movements for purging reactionaries. The State Council itself often presented something to the Political Consultative Committee and the People's Congress for observations and comments, and Zhang suggested the Political Consultative Committee and the People's Congress should be included in the decision-making process.

Chu suggested that since non-CCP members also had good ideas, self-esteem, and a sense of responsibility as well, there was no need to assign a CCP member across the nation as the head of every work unit, big or small, or even for the teams under each work unit. There was also no need that everything, major or minor, had to be done the way the CCP members suggested. All three had expressed their willingness to follow the CCP and none of their suggestions had exceeded the boundaries demarcated by the famous words of writer and critic Lu Xun,[6] "My master, your gown has become dirty. Please take it off and I will wash it for you." Like Lu Xun, these rightists expressed docility, submissiveness and respect.

None of the condemned rightists suggested that the CCP should be overthrown; all they had offered was constructive criticism. Yet precisely because of these suggestions, tens of thousands of people lost their freedom, and millions of families suffered. What followed were more movements such as confiding to the CCP, digging out the hardliners, the new Three Anti Campaign, sending intellectuals to the countryside to do hard labor, and catching the rightists who were missed the first time around. Whoever had a disagreement with the leader of the workplace, especially the party secretaries, would be labeled anti-CCP. The CCP would often subject them to constant criticism, or send them to labor camps for forced reeducation. Sometimes the Party relocated whole families to rural areas, and barred their children from going to college or joining the army. They couldn't apply for jobs in cities or towns either. The families would lose their job security and public health benefits. They became lowly members of the peasant rank and outcasts even among second-class citizens.

After the persecution of the intellectuals, some scholars developed a two-faced personality. They followed closely the Red Sun (i.e., Mao) and became the CCP's court-appointed intellectuals, doing or saying whatever the CCP asked. Some others became aloof and distanced themselves from political matters. Chinese intellectuals, who have traditionally had a strong sense of responsibility towards the nation, have been silenced ever since.

V. THE GREAT LEAP FORWARD—CREATING FALSEHOODS TO TEST PEOPLE'S LOYALTY

After the Anti-Rightist Movement, China became afraid of truth. Everyone joined in listening to false words, telling false tales, making up false stories, and avoiding and covering up the truth through lies and rumors. The Great Leap Forward was a nationwide collective exercise in lying. The people of the entire nation, under the direction of the CCP's evil specter, did many ridiculous things. Both liars and those being lied to were betrayed. In this campaign of lies and ridiculous actions, the CCP implanted its violent, evil energy into the spiritual world of the Chinese people. At the time, many people sang songs promoting the Great Leap Forward, "I am the Great Jade Emperor, I am the Dragon King, I can move the mountains and rivers, here I come."[7] Policies such as achieving a grain production of 75,000 kg per hectare, doubling steel production, and surpassing Britain in ten years and the United States in 15 years were attempted year after year. These policies resulted in a grave, nationwide famine that cost millions of lives.

During the eighth plenum of the Eighth CCP Central Committee meeting held in Lushan in 1959, who among the participants disagreed with General Peng Dehuai's[8] view that the Great Leap Forward initiated by Mao Zedong was foolish? However, supporting Mao's policy or not marked the line between loyalty or betrayal, or the line between life and death. In a story from Chinese history, when Zhao Gao[9] claimed that a deer was a horse, he knew the difference between a deer and a horse, but he purposefully called a deer a horse to control public opinion, silence debates, and expand his own power. The result of the Lushan Plenum was that even Peng Dehuai was forced to sign a resolution condemning and purging himself from the central government. Similarly, in the later years of the Cultural Revolution, Deng Xiaoping was forced to promise that he would never appeal against the government's decision to remove him from his posts.

Society relies on past experience to understand the world and expand its horizons. The CCP, however, has taken away opportunities from the people to learn from historical experience and lessons. The official censorship of the media has only helped further lower people's capacity to discern good from bad. After each political movement, the younger generations have only been given the Party's uplifting accounts, but have been deprived of the analyses, ideals, and experiences of the insightful people from older generations. As a result, people have only scattered information as the basis for understanding history and judging new events, thinking themselves correct while deviating thousands of miles from the truth. Thus the CCP's policy of keeping people ignorant has been carried out thoroughly.

VI. THE CULTURAL REVOLUTION—THE WORLD TURNED UPSIDE DOWN BY EVIL POSSESSION

The Cultural Revolution was a grand performance put on by the communist specter as it possessed all of China. In 1966, a new wave of violence rolled onto China's land, and an uncontrollable red terror shook the mountains and froze the rivers. Writer Qin Mu described the Cultural Revolution in bleak terms:

It was truly an unprecedented calamity: [the CCP] imprisoned millions due to their association with a [targeted] family member, ended the lives of millions more, shattered families, turned children into hoodlums and villains, burned books, tore down ancient buildings, and destroyed ancient intellectuals' gravesites, committing all kinds of crimes in the name of revolution.[10]

Conservative figures place the number of unnatural deaths in China during the Cultural Revolution at 7.73 million.

People often mistakenly think that the violence and slaughter during the Cultural Revolution happened mostly during the rebel movements, and that it was the Red Guards[11] and rebels who committed the killing. However, thousands of officially published Chinese county annuals indicate that the peak of unnatural deaths during the Cultural Revolution was not in 1966, when the Red Guards controlled most of the government organizations, or in 1967 when the rebels fought among different groups with weapons, but rather in 1968 when Mao regained control over the entire country. The murderers in those infamous cases were often army officers and soldiers, armed militiamen, and CCP members at all levels of the government.

The following examples illustrate how the violence during the Cultural Revolution was the policy of the CCP and the regional government, not the extreme behavior of the Red Guards. The CCP has covered up the direct instigation of and involvement in the violence by party leaders and government officials.

In August 1966, the Red Guards expelled Beijing residents who had been classified in past movements as landlords, rich farmers, reactionaries, bad elements, and rightists and forced them to the countryside. Incomplete official statistics showed that 33,695 homes were searched and 85,196 Beijing residents were expelled out of the city and sent back to where their parents had originally come from. Red Guards all over the country followed suit, expelling over 400,000 urban residents to the countryside. Even high-ranking officials, whose parents were landlords, faced exile to the country.

Actually, the CCP planned the expulsion campaign even before the Cultural Revolution began. Former Beijing mayor Peng Zhen declared that the residents of Beijing City should be as ideologically pure as glass panels and crystals, meaning that all residents with a bad class background would be expelled out of the city. In May of 1966, Mao commanded his subordinates to protect the capital. A capital working team was set up, led by Ye Jianying, Yang Chengwu and Xie Fuzhi. One of the tasks of this team was to use the police to expel Beijing residents of bad class background.

This history helps make clear why the government and police departments did not intervene but rather supported the Red

Guards in searching homes and expelling more than two percent of Beijing residents. The Minister of Public Security, Xie Fuzhi, required the police not to intervene in the Red Guards' actions but rather to provide advice and information to them. The Red Guards were simply utilized by the Party to carry out a planned action, and then, at the end of 1966, these Red Guards were abandoned by the CCP. Many were labeled counterrevolutionaries and imprisoned, and others were sent to the countryside, along with other urban youth, to labor and reform their thoughts. The West Town Red Guard organization, which led the expulsion of city residents, was established under the "caring" guidance of the CCP leaders. The order to incriminate these Red Guards was also issued after being revised by the secretary-general of the State Council.

Following the removal of the Beijing residents of bad class background, the rural areas started another round of persecution of bad class elements. On August 26, 1966, a speech of Xie Fuzhi was passed down to the Daxing Police Bureau at their work meeting. Xie ordered the police to assist the Red Guards in searching the homes of the "five black classes" (landlords, rich peasants, reactionaries, bad elements, and rightists) by providing advice and information and helping in their raids. The infamous Daxing Massacre[12] occurred as a result of direct instructions by the police department. The organizers were the director and the CCP secretary of the police department, and the killers were mostly militiamen who did not even spare the children.

Many were admitted into the CCP for their "good behavior" during similar slaughters. According to incomplete statistics for Guangxi Province, about 50,000 CCP members engaged in killing. Among them more than 9,000 were admitted into the Party shortly after killing someone, more than 20,000 committed murder after being admitted into the Party, and more than 19,000 other Party members were involved in killing in one way or another.

During the Cultural Revolution, class theory would also be applied to beatings. The bad deserved it if they were beaten by the good. It was honorable for a bad person to beat another bad person. It was a misunderstanding if a good person beat another good person. Such a theory invented by Mao was spread widely in the rebel movements. Violence and slaughter were widespread following the logic that the enemies of the class struggle deserved any violence against them.

From August 13 to October 7 of 1967, militiamen in Dao County of Hunan Province slaughtered members of the Xiangjiang Wind and Thunder organization and those of the five black classes. The slaughter lasted 66 days; more than 4,519 people in 2,778 households were killed in 468 brigades (administrative villages) of 36 people's communes in ten districts. In the entire prefecture consisting of ten counties, a total of 9,093 people were killed, of which 38 percent were of the five black classes and 44 percent were their children. The oldest person killed was 78 years old, and the youngest was only ten days old.

This is only one case of violence in one small area during the Cultural Revolution. In Inner Mongolia, after the establishment of the "revolutionary committee" in early 1968, the cleansing of class rank and purging of the fabricated Inner Mongolia People's Revolutionary Party resulted in the deaths of more than 350,000 people. In 1968, tens of thousands of people in Guangxi Province participated in the mass slaughter of a public faction known as "4.22" organization, killing more than 110,000.

These cases point out that those major acts of violent killing during the Cultural Revolution were all under the direct instigation and instruction of CCP leaders who encouraged and utilized violence to persecute and kill citizens. Those killers directly involved in instructing and executing the killing were mostly from the military, police, armed militia, and key members of the Party and the Youth League.

If during the Land Reform the CCP used peasants to overthrow landlords to obtain land, during the Industrial and Commercial Reform the CCP used the working class to overthrow capitalists to gain assets, and during the Anti-Rightist Movement the CCP eliminated all intellectuals who held opposing opinions, then what was the purpose of all the killing during the Cultural Revolution? The CCP used one group to kill another, and no one class was relied upon. Even if you were from the workers and peasants, two classes upon which the Party relied in the past, if your viewpoint differed from that of the Party, your life would be in danger. So in the end, what was it all for?

The purpose was to establish communism as the one and only religion dominating the entire country, controlling not just the state but every individual's mind.

The Cultural Revolution pushed the CCP and Mao Zedong's cult of personality to a climax. Mao's theory had to be used to dictate everything and one person's vision had to be embedded in tens of millions of people's minds. The Cultural Revolution, in a way unprecedented and never again to be matched, intentionally did not specify what could not be done. Instead, the Party emphasized what can be done and how to do it. Anything outside this boundary could not be done or even considered.

During the Cultural Revolution, everyone in the country carried out a religious-like ritual: ask the Party for instructions in the morning and report to the Party in the evening, salute Chairman

Mao several times a day, wishing him boundless longevity, and conduct morning and evening political prayers every day. Nearly every literate person had the experience of writing self-criticism and thought reports. Mao's quotations such as the following were frequently recited. "Fight ferociously against every passing thought of selfishness." "Execute the Party's command whether or not you understand it. Even if you do not understand, carry it out anyway and your understanding should deepen in the process of execution."

Only one god (Mao) was allowed to be worshiped; only one kind of scripture (Mao's teaching) was allowed to be studied. Soon the "god-making" process progressed to such a degree that people could not buy food in canteens if they did not recite a quotation or make a greeting to Mao. When shopping, riding the bus, or even making a phone call, one had to recite one of Mao's quotations, even if it was totally irrelevant. In these rituals of worship, people were either fanatical or cynical, and in either case were already under the control of the communist evil specter. Producing lies, tolerating lies, and relying on lies became Chinese people's lifestyle.

VII. THE REFORM AND OPENING UP—THE VIOLENCE PROGRESSES WITH TIME

The Cultural Revolution was a period full of bloodshed, killings, grievances, loss of conscience, and confusion of right and wrong. After the Cultural Revolution, the CCP leadership changed its banners frequently, as the government changed hands six times within 20 years. Private ownership has returned to China, disparities in the standard of living between cities and rural areas have widened, the desert area has quickly expanded, river water has been drying up, and drug-use and prostitution have increased. All the "crimes" the CCP fought against are now permitted again.

The CCP's ruthless heart, devious nature, evil actions, and ability to bring ruin to the country increased. During the Tiananmen Square massacre in 1989, the Party mobilized armies and tanks to kill students protesting on Tiananmen Square. The vicious persecution against Falun Gong practitioners is even worse. In October of 2004, to take land from the peasants, Yulin City of Shaanxi Province mobilized over 1,600 riot police to arrest and shoot more than 50 peasants. The political control of the Chinese government continues to rely on the CCP's philosophy of struggle and violence. The only difference from the past is that the Party has become even more deceptive.

LAW MAKING

The CCP has never stopped creating conflicts among the people. They have persecuted large numbers of citizens for being reactionaries, anti-socialists, bad elements, and evil cult members. The totalitarian nature of the CCP continues to conflict with all other civil groups and organizations. In the name of "maintaining order and stabilizing society," the Party has kept changing constitutions, laws and regulations, and has persecuted as reactionaries anyone who disagrees with the government.

In July 1999, Jiang Zemin made a personal decision, against most other Politburo members' wills, to eliminate Falun Gong in three months; slander and lies quickly enveloped the country. After Jiang Zemin denounced Falun Gong as an "evil cult" in an interview with the French newspaper *Le Figaro,* Chinese official propaganda followed up by quickly publishing articles pressuring everyone in the country to turn against Falun Gong. The National People's Congress was coerced into passing a non-descript decision dealing with evil cults; soon after that the Supreme People's Court and Supreme People's Procuratorate jointly issued an "explanation" of the "decision."

On July 22, 1999, the Xinhua News Agency published speeches by the CCP's organization department and propaganda department leaders publicly supporting Jiang's persecution against Falun Gong. The Chinese people became enmeshed in the persecution simply because it was a decision made by the Party. They can only obey orders and dare not raise any objections.

Over the past five years, the government has utilized one-fourth of the nation's financial resources to persecute Falun Gong. Everyone in the country has had to pass a test. Most who admitted to practicing Falun Gong but refused to give up the practice have lost their jobs; some are sentenced to forced labor. The Falun Gong practitioners have not violated any laws, nor have they betrayed the country or opposed the government; they have only believed in Truthfulness, Compassion, and Tolerance. Yet hundreds of thousands were imprisoned. While the CCP has enforced a tight blockade of information, more than 1,143 people[13] have been confirmed by their families to have been tortured to death. The true number of deaths is much higher.

NEWS REPORTING

On October 15, 2004, Hong Kong-based *Wenweipao* reported that China's 20th satellite returned to earth, falling on and destroying the house of Huo Jiyu in Penglai Township, located in Dayin County, Sichuan Province. The report quoted Dayin County government office director Ai Yuqing saying that the "black lump" was confirmed to be the satellite. Ai was the on-site deputy director of the satellite recovery project. However, Xinhua News only reported the time of the satellite's recovery, emphasizing that this was the 20th scientific and technical experimental satellite recovered by China. Xinhua News did not mention a word about the satellite destroying a house. This is a typical example of the Chinese news media's consistent practice of reporting only the good news and covering up the bad news, as instructed by the Party.

Lies and slander published by newspapers and broadcast on television have greatly assisted the execution of the CCP's policies in all past political movements. The Party's command would be instantly executed by the media in the country. When the Party wanted to start an Anti-Rightist Movement, media all over China reported with one voice the crimes of rightists. When the Party wanted to set up the people's communes, every newspaper in the nation started to praise the superiority of people's communes. Within the first month of the persecution of Falun Gong, all television and radio stations slandered Falun Gong repeatedly in their prime time broadcasting in order to brainwash people. Since then, Jiang has utilized all media repeatedly to fabricate and spread lies and slander about Falun Gong. This includes the effort to incite nationwide hatred against Falun Gong by reporting false news about Falun Gong practitioners' committing murder and suicide. An example of such false reporting is the staged Tiananmen self-immolation incident, which was criticized by the NGO International Educational Development as a government-staged action to deceive people. In the past five years, no mainland Chinese newspaper or TV station has reported the truth about Falun Gong.

Chinese people are used to the false news reports. A senior reporter of Xinhua News Agency once said, "How could you trust a Xinhua report?" People have even described Chinese news agencies as the Party's dog. A folk song has it: "It is a dog raised by the Party, guarding the Party's gate. It would bite anyone the Party wants it to bite, and bite however many times the Party wants it to."

EDUCATION

In China, education became another tool used to control people. The original purpose of education was to develop intellectuals to have both knowledge and correct judgment. Knowledge refers to the understanding of information, data and historical events; judgment refers to the process of analyzing, investigating, critiquing, and reproducing such knowledge—a process of spiritual development. Those who have knowledge without proper judgment are referred to as bookworms, not true intellectuals with a social conscience. This is why in Chinese history it is the intellectuals with righteous judgment, not those having merely knowledge, who have been highly respected. Under the CCP's control, however, China is filled with intellectuals who have knowledge but not judgment, or who dare not exercise judgment. Education in schools focused on teaching students not to do things that the Party did not want them to do. In recent years, all schools started to teach politics and CCP history with unified textbooks. The teachers did not believe the content of the text, yet they were forced by the Party discipline to teach it against their wills. The students did not believe the text or their teachers, yet they had to remember everything in the text in order to pass the exams. Recently, questions about Falun Gong were included in term and entrance exams for colleges and high schools. Students who do not know the standard answers do not get high scores to enter good colleges or high schools. If a student dares to speak the truth, he will be expelled from school immediately and lose any chance of formal education.

In the public education system, due to the influence of the newspapers and government documents, many well-known sayings or phrases have been spread as truth, such as Mao's quotation, "We should support whatever the enemy opposes and oppose whatever the enemy supports." The negative effect is widespread: it has poisoned people's hearts, supplanting benevolence and destroying the moral principle of living in peace and harmony.

In 2004, the China Information Center analyzed a survey done by the China Sina Net, and the results show that 82.6 percent of Chinese youth agreed that one can abuse women, children and prisoners during a war. This result is shocking. But it reflects the Chinese people's mindset, and especially that of the younger generation, who lack a basic understanding of either the traditional cultural concept of benevolent rule or the notion of universal humanity.

On September 11, 2004, a man fanatically slashed 28 children with a knife in Suzhou City. On the 20th of the same month, a man in Shandong Province injured 25 elementary school students with a knife. Some elementary school teachers forced students to make firecrackers by hand to raise funds for the school, resulting in an explosion in which students died.

IMPLEMENTING POLICIES

The CCP leaders have often used threats and coercion to ensure the implementation of their policies. One of the means they used was the political slogan. For a long time, the CCP used the number of slogans posted as a criterion to assess one's political achievements. During the Cultural Revolution, Beijing became a red sea of posters overnight, with the slogan "Down with the ruling capitalists in the Party" everywhere. In the countryside, ironically, the signs were shortened to "Down with the ruling Party."

Recently, to promote the forest law, the State Bureau of Forestry and all its stations and forest protection offices strictly ordered a standard amount of slogans to be put out. Not reaching the quota would be treated as not accomplishing the task. As a result, local government offices posted a large number of slogans, including "Whoever burns the mountains goes to prison." In the administration of birth control in recent years, there have been even scarier slogans such as, "If one person violates the law, the whole village will be sterilized," "Rather another tomb than another baby," or, "If he did not have a vasectomy as he should, his house will be torn down; if she did not have an abortion as she should, her cows and rice fields will be confiscated." There were more slogans that violate human rights and the Constitution, such as, "You will sleep in prison tomorrow if you don't pay taxes today."

A slogan is basically a way of advertising, but in a more straightforward and repetitive manner. Hence, the Chinese government often uses slogans to promote political ideas, beliefs and positions. Political slogans can also be viewed as words the government speaks to its people. However, in the CCP's policy-promoting slogans, it is not hard for one to sense the tendency of violence and cruelty.

VIII. BRAINWASH THE WHOLE COUNTRY AND TURN IT INTO A "MIND PRISON"

The most effective weapon the CCP uses to maintain its tyrannical rule is its system of control. In a well-organized fashion, the CCP imposes a mentality of obedience on every one of its citizens. Whether the Party contradicts itself or constantly changes policies doesn't matter, so long as it can systematically organize a way to deprive people of their naturally endowed human rights. The government's tentacles are omnipresent. Whether it is in rural or urban areas, citizens are governed by the so-called street or township committees. Until recently, getting married or divorced, and having a child all needed the approval of these committees. The Party's ideology, way of thinking, organizations, social structure, propaganda mechanisms and administrative systems serve only its dictatorial purposes. The Party, through the systems of government, strives to control every individual's thoughts and actions.

The brutality with which the CCP controls its people is not limited to the physical torture it inflicts. The Party also forces people to lose their ability to think independently, and makes them into fearful, self-protective cowards daring not to speak up. The goal of the CCP's rule is to brainwash each of its citizens so that they think and talk like the CCP, and do what it promotes.

There is a saying that, "Party policy is like the moon, it changes every 15 days." No matter how often the Party changes its policies, everyone in the nation needs to follow them closely. When you are used as a means of attacking others, you need to thank the Party for appreciating your strength; when you are hurt, you have to thank the Party for "teaching you a lesson"; when you are wrongfully discriminated against and the Party later gives you redress, you have to thank the Party for being generous, open-minded and able to correct its mistakes. The Party runs its tyranny through continuous cycles of suppression followed by redress.

After 55 years of tyranny, the CCP has imprisoned the nation's mind and enclosed it within the range allowed by the CCP. For someone to think outside this boundary is considered a crime. After repeated struggles, stupidity is praised as wisdom; being a coward is the way to survive. In a modern society with the Internet as the mainstream of information exchange, the CCP even asks its people to exercise self-discipline and not read news from outside or log onto websites with keywords like "human rights" and "democracy."

The CCP's movement to brainwash its people is absurd, brutal, and despicable, yet ubiquitous. It has distorted the moral values and principles of Chinese society and completely rewritten the nation's behavioral standards and lifestyle. The CCP continuously uses mental and physical torture to strengthen its absolute authority to rule China with the all-encompassing CCP religion.

CONCLUSION

Why does the CCP have to fight incessantly to keep its power? Why does the CCP believe that as long as life exists, strife is endless? To achieve its goal, the CCP does not hesitate to murder people or to destroy the ecological environment, nor does the CCP care that the majority of farmers and many urban citizens are living in poverty.

Is it for the ideology of communism that the CCP goes through an endless strife? The answer is "No." One of the principles of the Communist Party is to get rid of private ownership, which the CCP tried to do when it came to power. The CCP believed that private ownership was the root cause of all evil. However, after the economic reform in the 1980s, private ownership was allowed again in China and protected by the Constitution. Piercing through the CCP's lies, people will see clearly that in its 55 years of rule, the CCP merely stage-managed a drama of property redistribution. After several rounds of such distribution, the CCP simply converted the capital of others into its own private property.

The CCP claims itself to be the pioneer of the working class. Its task is to eliminate the capitalist class. However, the CCP bylaws now unequivocally allow capitalists to join the Party. Members of the CCP no longer believe in the Party and communism, and the CCP's existence is unjustifiable. What is left of the Communist Party is only a shell void of its alleged content.

Was the long-term struggle to keep the CCP members free from corruption? No. Fifty-five years after the CCP came to power, corruption, embezzlement, unlawful conduct, and acts that damage the nation and the people are still widespread among the CCP officials throughout the country. In recent years, among the total number of approximately 20 million party officials in China, eight million have been tried and punished for crimes related to corruption. Each year, about one million people complain to higher authorities about the corrupt officials who have not been investigated. From January to September of 2004, the China Foreign Exchange Bureau investigated cases of illegal foreign exchange clearance in 35 banks and 41 companies, and found US$120 million in illegal transactions. According to statistics in recent years, no less than 4,000 CCP officials have escaped China with embezzled money, and their stolen funds from the state add up to tens of billions of U.S dollars.

Were the struggles aiming to improve people's education and consciousness and keep them interested in national affairs? The answer is another resounding "No." In today's China, materialistic pursuits are rampant, and people are losing the traditional virtue of honesty. It has become common for people to deceive relatives and swindle friends. Many Chinese either are unconcerned or refuse to speak about many important issues such as human rights or the persecution of Falun Gong. Keeping one's thoughts to oneself and choosing not to speak the truth have become a basic survival skill in China. In the meantime, the CCP has repeatedly excited the public sentiment of nationalism on opportune occasions. The CCP may, for example, organize Chinese people to throw rocks at the U.S. embassy and burn U.S. flags. The Chinese people have been treated as either an obedient mass or a violent mob, but never citizens with guaranteed human rights. Cultural improvement is the basis for raising the consciousness of the people. The moral principles of Confucius and Mencius have, for thousands of years, established moral standards and principles. "If all these [moral] principles are abandoned, then people would have no laws to follow and discern no good and evil. They would lose their directions…the Tao would be destroyed."[14]

The purpose of the CCP's class struggle is continuously to generate chaos, through which it can firmly establish itself as the one and only ruling party and religion in China, using the party's ideology to control the Chinese people. Government institutions, the military, and news media are all tools used by the CCP to exercise its violent dictatorship. The CCP, having brought incurable diseases to China, is itself on the edge of demise, and its collapse is inevitable.

Some people worry that the country will be in chaos if the CCP falls apart. Who will replace the CCP's role in governing China? In China's 5,000-year history, a mere 55 years ruled by the CCP is as short as a fleeting cloud. Unfortunately, however, during this short period of 55 years, the CCP has shattered traditional beliefs and standards; destroyed the traditional moral principles and social structures; turned caring and love among human beings into struggle and hatred; and replaced the reverence for heaven, the earth and nature with the arrogance of humans conquering nature. With one act of destruction after another the Party has ravaged the social, moral and ecological systems, leaving the Chinese nation in deep crisis.

In Chinese history, every benevolent leader viewed loving, nourishing, and educating the people as the duties of government. Human nature aspires to kindness, and the government's role is to bring about this innate human capacity. Mencius said, "This is the way of the people: those with constant means of support will have constant hearts, while those without constant means will not have constant hearts." Education without prosperity has been ineffective;

the tyrannical leaders who have had no love for the people but who have killed the innocent have been despised by the Chinese people.

In the 5,000 years of Chinese history, there have been many benevolent leaders, such as Emperor Yao and Emperor Shun in ancient times, Emperor Wen and Emperor Wu of the Zhou Dynasty, Emperor Wen and Emperor Jing in the Han Dynasty, Emperor Tang Taizong in the Tang Dynasty, and Emperor Kangxi and Emperor Qianlong in the Qing Dynasty. The prosperity enjoyed in these dynasties was all a result of the leaders' practicing the heavenly Tao, following the doctrine of the mean, and striving for peace and stability. The characteristics of a kind leader are to make use of virtuous and capable people, be open to different opinions, promote justice and peace, and give the people what they need. This way, citizens will obey the laws, maintain a sense of decorum, live happily and work efficiently.

Looking at world affairs, we often ask who determines whether a state will prosper or disappear, even though we know that the rise and fall of a nation has its reasons. When the CCP is gone, we can expect that peace and harmony will return to China. People will return to being truthful, benevolent, humble, and tolerant, and the nation will again care for the people's basic needs, and all professions will prosper.

COMMENTARY FOUR

打碎旧世界
创立新世界

ON HOW THE COMMUNIST PARTY IS AN ANTI-UNIVERSE FORCE

COMMENTARY FOUR

ON HOW THE COMMUNIST PARTY IS AN ANTI-UNIVERSE FORCE

FOREWORD

Chinese people value greatly the Tao, or the Way. In ancient times a brutal emperor would be called "a decadent ruler who lacks the Tao." Any behavior not conforming to the standard of morality, which, in Chinese, is denoted by the two characters *Dao De*, meaning Tao and virtue respectively, was said "not to follow the principle of Tao." Even farmers in revolt put out banners proclaiming "achieve the Way on behalf of heaven." Lao Zi[1] said, "There is something mysterious and whole, which existed before heaven and earth. Silent, formless, complete, and never changing. Living eternally everywhere in perfection, it is the mother of all things. I do not know its name; I call it the Way." This suggests that the world is formed from Tao.

In the last hundred years, the sudden invasion by the communist specter has created a force against nature and humanity, causing limitless agony and tragedy. It has also pushed civilization to the brink of destruction. Having committed all sorts of atrocities that violate the Tao and oppose heaven and the earth, it has become an extremely malevolent force against the universe.

"Man follows the earth, the earth follows heaven, heaven follows the Tao, and the Tao follows what is natural."[2] In ancient China people believed in complying with, harmonizing and co-existing with heaven. Humankind integrates with heaven and earth, and exists in mutual dependence with them. The Tao of the universe does not change. The universe runs according to the Tao in an orderly manner. The earth follows the changes of heaven, therefore it has four distinct seasons. By respecting heaven and the earth, humankind enjoys a harmonious life of gratitude and blessings. This is reflected in the expression "heaven's favorable timing, earth's advantageous terrain, and harmony among the people."[3] According to Chinese thought, astronomy, geography, the calendar system, medicine, literature, and even social structures all follow this understanding.

But the Communist Party promotes humans over nature and a philosophy of struggle in defiance of heaven, the earth, and nature. Mao Zedong said, "battling with heaven is endless joy, fighting with the earth is endless joy, and struggling with humanity is endless joy." Perhaps the Communist Party did acquire real joy from these struggles, but the people have paid tremendously painful costs.

I. STRUGGLE WITH PEOPLE AND EXTERMINATE HUMAN NATURE

CONFOUND GOOD AND EVIL AND ELIMINATE HUMANITY

A human being is first a natural being, and then a social being. "Men at their birth are naturally good"[4] and "The heart of compassion is possessed by all people alike"[5] are among the many guidelines that human beings bring with them at birth, guidelines that enable them to distinguish right from wrong, and good from evil. However, for the CCP, human beings are animals or even machines. According to the CCP, the bourgeoisie and the proletariat are just material forces.

The CCP's purpose is to control people and gradually change them into rebellious, revolutionary ruffians. Marx said, "Material forces can only be overthrown by material force"; "Theory also becomes a material force as soon as it has gripped the masses."[6] He believed that the entire human history is nothing but the continuous evolution of human nature, and that human nature is in fact class nature; he posited that there is nothing inherent and inborn but products of the environment. He argued that a human being is a social man, disagreeing with the natural man concept postulated by Feuerbach. Lenin believed that Marxism cannot be generated naturally among the proletariat, but must be infused from outside. Lenin tried his best but still could not cause workers to shift from the economic struggle to the political battle for power. So he pinned his hopes on the Conditioned Reflex Theory put forth by Nobel Prize winner Ivan Petrovich Pavlov. Lenin said this theory "has significant meaning for the proletariat all around the world." Trotsky[7] even vainly hoped that conditioned reflex would not only psychologically change a person, but also physically change the person. In the same way that a dog drools once it hears the lunch bell ringing, soldiers would be expected to rush ahead bravely upon hearing gunshots, thus devoting their lives to the Communist Party.

Since ancient times, people have believed that rewards come from effort and labor. Through hard work one gains a prosperous life. People have contempt for indolence and consider reaping benefits without laboring as immoral. After the Communist Party spread to China like a plague, however, it encouraged social scum and idlers to divide land, rob private property, and tyrannize men and women—all were done publicly under the color of law.

Everyone knows that it is good to respect one's elders and care for the young, and bad to disregard elders and teachers. The ancient Confucian education had two parts: *Xiao Xue* (Small Learning) and *Da Xue* (Great Learning). *Xiao Xue* education, received by children below 15, mainly focused on manners regarding cleanliness, social interactions and etiquette (education on hygiene, social behavior, speech, and so on). *Da Xue* education emphasized virtue and acquiring the Tao.[8] During the CCP's campaigns to criticize Lin Biao and Confucius and to denounce respect for teachers, the Party erased all moral standards from the minds of the younger generation.

An ancient saying goes, "One day as my teacher, and I should respect him as my father for my entire life."

On August 5, 1966, Bian Zhongyun, a teacher of the Affiliated Girls High School of Beijing Normal University, was paraded by her female students on the street, wearing a tall dunce hat and clothes stained with black ink, carrying an insulting black board around her neck, in the midst of the students' drumming on dustbins. She was forced to her knees on the ground, beaten with a wooden stick spiked with nails, and burned with boiling water. She was tortured to death.

The female principal of the Affiliated High School of Peking University was forced by students to knock on a broken washbasin and yell "I am a bad element." Her hair was cut messily to humiliate her. Her head was beaten until it gushed blood, as she was forced down to crawl on the ground.

Everyone thinks to be clean is good and to be dirty is bad. But the CCP promotes "getting mud all over the body and covering your hands with calluses," and praises as good that your "hands are dirty and feet smeared with cow-dung."[9] People like this were considered to be the most revolutionary, and could attend universities, join the Party, be promoted, and eventually become Party leaders.

Humankind has progressed because of the accumulation of knowledge, but, under the CCP, gaining knowledge was considered bad. Intellectuals were classified as the stinky ninth category—worst on a scale of one to nine. Intellectuals were told to learn from illiterates, and to be re-educated by poor peasants in order to be reformed and start new lives. In the re-education of intellectuals, professors from Tsinghua University were banished to Carp Island in Nanchang, Jiangxi Province. Schistosomiasis[10] was a common disease in this area, and even a labor camp originally located there had to move. Upon touching the river water, these professors were immediately infected and developed cirrhosis, thus losing their ability to work and live.

Under former Chinese Premier Zhou Enlai's instigation, the Cambodian Communist Party (Khmer Rouge) carried out the cruelest persecution of intellectuals. Those who had independent thoughts were subjected to reform and extermination, both spiritually and physically. From 1975 to 1978, one-quarter of the Cambodian population was killed; some met their death simply on account of marks left on their faces after wearing glasses.

After the Cambodian communists' victory in 1975, Pol Pot prematurely started to establish socialism—"a heaven in human society" that has no class differences, no urban and rural divides, no currency or commercial trade. In the end, families were torn apart and replaced with male labor teams and female labor teams. They were all forced to work and eat together, and wear the same black revolutionary or military uniform. Husbands and wives could only meet each other once a week with approval.

The Communist Party claims to fear no heaven or earth, but has attempted with arrogance to reform heaven and earth. This is a complete disregard for all the righteous elements and forces in the universe. Mao Zedong wrote while a student in Hunan,

In all centuries, nations have conducted great revolutions. The old is washed away and things are imbued with the new; great changes have occurred, involving life and death, success and ruin. It is the same with the destruction of the universe. The destruction is definitely not the final destruction, and there is no doubt that destruction here will be birth over there. We all anticipate such destruction, because in destroying the old universe we bring about the new universe. Isn't that better than the old universe![11]

Affection is a natural human emotion. Affection between husbands and wives, between children and parents, and between friends is generally normal in the human society. Through incessant political campaigns, the CCP has changed humans to wolves, or even an animal that is fiercer and crueler than the wolf. Even the fiercest tigers would not eat their young. But under the rule of the CCP, it has been common for parents and children to report on each other, or husbands and wives to expose each other; familial relations were frequently renounced.

In the mid-1960s, a female teacher in an elementary school in Beijing accidentally put "socialism" and "fall down" together when she drilled her students in Chinese characters. Students reported her. After that, she was criticized everyday, and slapped by male students. Her daughter severed the relationship with her. Whenever the revolutionary struggle in her school became more intense, her daughter would criticize her mother's "new movement in class struggles" during political sessions. For several years following the mishap, the teacher's only work was the daily cleaning of the school, including its toilets.

People who went through the Cultural Revolution will never forget Zhang Zhixin, who was sent to jail because she criticized Mao for his failure in the Great Leap Forward. Many times, prison guards stripped off her clothes, handcuffed her hands behind her back and threw her into male prison cells, letting male prisoners gang rape her. She became insane in the end. When she was being executed, prison guards feared she would shout slogans in protest. They pressed her head on a brick and cut her trachea without any anesthesia.

In the persecution of Falun Gong in recent years, the CCP continues to use the same old methods of inciting hate and instigating violence.

The Communist Party suppresses human beings' virtuous nature, and promotes, encourages, and uses the evil side of humanity to strengthen its rule. In one campaign after another, people with conscience are forced into silence for fear of violence. The Communist Party has systematically destroyed universal moral standards in an attempt to completely demolish the concepts of good and evil and of honor and shame that have been maintained by humankind for thousands of years.

THE EVIL THAT TRANSCENDS THE LAW OF MUTUAL GENERATION AND MUTUAL INHIBITION

Lao Zi said,

Under heaven all can see beauty as beauty only because there is ugliness.

All can know good as good only because there is evil.

Therefore having and not having arise together.

Difficult and easy complement each other.

Long and short contrast each other;

High and low rest upon each other;

Voice and sound harmonize each other;

Front and back follow one another.[12]

Simply put, the law of mutual generation and mutual inhibition exists in the human world. Not only are humans divided into good and bad individuals, but good and evil also co-exist within a single person.

Dao Zhi, an icon of bandits in ancient China, told his followers, "Bandits should follow the Way as well." He went on and elaborated that in being a bandit one should also be "honorable, courageous, righteous, wise, and benevolent." That is to say, even a bandit cannot do whatever pleases him, but has to follow certain rules.

The history of the CCP can be said to be full of trickery and betrayal without constraint. For example, what bandits honor the most is "righteousness." Even their place to share the booty is called "the hall of righteousness for dividing the spoils." But whenever a crisis arises among comrades within the CCP, they expose and accuse one another, and even fabricate false charges to frame one another, adding insult to injury.

Take General Peng Dehuai for example. Mao Zedong, coming from a peasant background, of course knew that it was impossible to produce 130,000 *jin* of grain per *mu*[13] and that what Peng said was all true[14]. He also knew that Peng had no intention of taking his power, let alone the fact that Peng has saved his life several times when Peng fought Hu Zongnan's 200,000 troops with only 20,000 troops of his own during the CCP-KMT war.

Nevertheless, as soon as Peng expressed his disagreement with Mao, Mao immediately burst into a rage and threw into a garbage can the poem he wrote in praise of Peng—"Who dares to ride ahead on horseback with sword drawn—only our General Peng!" Mao was determined to put Peng to death, despite the nobility of Peng's life-saving comradeship.

The CCP kills brutally rather than governs with benevolence; it persecutes its own members in contempt of comradeship and personal loyalty; it barters away China's territory, acting cowardly; it makes itself an enemy of righteous belief, lacking wisdom; it launches mass movements, violating the sage's way to govern the nation. All in all, the CCP has gone so far as to abandon the minimal moral standard that "even bandits should follow the Way as well." Its evilness has reached well beyond the law of mutual generation and mutual inhibition in the universe. The CCP completely opposes nature and humanity for the purpose of confounding the criteria for good and evil and overturning the law of the universe. Its unrestrained arrogance has reached its zenith, and it is doomed to come to collapse completely.

II. FIGHT WITH THE EARTH IN VIOLATION OF THE LAW OF NATURE, BRINGING ENDLESS DISASTER

EXTEND CLASS STRUGGLE TO NATURE

Jin Xunhua was a 1968 high school graduate from the Wusong No.2 Middle School of Shanghai and a member of the Standing Committee of the Middle School Red Guards in Shanghai. He was sent to the countryside of Heilongjiang Province in March, 1969. On August 15, 1969, fierce floods rushed down from a mountain range and soon inundated the areas surrounding the

Shuang River. Jin jumped into the swift currents in order to retrieve two drifting electric wire poles for his production team and was drowned.

The following are two of Jin's diary entries[15] before he died.

July 4

I am beginning to feel the severity and intensity of the class struggle in the countryside. As a red guard of Chairman Mao, I stand fully prepared to fight head on against the reactionary forces with the invincible Mao Zedong Thought as my weapon. I'm willing to do that even if it means I have to sacrifice my life. I will fight, fight, and fight to the best of my ability to consolidate the dictatorship of the proletariat.

July 19

The class enemies in that production brigade are still arrogant. Educated youth came to the countryside precisely to participate in the three major revolutionary movements in the countryside. First and foremost, the class struggle. We should rely on the class of poor and the lower-middle peasants, mobilize the masses and suppress the arrogance of the enemies. We educated youth should always uphold the great banners of Mao Zedong Thought, never forget the class struggle, and never forget the dictatorship of the proletariat.

Jin went to the countryside with the thought of fighting heaven and earth and reforming humanity. His diaries reveal that his mind was full of fights. He extended the idea of struggling with humans to fighting with heaven and earth, and eventually lost his life for it. Jin is a typical case of the philosophy of struggle and, at the same time, undoubtedly became its victim.

Engels once said that freedom is the recognition of inevitability. Mao Zedong added "and the reformation of the world." This final touch fully brought to light the CCP's view of nature, namely, as something to be changed. The "inevitability" as understood by the communists is the matter out of their eyesight and the pattern whose origin is beyond their exposition. They believe that nature and humanity can be conquered by mobilizing subjective human consciousness to understand objective laws. The communists have made a mess of both Russia and China, their two pilot fields, in their efforts to change nature.

The folk songs during the Great Leap Forward show the arrogance and stupidity of the CCP: "Let the mountains bow and let the rivers step aside"; "There's no Jade Emperor in the heaven and there's no Dragon King on the earth. I am the Jade Emperor and I am the Dragon King. I order the three mountains and five gorges to step aside, here I come!"[16]

The Communist Party has come! So with it comes the destruction of balance in nature and the originally harmonious world.

DISRUPTING NATURE CAUSES THE CCP TO REAP WHAT IT HAS SOWN

Under its agricultural policy of keeping the grain as a key link, the CCP at will converted to farmland large areas of mountain slopes and grasslands that were unsuitable for farming, and filled rivers and lakes in China to make cropland. What was the result? The CCP claimed that the grain production in 1952 exceeded that of the nationalist period, but what the CCP did not reveal was that not until 1972 did the total grain production in China exceed that of the peaceful Qianlong reign of the Qing Dynasty. Even up to this day, China's per capita grain production is still far below that of the Qing Dynasty, and is a mere one third of that of the Song dynasty, when agriculture was at its peak in Chinese history.

Indiscriminate cutting of trees, leveling of rivers and filling of lakes have resulted in drastic ecological deterioration in China. Today, China's ecosystem is on the brink of collapse. The drying-up of the Hai River and the Yellow River and the pollution of the Huai River and the Yangtze River sever the life line on which the Chinese nation has depended for its survival. With the disappearance of grasslands in Gansu, Qinghai, Inner Mongolia, and Xinjiang, sandstorms have made their way into the central plains.

In the 1950s, under the guidance of the Soviet experts, the CCP built the Sanmenxia hydraulic power station on the Yellow River. To this day, this power station only gives a generating capacity at the level of a medium-sized river, despite the fact that the Yellow River is the second largest river in China. To make matters worse, this project has caused an accumulation of mud and sand at the river's upper reaches and raised the height of the riverbed. Because of this, even a moderate flood brings enormous losses in life and property to people on both sides of the riverbank. In the 2003 flood of the Wei River, the peak water flux was 3,700 cubic meters per second, a level that may occur every three to five years. Yet that flood caused a disaster unprecedented in the past 50 years.

There have been a multitude of large-scale reservoirs built in the locality of Zhumadian in Henan Province. In 1975, the dams of these reservoirs collapsed one after another. Within a short duration of two hours, 60,000 people drowned. The total death toll reached as high as 200,000.

The CCP continues wanton acts of destruction on the land of China. The Three Gorges Dam on the Yangtze River and the

South-to-North Water Transfer Project are all attempts by the CCP to change the natural ecosystems with investments amounting to hundreds of billions of dollars, not to mention those small and medium-sized projects to "fight with the earth." Furthermore, it was once suggested within the CCP that an atomic bomb be used to blast open a passage on the Qinghai-Tibet Plateau to change the natural environment in western China. Although the CCP's arrogance and contempt for the land have shocked the world, they are not unexpected.

In the hexagrams (*Ba Gua*) of *The Book of Changes*, China's ancestors regarded heaven as *Qian* or the creative, and revered it as the heavenly Tao. They considered the earth as *Kun* or the receptive, and respected receptive virtues.

Kun, the hexagram following Qian, is explained in *The Book of Changes* as such: "Being in the hexagram of *Kun*, Earth's nature is to extend and respond. In correspondence with this, superior persons handle and sustain all things with bountiful virtues."

The Confucian commentary on *The Book of Changes*[17] says, "Perfect is *Kun's* greatness; it brings birth to all beings."

Confucius further commented on the nature of *Kun*,

Kun is the most soft, yet in motion it is firm. It is most still, yet in nature, square. Through following she obtains her lord, yet still maintains her nature and thus endures. She contains all things, and is brilliant in transforming. This is the way of *Kun*—how docile it is, bearing heaven and moving with time.

Clearly, only in the earth mother's receptive virtues of softness, stillness, and endurance in following heaven can all things sustain and flourish on earth. *The Book of Changes* teaches us the proper attitude toward the heavenly Tao and earthly virtues: to follow heaven, abide by the earth, and respect nature.

The CCP, however, in violation of *Qian* and *Kun*, promotes "battling with heaven and fighting with the earth." It has plundered the earth's resources at will. In the end, it will inevitably be punished by heaven, the earth and the law of nature.

III. BATTLING WITH HEAVEN, SUPPRESSING FAITH AND REJECTING BELIEF IN GOD

HOW CAN A LIMITED LIFE UNDERSTAND LIMITLESS SPACE-TIME?

Einstein's son, Edward, once asked him why he was so famous. Einstein, pointing at a blind beetle on a leather ball, replied that it did not know the path it crawled is curved, but "Einstein knows." Einstein's answer truly has deep implications. A Chinese saying conveys a similar meaning, "You do not know the true face of Mountain Lu precisely because you are in the mountain." To understand a system, one must step out of that system to observe it. However, using limited notions to observe the limitless space-time of the universe, mankind will never be able to understand the complete make-up of the universe, and thus the universe will remain forever a mystery for humankind.

The realm non-traversable by science belongs to spirituality or metaphysics, which falls naturally in the realm of faith.

Faith, a mental activity that involves experience and the understanding of life, space-time and the universe, lies beyond that which can be managed by a political party. "Render therefore unto Caesar the things that are Caesar's, and unto God the things that are

God's."[18] However, based on its pitiful and absurd understanding of the universe and life, the Communist Party calls everything outside of it own theories "superstitions," and subjects believers of God to brainwashing and conversion. Those unwilling to change their faith have been insulted or even killed.

Real scientists hold a very broad outlook of the universe, and will not deny the unlimited "unknown" with an individual's limited notions. The renowned scientist Newton, in his seminal book *Principles of Mathematics* published in 1678, explained in detail the principles of mechanics, tidal formation, and planetary movement, and calculated the movements of the solar system. Newton, who was so eminently accomplished, said repeatedly that his book offered a mere description of surface phenomena, and that he absolutely did not dare to speak about the real meaning of the ultimate God in creating the universe. In the second edition of *Principles of Mathematics*, in expressing his faith Newton wrote, "This most beautiful system of the sun, planets, and comets could only proceed from the counsel and dominion of an intelligent and powerful being... As a blind man has no idea of colors, so we have no idea of the manner by which the all-wise God perceives and understands all things."

Let us put aside the questions of whether there are heavenly kingdoms that transcend this space-time and whether those seeking the Way can return to their divine origins and true selves. One thing we can all agree on: Followers of a righteous faith all believe in the causal relationship that goodness begets goodness and that evil will be punished. Righteous faiths play a very important role in maintaining human morality at a certain level. From Aristotle to Einstein, many believe in the existence of a prevailing law in the universe. Humanity has never stopped probing for the truth of the universe through various means. In addition to scientific exploration, why cannot religion, faith, and cultivation be accepted as other approaches through which to uncover universal truth?

THE CCP DESTROYS HUMANITY'S RIGHTEOUS FAITH

All nations have historically believed in God. Precisely because of belief in God and the karmic causality of good and evil, humans would restrain themselves and maintain the moral standard of the society. At all times and across the world, the orthodox religions in the west and Confucianism, Buddhism, and Taoism in the east have all taught people that true happiness comes from having faith in God, worshipping heaven, being compassionate, cherishing what one has, being grateful for one's blessings, and paying back others' kindness.

A guiding premise of communism has been atheism—the belief that there is no Buddha, no Tao, no past lives, no afterlife, and no causal retribution. Therefore, communists in different countries have all told the poor and the lumpen proletariat[19] that they do not need to believe in God; they do not need to pay for what they do; and they do not need to abide by the laws and behave themselves. On the contrary, they should use trickery and violence to acquire wealth.

In ancient China, emperors, considered to be of supreme nobility, still placed themselves below heaven, calling themselves "sons of heaven." Controlled and restrained by "heaven's will," they would, from time to time, issue imperial edicts to blame themselves and repent to heaven. The communists, however, take it upon themselves to represent the will of heaven. Unrestricted by laws or heaven, they are free to do anything they want. As a result, they have created one hell after another on earth.

Marx, the patriarch of communism, believed that religion is the spiritual opium for the people. He was afraid that people would believe in divinity and God and refuse to accept his communism. The very first chapter of Engels's *Dialectics of Nature* contains a criticism of Mendeleyev and his group's study of mysticism.

Engels stated that everything during or before the Middle Ages had to justify its existence before the trial of human rationality. As he made this remark, he regarded himself and Marx to be judges in such a trial. Mikhail Bakunin, an anarchist and friend of Marx, commented on Marx this way, "He appeared to be God to people. He cannot tolerate anyone else as God except himself. He wanted people to worship him as they would God, and pay homage to him as their idol. Otherwise, he would subject them to verbal attack or persecution."

Traditional orthodox faith constitutes natural obstacles to communist arrogance.

The CCP has lost all composure in its frantic persecution of religion. During the Cultural Revolution, numerous temples and mosques were torn down, and monks were paraded in humiliation through the streets. In Tibet, 90 percent of the temples were damaged. Even today, the CCP continues religious persecution, jailing tens of thousands of house church Christians. Gong Pinmei, a Catholic priest in Shanghai, was imprisoned for more than 30 years by the CCP. He came to the US in the 1980s. Before he died at an age over 90, he made a will that said, "Move my grave back to Shanghai when the CCP no longer rules China." In more than 30 years of solitary confinement because of his belief, the CCP pressured him many times to renounce his faith and to accept the leadership of the CCP's Three-Self Patriotic Committee[20] in exchange for his release.

In recent years, the CCP's crackdown on Falun Gong practitioners, who stand for the principles of Truthfulness, Compassion, and Tolerance, has been an extension of its doctrine of "battling with heaven," as well as an inevitable outcome of its forcing people against their will.

The atheist communists attempt to channel and control people's belief in God; they derive joy from battling with heaven. Their absurdity cannot be described in words; descriptions such as arrogance or hubris cannot even begin to depict a fraction of it.

CONCLUSION

In practice, communism has completely failed across the globe. Jiang Zemin, a former leader of the last major communist regime in the world, said to a correspondent of *The Washington Post* in March 2001, "When I was young I thought communism would come very quickly, but now I don't feel like this."[21] At present those who truly believe in communism are few and far between.

The communist movement is destined to fail since it violates the law of the universe and runs counter to heaven. Such an anti-universe force will surely be punished by the heaven's will and divine spirits.

Though the CCP has survived crises by frequently changing its appearance and clinging to its last desperate contrivances, its inevitable doom is clear to the whole world. Shedding its beguiling masks one by one, the CCP is revealing its true nature of greed, brutality, shamelessness, wickedness and opposition to the universe. But it continues to control people's minds, twist human ethics and thus bring ravages to human morality, peace and progress.

The vast universe carries with it the irrefutable will of heaven, which can also be called the will of the divine, or the law and force of nature. Humanity will have a future only if it respects heaven's will, follows the course of nature, observes the law of the universe, and loves all beings under heaven.

COMMENTARY FIVE

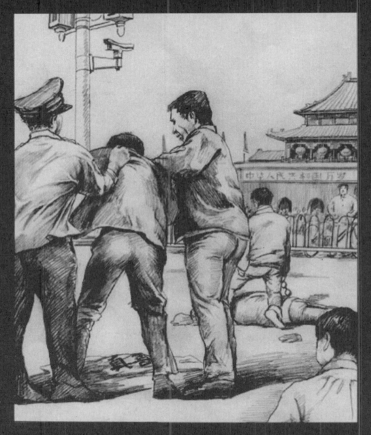

ON THE COLLUSION OF JIANG ZEMIN
AND THE CHINESE COMMUNIST PARTY
TO PERSECUTE FALUN GONG

COMMENTARY FIVE

ON THE COLLUSION OF JIANG ZEMIN AND THE COMMUNIST PARTY TO PERSECUTE FALUN GONG

FOREWORD

Ms. Zhang Fuzhen, about 38 years old, was an employee of Xianhe Park, Pingdu City, Shandong Province, China. She went to Beijing to appeal for Falun Gong in November 2000 and was later abducted by the authorities. According to people with knowledge of the case, the police tortured and humiliated Zhang Fuzhen, stripping her naked and shaving her whole head. They tied her to a bed with her four limbs stretched out, and she therefore was forced to relieve herself on the bed. Later, the police gave her an injection of an unknown poisonous drug. After the injection, Zhang was in so much pain that she nearly went insane. She struggled in great pain on the bed until she died. The whole process was witnessed by the local officials of the 610 Office. (From a July 23, 2004 report on the Clearwisdom website.)[1]

Ms. Yang Lirong, 34, was from Beimen Street, Dingzhou City, Baoding Prefecture, Hebei Province. Her family was often harassed and intimidated by the police because she practiced Falun Gong. On February 8, 2002, after a nighttime police raid, Ms. Yang's husband, a driver in the Bureau of Standards and Meteorology, was traumatized and afraid of losing his job. He could not withstand the tremendous pressure the authorities exerted on him. Early the next morning, taking advantage of the time when their elderly parents had stepped out of the house, he strangled his wife. Yang Lirong died tragically, leaving behind a 10-year-old son. Soon afterwards, her husband reported the

119

incident to the authorities, and the police hurried to the scene to conduct an autopsy on Ms. Yang's body, which was still warm. They removed many organs from her body while the organs were still radiating heat and blood gushed out. A Dingzhou Public Security Bureau staff member said, "This is no autopsy; it is vivisection!" (From a September 25, 2004 report on the Clearwisdom website)[2]

In the Wanjia Forced Labor Camp in Heilongjiang Province, a woman who was about 7 months pregnant was hung up from a beam. Both of her hands were tied with a coarse rope that was hung over a pulley attached to the beam. The stool that supported her was removed, and she was suspended in the air. The beam was 3 to 4 meters (10 to 12 feet) above the ground. The rope went through the pulley, and one end of the rope was held by the prison guards. When the guards pulled on the rope, she would be suspended in the air; as soon as the police let go of the rope, she would quickly fall to the ground. This pregnant woman suffered painful torture like this until she had a miscarriage. Even crueler was that her husband was forced to watch his wife endure the torture (from a November 15, 2004 report on the Minghui website, an interview with Ms. Wang Yuzhi who was tortured for over 100 days in the Wanjia Forced Labor Camp).[3]

These startling tragedies occurred in modern-day China. They happened to Falun Gong practitioners, who are being brutally persecuted, and they are just a few of the countless torture cases that have taken place over the past five years of continuous persecution.

Since China began economic reforms in the late 1970s, the CCP has endeavored to build a positive, liberal image in the international community. However, the persecution of Falun Gong over the last five years, which has been bloody, irrational, widespread, vehement and brutal, has enabled the international community to once again witness the true face of the CCP and the biggest disgrace on the CCP's human rights record. The general public in China, under the delusion that the CCP has been improving and progressing, has become used to blaming the low morality of the police for the atrocities committed by the Chinese legal system and law enforcement. However, the brutal, systematic persecution of Falun Gong is ubiquitous throughout every level of Chinese society and has completely burst the illusion of improved human rights. Many people are now pondering how such a bloody and outrageous persecution could have happened in China. The social order was stabilized after the chaos of the Cultural Revolution 20 years ago. Why has China entered another similar cycle of nightmarish events? Why is Falun Gong, which upholds the principles of "Truthfulness, Compassion and Tolerance" and has been promulgated in over 60 countries worldwide, being persecuted only in China, not anywhere else in the world? In this persecution, what is the relationship between Jiang Zemin and the CCP?

Jiang Zemin lacks both ability and moral integrity. Without a finely-tuned machine of violence like the CCP, which is based on slaughter and lies, he would never have been capable of launching this genocide, a genocide that is widespread throughout China and that even penetrates overseas. Similarly, the CCP would not have easily gone against the current of the historic trends and the environment created by the CCP's recent economic reforms and attempts to connect to the world; only a self-willed dictator like Jiang Zemin who was determined to have his way could make this happen. The collusion and resonance between Jiang Zemin and the evil specter of the CCP have amplified the atrocities of the persecution to an unprecedented level. It is similar to how the resonance between the sound of a mountain climber's equipment on accumulated snow can cause an avalanche and bring about disastrous consequences.

I. SIMILAR BACKGROUNDS GENERATE THE SAME SENSE OF CRISIS

Jiang Zemin was born in the restless year of 1926. Just as the CCP conceals its bloody history, Jiang Zemin, in front of the Party and the Chinese people, has also covered up his history of being a traitor to China.

In the year when Jiang Zemin was 17, the worldwide anti-fascist war was in full swing. While patriotic youths went one after another to the frontline to fight Japan and save China, Jiang Zemin chose to pursue higher education. In 1942 he attended the Central University in Nanjing established by the puppet regime of Wang Jingwei under the control of the Japanese. Investigations from various sources suggest the true reason was that Jiang Zemin's biological father, Jiang Shijun, was once a high-ranking officer in the anti-China propaganda department of the Japanese army after Japan occupied Jiangsu Province during its invasion of China. Jiang Shijun was truly a traitor to China.

In terms of betrayal and treachery, Jiang Zemin and the CCP are the same: they are so devoid of feelings and affection for the Chinese people that they dare recklessly to kill innocent people.

In order to infiltrate the CCP to raise his own wealth and rank after the CCP won the civil war, Jiang Zemin fabricated the lie that he was adopted and raised by his uncle Jiang Shangqing, who had joined the CCP at an early age and was later shot dead by bandits.

Because of his fabricated family history, he was able to be promoted from a low-ranking official to deputy minister of the Electronics Industry in only a few years time. Jiang's promotion was not due to his ability, but to personal connections and favors. In his tenure as the CCP Secretary of the City of Shanghai, Jiang Zemin spared no effort in currying favor with CCP magnates like Li Xiannian and Chen Yun[4] who came to Shanghai every year for the Spring Festival. Even as the party secretary of the City of Shanghai, he once stood and waited in the deep snow for several hours in order personally to deliver a birthday cake to Li Xiannian.

The Tiananmen Square massacre on June 4, 1989 was another turning point in Jiang Zemin's life. He became the general secretary of the CCP through suppressing a liberal newspaper, the *World Economic Herald,* putting the leader of the People's Congress, Wan Li, under house arrest, and supporting the massacre. Even before the massacre took place, Jiang Zemin had delivered a secret letter to Deng Xiaoping, requesting that "resolute measures" be taken against the students; otherwise "both the nation and the Party would be subjugated." Over the past 15 years, Jiang has conducted wanton suppression and killing of all dissidents and groups who hold independent beliefs, in the name of "stability as the overriding priority."

Since both Russia and China started to survey their common border in 1991, Jiang Zemin has fully acknowledged the results of the invasions of China by the Tsar and the former Soviet Union, and completely accepted all the unequal treaties between Russia and China since the Aigun Treaty. Chinese lands covering over one million square kilometers have thus been permanently forfeited by him.

With Jiang Zemin's personal history, pretending to be the orphan of a CCP martyr while in fact he was the eldest son of a Chinese traitor, he personally followed the CCP's example of deceit; with his support of the June 4 massacre and suppression of democratic movements and religious beliefs, he has personally adopted the CCP's practice of killing; just as the CCP used to be under the Soviet Union's command as a Far East branch of the Communist International so Jiang Zemin now gives out land for free; he is practiced in the betrayal so characteristic of the CCP.

Jiang Zemin and the CCP share similar disgraceful origins and history. Because of this, both share an acute sense of insecurity regarding their power.

II. BOTH JIANG ZEMIN AND THE CCP EQUALLY FEAR TRUTHFULNESS, COMPASSION AND TOLERANCE

The history of the international communist movement was written with the blood of hundreds of millions of people. Nearly every communist country went through a process similar to the counter-revolutionary suppression by Stalin in the former Soviet Union. Millions or even tens of millions of innocent people were slaughtered. In the 1990s, the former Soviet Union dissolved and Eastern Europe went through drastic changes. The communist bloc lost more than half of its territory overnight. The CCP learned from this lesson and realized that stopping suppression and allowing the right to free speech was the equivalent to seeking its own doom. If people were allowed to express themselves freely, how could the CCP cover up its bloody atrocities? How could it justify its deceptive ideology? If suppression was stopped and people were free of threats and fears, wouldn't they dare to choose a lifestyle and a belief other than communism? Then, how would the Communist Party maintain the social basis essential to its survival?

The CCP remains essentially the same regardless of any surface changes it might have made. After the June 4 massacre, Jiang Zemin cried out to "eliminate any unstable factors in their embryonic stage." Extremely afraid, he concluded that he would never give up lying to the public, and he would continue to suppress the people until they were completely immobilized.

During this period Falun Gong was introduced in China. At first, Falun Gong was regarded by many as a type of qigong[5] with an especially powerful ability to keep people healthy and fit. Later, people gradually realized the essence of Falun Gong was not its five easy exercises. Instead, Falun Gong's essence is to teach people to become better based upon the principles of Truthfulness, Compassion and Tolerance.

FALUN GONG TEACHES "TRUTHFULNESS, COMPASSION AND TOLERANCE;" THE COMMUNIST PARTY BREWS "FALSEHOOD, HATRED AND STRUGGLE"

Falun Gong promotes "Truthfulness," including only telling the truth and doing truthful things. The CCP relies on lies to brainwash people. If everyone began telling the truth, the public would learn that the CCP grew by ingratiating itself with the Soviet Union, murdering, kidnapping, taking flight when convenient, planting opium, usurping the cause of fighting against the Japanese invasion, and so on. The CCP once claimed, "Nothing significant can be accomplished without lying." After the CCP seized power, it initiated successive political movements and incurred countless bloody debts. Promoting truthfulness would thus spell certain doom to the CCP.

Falun Gong promotes "Compassion," including considering others first and being kind to others in all circumstances. The CCP has always advocated "brutal struggle and merciless crackdown." The CCP's model hero, Lei Feng, once said, "We should treat our enemies mercilessly, being as cold as the severe winter." Actually, the CCP treated not only their enemies like that, they haven't treated their own members any better. The founders of the Communist Party, the supreme commanders and marshals, and even a chairman of the country were all mercilessly interrogated, brutally beaten and miserably tortured by their own Party. The slaughter of the so-called "class enemies" was so brutal it could make one's hair stand on end. If "compassion" had dominated society, the mass movements based upon "vice," as initiated by the Communist Party, would have never been able to take place.

The *Communist Manifesto* states "the history of all hitherto existing society is the history of class struggle." This represents the Communist Party's concept of history and the world. Falun Gong promotes searching inside oneself for one's own shortcomings in the face of conflict. This introspective and self-restrained outlook is the complete opposite of the CCP's philosophy of struggle and attack.

Struggle has been the major means for the Communist Party to gain political power and survive. The Communist Party periodically initiated political movements to suppress certain groups of people in order to recharge itself and revive its revolutionary fighting spirit. The process was repeated with violence and lies, in order to strengthen and renew people's fear, so as to maintain its power.

From the ideological point of view, the philosophy that the Communist Party has relied on for its survival is completely opposite to what Falun Gong teaches.

PEOPLE WITH RIGHTEOUS BELIEFS ARE FEARLESS, WHILE THE CCP RELIES ON PEOPLE'S FEAR TO MAINTAIN ITS POLITICAL POWER

People who understand the truth are fearless. Christianity was persecuted for nearly 300 years. Numerous Christians were beheaded, burned to death, drowned or even fed to lions, but the Christians did not give up their belief. When Buddhism experienced the Dharma tribulation in history, Buddhists also behaved faithfully in a similar manner.

The atheists' propaganda aims to make people believe there are no heaven or hell and no karmic retribution, so that people would no longer be restrained by their conscience. Instead, they would focus on wealth and comfort as being the reality of this world. The weaknesses in human nature can then be manipulated, and intimidation and temptation can be used to control people fully. However, those with strong belief are able to see through life and death. The illusions of the secular world do not move them. They take the temptations of the earthly world and the threats to their lives lightly, thus rendering the Communist Party feeble in any efforts to manipulate them.

THE HIGH MORAL STANDARDS OF FALUN GONG EMBARRASSES THE CCP

After the June 4 massacre in 1989, the ideology of the CCP has gone completely bankrupt. In August 1991, the Communist Party of the former Soviet Union collapsed, followed by drastic changes in Eastern Europe. This brought enormous fear and pressure to the CCP. The legitimacy of its rule and the prospect of its survival faced unprecedented challenges as it encountered great crises both at home and abroad. At that time, the CCP was no longer able to unite its members with its original doctrines of Marxism,

127

Leninism and Maoism. Instead, it turned to total corruption in exchange for Party members' loyalty. In other words, whoever followed the Party would be allowed to gain personal benefits through corruption and embezzlement, an advantage impossible to non-party members. Especially after Deng Xiaoping's tour of southern China in 1992[6], government officials' profiteering and corruption in real estate and the stock market have run wild in China. Illegal second wives and smuggling are everywhere. Pornography, gambling and drugs have become rampant all over China. Although it may not be fair to say that there was not a single good person in the Communist Party, the general public long ago lost confidence in the Party's anti-corruption efforts, and holds that more than half of the middle or high ranking government officials are involved in corruption.

At the same time, the high moral standards demonstrated by Falun Gong practitioners, who practice Truthfulness, Compassion and Tolerance, resonated with kindness in the hearts of the public. More than 100 million people were attracted to Falun Gong and started the practice. Falun Gong is a mirror of righteousness which by its very nature reveals all the unrighteousness of the CCP.

THE CCP WAS EXTREMELY JEALOUS OF THE WAY FALUN GONG WAS SPREAD AND MANAGED

The unique way Falun Gong propagates is person to person and heart to heart. Falun Gong has a loose management structure, and anyone can come and go freely as he wishes. It is very different from the strict organization of the CCP. Despite the strict organization, the political study and group activities conducted weekly or more frequently in the CCP branches existed only in form. Few Party members agreed with the Party ideology. On the contrary, Falun Gong practitioners conscientiously followed the principles of Truthfulness, Compassion and Tolerance. Because of the powerful effect of Falun Gong on improving people's mental and physical health, the number of people who practiced Falun Gong grew exponentially. Practitioners voluntarily studied Mr. Li Hongzhi's series of books and promoted Falun Gong at their own expense. In a short seven years time, the number of Falun Gong practitioners grew from none to 100 million. When they practiced the exercises in the morning, Falun Gong exercise music could be heard in almost every park in China.

The Communist Party said that Falun Gong competes for the masses with the CCP and that it was a religion. In fact, what Falun Gong brings to people is a culture and a way of life. It is an ancestral culture and the root of Chinese traditions, which the Chinese people had lost long ago. Jiang Zemin and the Communist Party feared Falun Gong, because once this traditional morality was accepted by the public, nothing could prevent it from spreading rapidly. The Chinese traditional beliefs have been forcibly shut off and tampered with by the Communist Party for decades. It would be the choice of history to return to tradition. It would be the path of return chosen by the vast majority of people after tribulations and misery. When given such a choice, people would certainly distinguish between right and wrong and are likely to leave wickedness behind. This would certainly be a fundamental denial and abandonment of what the Communist Party has promoted. This was like striking at the mortal weakness of the CCP. When the number of people who practiced Falun Gong exceeded that of the Communist Party members, one could imagine the deep fear and jealousy of the CCP.

In China, the CCP exerts total control over every part of society. In the countryside, there are Communist Party branches in every single village. In urban areas, branch offices of the CCP are found in every administrative office in the neighborhoods. In the army, government and enterprises, the Party branches reach to the very roots. Absolute monopoly and exclusive manipulation are essential measures that the CCP takes to maintain its regime. The Chinese Constitution euphemistically termed this phenomenon as "persisting in the leadership of the Party." Falun Gong practitioners, on the other hand, were obviously more inclined to take Truthfulness, Compassion and Tolerance as their principles. The CCP saw this as nothing short of denying the leadership of the Party, which was absolutely unacceptable to the Party.

THE COMMUNIST PARTY CONSIDERS FALUN GONG'S THEISM A THREAT TO THE LEGITIMACY OF THE COMMUNIST REGIME

A true theistic belief is bound to be a significant challenge to the Communist Party. Because the legitimacy of the Communist regime was based upon the so-called dialectical materialism and the wish to build a heaven on earth, it could only rely on the leadership of the vanguard in the world, namely, the Communist Party. Meanwhile, the practice of atheism enabled the Communist Party to interpret freely what is virtuous and what is good or bad. As a result, there has been virtually no morality or distinction between good or bad to speak of. All that people have to remember is that the Party is always "great, glorious and correct."

However, theism gives people an unchanging standard of good and bad. Falun Gong practitioners evaluate right or wrong based on Truthfulness, Compassion and Tolerance. This obviously hinders the CCP's consistent efforts to unify people's thinking.

Continuing with this analysis, there are still many other reasons. However, any one of the above five reasons is fatal to the CCP. Actually, Jiang Zemin suppresses Falun Gong for the same reasons. Jiang Zemin started his career by lying about his past, so of course he is afraid of the truth. Through suppressing people, he quickly became successful and powerful, so of course he dislikes compassion. He maintained his power through political struggles inside the Party, so of course he dislikes tolerance.

From a small incident we can tell how extremely petty and jealous Jiang Zemin is. The Museum of Hemudu Cultural Ruins[7] in Yuyao County (now reclassified as a city), Zhejiang Province is a major historical and cultural site under state conservation. Originally, it was Qiao Shi[8] who wrote the signature inscription for the Museum of Hemudu Cultural Ruins. In September 1992, Jiang Zemin saw Qiao Shi's inscription when he visited the museum and his face turned dark and gloomy. The accompanying personnel were very nervous, as they knew that Jiang could not stand Qiao Shi and that Jiang liked to show off so much that he would write an inscription wherever he went, even when he went to visit the traffic police division of the Public Security Bureau in Jinan City and Zhengzhou City's Retired Engineers Association. The museum staff dared not slight the petty Jiang Zemin. Consequently, in May 1993, under the excuse of renovation, the museum replaced Qiao Shi's inscription with one of Jiang's before the re-opening.

Mao Zedong is said to have "four volumes of profound and powerful writing," whereas the *Selected Works of Deng Xiaoping* has a "cat theory"[9] with a flavor of practicality. Jiang Zemin exhausted his brain but could only come up with three sentences, yet he claimed to have come up with Three Represents. It was published into a book and promoted by the CCP through level after level of government organizations, yet it only sold because people were forced to buy it. Nevertheless, the Party members still didn't respect Jiang Zemin even a little bit. They spread gossip about his affair with a singer, the embarrassing episodes of his singing "O Sole Mio" when he traveled abroad, and combing his hair in front of the King of Spain. When the founder of Falun Gong, Mr. Li Hongzhi, who was born an ordinary civilian, gave a lecture, the lecture hall would be filled with professors, experts and Chinese students studying abroad. Many people with doctorates or masters degrees flew thousands of miles to listen to his lectures. When Mr. Li lectured eloquently on the stage for several hours, he did it without using any notes. Afterwards, the lecture could be transcribed on paper and made into a book to be published. All these things were unbearable to Jiang Zemin, who is vain, jealous and petty.

Jiang Zemin lives an extremely lavish, lustful and corrupt life. He spent 900 million yuan ($US 110 million) to buy a luxurious plane for his own use. Jiang often drew money from public funds, by the tens of billions, for his son to do business. He used nepotism to promote his relatives and minions to high-ranking posts above the ministerial level, and he resorted to desperate and extreme measures in covering up for his cronies' corruption and crimes. For all these reasons, Jiang is afraid of Falun Gong's moral authority, and even more afraid that the topics of heaven, hell, and the principle of good and bad being rewarded accordingly, as addressed by Falun Gong, are indeed real.

Although Jiang held the greatest power in the CCP in his hands, since he lacked political achievement and talent, he often worried that he would be forced out of the power amidst the CCP's ruthless power struggles. He is very sensitive about his status as the "core" of the power. In order to eliminate dissension, he plotted underhanded schemes to get rid of his political enemies Yang Shangkun and Yang's brother Yang Baibing. At 15th National Congress of the Communist Party Committee (CPC) in 1997 and the 16th National Congress of the CPC in 2002, Jiang forced his opponents to leave their posts. Yet, he, on the other hand, ignored the relevant regulations and clung dearly to his post.

In 1989, the new Secretary General of the CCP Jiang Zemin held a press conference for both domestic and foreign reporters. A French reporter asked about the story of a female college student who, because of her involvement in the June 4 student movement in Tiananmen Square, was transferred to a farm in Sichuan Province to carry bricks from one place to another and was raped repeatedly by the local peasants. Jiang replied, "I don't know if what you said is true or not, but that woman is a violent rioter. Even if it were true, she deserved it." During the Cultural Revolution, Zhang Zhixin[10] was subjected to gang rape and her trachea was cut (so that at her execution she could not shout out the truth) when she was detained in prison. Jiang Zemin would probably also think that she deserved it. We can easily see Jiang Zemin's scoundrel-like deviant mentality and cruelty.

In summary, Jiang Zemin's hunger for dictatorial power, cruelty, and fear of Truthfulness, Compassion and Tolerance are the causes for his irrationally launching the campaign to suppress Falun Gong. This is highly consistent with the way the CCP operates.

III. JIANG ZEMIN AND THE CCP COLLUDED WITH EACH OTHER

Jiang Zemin is known for showing off and employing political trickery. His incompetence and ignorance are well known. Although he wholeheartedly intended to exterminate Falun Gong out of personal spite, he was incapable of doing much, as Falun Gong is rooted in traditional Chinese culture and has become so popular as to gain a broad social basis. However, the mechanisms of tyranny employed by the CCP, perfected through numerous movements, were in full operation, and the CCP intended to uproot Falun Gong. Jiang Zemin took advantage of his position as the

133

general secretary of the CCP and personally launched the crackdown against Falun Gong. The effect of collusion and resonance between Jiang Zemin and the CCP was like an avalanche caused by the shouts of a mountain climber.

Before Jiang officially issued orders for the crackdown against Falun Gong, the CCP had already begun its suppression, monitoring, investigation and fabrications for framing accusations against Falun Gong. The evil specter of the CCP instinctively felt threatened by Truthfulness, Compassion and Tolerance, not to mention the unprecedented rapid growth of the practice. Undercover public security personnel in the CCP infiltrated Falun Gong as early as 1994, but they failed to discover any faults, and some even began to practice Falun Gong in earnest. In 1996, *Guangming Daily* violated the Three Restrictions (a state policy regarding qigong that rules that the state does not advocate, intervene in, or condemn qigong activities), publishing an article denouncing Falun Gong's ideology. After that, politicians with backgrounds in public security or with the title of "scientists" continually harassed Falun Gong. At the beginning of 1997, Luo Gan, secretary of the Political and Judiciary Committee of the Central Committee of the CCP took advantage of his power and ordered the Public Security Bureau to carry out a nationwide investigation of Falun Gong with the intention of finding charges to justify a ban on Falun Gong. After it was reported from around the country that no evidence had been found, Luo Gan issued a circular, No. 555: "Notification Regarding Starting an Investigation of Falun Gong" through the First Bureau of the Public Security Ministry (also called the Political Security Bureau). He first charged Falun Gong with being an "evil cult" and then ordered the police departments across the country to investigate Falun Gong systematically, using undercover personnel to collect evidence. The investigation found no evidence to support his accusation.

Before the CCP, an organization of an evil specter, could begin to crack down on Falun Gong, it needed the right person to initiate the mechanisms for suppression. How the head of the CCP handled the issue was crucial. As an individual, the CCP's head could possess both goodness and evil—two opposite aspects of human nature. If he chose to follow his good side, then he could temporarily restrain an eruption of the vile Party nature; otherwise, the evil nature of the CCP would manifest fully.

During the pro-democracy student movement in 1989, Zhao Ziyang, then General Secretary of the CCP Central Committee, had no intention of suppressing the students. It was the eight party elders controlling the CCP who insisted on suppressing the students. Deng Xiaoping said at that time, "(We would) kill 200,000 people in exchange for 20 years of stability." The so-called "20 years of stability" actually meant 20 years of rule by the CCP. This idea conformed to the CCP's fundamental goal of being a dictatorship, so it was accepted by the CCP.

Regarding the Falun Gong issue, out of the seven members of the Politburo Standing Committee of the CCP Central Committee, Jiang Zemin was the only one who insisted on the suppression. The excuse Jiang provided was that it was related to "the survival of the Party and the country." This touched the most sensitive nerve of the CCP and provoked the CCP's tendency toward struggle. Jiang Zemin's attempt to maintain his personal power and the CCP's attempt to maintain dictatorship by a single party were highly unified on this point.

On the evening of July 19, 1999, Jiang Zemin chaired a conference of the CCP's highest-ranking officials. He overrode the law with his political power, personally "unified" the understanding of all members present, and personally decided to launch a massive crackdown on Falun Gong. He banned Falun Gong in the name of the Chinese government and deceived the public. The CCP, China's government, and the violent mechanisms employed by the CCP were used to their full extent in an overwhelming suppression of millions of innocent Falun Gong practitioners.

If the general secretary of the CCP at that time had been someone other than Jiang Zemin, the suppression of Falun Gong would not have taken place. In that respect, we can say that the CCP used Jiang Zemin.

On the other hand, if the CCP had not incurred so many bloody debts with its scoundrel, immoral and savage nature, it would not have considered Falun Gong to be a threat. Without the CCP's complete and pervasive control over every part of society, Jiang Zemin's intention to suppress Falun Gong would not have gained organization, financing, and propaganda; or the support of diplomats, personnel and equipment; or the support of prisons, police, the National Security Department, and army; or the so-called "support" from the circles of religions, science and technology, democratic parties, workers' unions. Youth Corps Committees, Women's Associations and so on. In this respect, we can say that Jiang Zemin used the CCP.

IV. HOW JIANG ZEMIN USES THE CCP TO PERSECUTE FALUN GONG

By taking advantage of the CCP's organizational principle that the entire membership of the Party must be subordinated to the Central Committee, Jiang Zemin exploited the state machinery controlled by the CCP to serve the objective of persecuting Falun Gong. The CCP-controlled apparatus includes the army, the media, public security personnel, the police, para-military police, state security forces, judicial system, the National People's Congress, diplomatic personnel as well as sham religious groups. The army and para-military police, all of whom are controlled by the CCP, have directly taken part in the abduction and arrest of Falun Gong practitioners. The news media in China have assisted Jiang's regime in spreading lies and smearing Falun Gong. The state security system has been exploited by Jiang Zemin personally in gathering and submitting information, fabricating lies, and falsifying intelligence. The National People's Congress and the judicial system have put on the "legal" appearance and the garb of "rule of law" to justify crimes committed by Jiang Zemin and CCP, effectively deceiving people from all walks of life. They have turned themselves into an instrument for the service and protection of Jiang Zemin. At the same time, the diplomatic system has spread lies in the international community and enticed foreign governments, senior officials and international media with political and economic incentives so that they will remain silent regarding the issue of the persecution of Falun Gong.

During the Central Committee's working conference, in which the suppression of Falun Gong was ordered, Jiang Zemin claimed, "I just don't believe that the CCP can't beat Falun Gong." In planning the strategy of the suppression, three policies were put in place regarding Falun Gong practitioners: "to ruin their reputation, bankrupt them financially, and destroy them physically." A suppression campaign subsequently went into full operation.

EXPLOITING THE MEDIA TO BLOCK THE FLOW OF INFORMATION

The policy of "ruining [Falun Gong practitioners'] reputations" has been carried out by the media, which are under the absolute control of the CCP. Starting on July 22, 1999, the third day into the campaign of arresting Falun Gong practitioners across the country, the CCP-controlled news media launched a full-scale anti-Falun Gong propaganda blitz. Take the Beijing-based China Central Television (CCTV) as an example. In the remaining months of 1999, CCTV spent seven hours a day broadcasting preprogrammed footage to spread lies about Falun Gong. Producers of these programs started by distorting and falsifying speeches by Mr. Li Hongzhi, founder of Falun Gong, then threw in cases of so-called suicide, murder, and death due to refusal of medical treatment. They did everything they could to smear and frame Falun Gong and its founder.

The most publicized case was removing the word *not* from what Mr. Li Hongzhi once said at a public event, that "The incident of the so-called explosion of the earth does not exist." The CCTV program turned this statement into "The explosion of the earth does exist," therefore claiming that Falun Gong spreads doomsday theories. Subterfuge is also employed in order to mislead the public, for example transferring the offences of ordinary criminals to Falun Gong practitioners. A murder committed by the mentally deranged Fu Yibin in Beijing and a fatal poisoning by a beggar in Zhejiang Province were both blamed on Falun Gong. The CCP then uses the media to instigate hatred among the deceived public, justifying and seeking support for the unpopular, bloody persecution.

Over 2,000 newspapers, over 1,000 magazines, and hundreds of local TV and radio stations under the absolute control of the CCP became overloaded in their all-out propaganda smear campaign of Falun Gong. These propaganda programs were further spread to every other country outside of China via the official Xinhua News Agency, China News Services, Hong Kong China News Agency, and other CCP-controlled overseas media organizations. Based on incomplete statistics, within only six months, over 300,000 news articles and programs smearing and targeting Falun Gong were published or broadcast, poisoning the minds of countless deceived people.

At overseas Chinese embassies and consulates, a large number of albums, CDs, and publications criticizing and pretending to "expose" Falun Gong were on display. Special columns were set up on the Ministry of Foreign Affairs' website to criticize and "expose" Falun Gong. In addition, at the end of 1999 during the Asia-Pacific Economic Cooperation (APEC) summit held in New Zealand, Jiang Zemin completely dispensed with any pretence and handed out a pamphlet defaming Falun Gong to every one of the heads of state of more than ten countries attending the conference. In France, Jiang Zemin, in violation of the Chinese constitution, labeled Falun Gong an "evil cult" in front of foreign media in order to ruin Falun Gong practitioners' reputations.

The black cloud of oppression choking the country signaled that something as drastic as the Cultural Revolution was about to start all over again.

The most despicable incident to frame Falun Gong was the so-called "self-immolation" staged in January 2001, which was reported worldwide at unprecedented speed via Xinhua News Agency. The incident has since been criticized by numerous international organizations, including the NGO International Education and Development Agency at the United Nations in Geneva, as a government-staged action meant to deceive people. During questioning, a member of the TV crew admitted that some of the footage shown on CCTV was in fact shot afterwards. The unscrupulous nature of the oppressors is obvious. One can't help but wonder how these "Falun Gong disciples facing death unflinchingly" (referring to the self-immolators) could be so cooperative with the CCP authorities as to let them shoot the footage of self-immolation again.

No lies can survive the light of day. While spinning out rumors and fabricating lies, the CCP also has done everything in its power to block the flow of information. It has relentlessly suppressed any overseas reports on Falun Gong activities as well as any reasonable defense by Falun Gong practitioners. All Falun Gong books and other documents have been destroyed without exception. Extreme measures have been taken to guard against any foreign media attempts to interview Falun Gong practitioners in China, including expelling journalists from China, pressuring foreign news media, or forcing them to be silent by threatening to ban them from China.

As for the Falun Gong practitioners in China who have tried to transmit overseas the facts about Falun Gong and materials documenting inhumane suppression by the authorities, the CCP has also adopted extreme and brutal measures in suppressing them. Li Yanhua, a woman about 60 years old, was from Dashiqian City, Lianning Province. She was kidnapped by the police when handing out materials with information about the persecution of Falun Gong on February 1, 2001, and was beaten to death by the police. To cover up their crimes, the police said that she died from being "entranced by Falun Gong."

At Tsinghua University alone, over a dozen teachers and students were given long prison terms for handing out materials on Falun Gong. After exposing the facts about the rape suffered in detention by Ms. Wei Xingyan, a Falun Gong practitioner and graduate student at Chongqing University, seven Falun Gong practitioners in Chongqing were charged and given long prison terms.

Imposing Fines and Ransacking Homes without Due Process

The entire state apparatus of the CCP has carried out a policy of "bankrupting [Falun Gong practitioners] financially." In the more than five years since the start of the suppression, hundreds of thousands of Falun Gong practitioners have been fined amounts ranging from thousands of yuan to tens of thousands of yuan in efforts to intimidate them and cause them severe financial loss. With no justification whatsoever, local governments, work units, police stations and public security departments have arbitrarily imposed these fines. Those who are forced to pay the fines are not issued any receipts or referred to any articles of law for explanation. There is no due process.

Ransacking homes is another form of robbery and intimidation inflicted on Falun Gong practitioners. Those who have held firm in their belief have had to face unwarranted searches with the police ransacking their residence at any moment. Their cash and other valuables have been confiscated without justification. In the countryside, even stored grain and other food products have not been spared. Likewise, none of the items taken away from Falun Gong practitioners have been documented nor any receipts ever issued. Usually those who confiscate the practitioners' property keep it for themselves.

At the same time, Falun Gong practitioners have also faced the penalty of being laid off. In the countryside the authorities have threatened to confiscate practitioners' land. The CCP has not overlooked the elderly who are retired. Their pension plans have been terminated and the government has evicted them from their residences. Some Falun Dafa practitioners in business have had their properties confiscated and bank accounts frozen.

In carrying out these policies, the CCP took the approach of guilt by association. That is, if there were Falun Gong practitioners

141

found in any particular work unit or state enterprise, the leaders and the employees of these units would not receive bonuses, nor would they get promoted. The goal is to instigate hatred towards Falun Gong practitioners in society. Family members and relatives of Falun Gong practitioners also face the threat of dismissal from work, of having their children expelled from school, and of being evicted from their residences. All these measures serve the same purpose: cutting off all possible sources of income for Falun Gong practitioners in order to force them to give up their belief.

BRUTAL ACTS OF TORTURE AND WANTON KILLING

The gruesome policy of "destroying [Falun Gong practitioners] physically" has been primarily carried out by the police, procuratorate[11] and the court system in China. Based on statistics gathered by the Clearwisdom website, at least 1,143[12] Falun Gong practitioners have died from persecution in the last five years. The deaths have occurred in over 30 provinces, autonomous regions, and municipalities under the direct leadership of the central government. By October 1, 2004, the province recording the greatest number of deaths was Heilongjiang, followed by Jilin, Liaoning, Hebei, Shandong, Sichuan, and Hubei. The youngest to die was only 10 months old, the oldest was 82 years old. 38.8 percent were over 50 years of age. 51.3 percent of deaths were women. CCP officials have admitted privately that the actual number of Falun Gong practitioners who have died from the persecution is much higher.

The brutal tortures used on Falun Gong practitioners are many and varied. Beating, whipping, electric shock torture, freezing, tying with ropes, handcuffing and shackling for extended periods, burning with open flames, lit cigarettes or hot irons, being cuffed and hung up, being forced to stand or kneel down for a long time, being jabbed with bamboo sticks or metal wires, sexual abuse and rape are just a handful of examples. In October 2000, guards at the Masanjia Forced Labor Camp in Liaoning Province stripped the clothes completely off 18 female Falun Gong practitioners and threw them into the prison cells for male inmates to rape and abuse at will. All these crimes have been documented in full and are too numerous to list.

Another common form, among many, of inhumane torture is the abusive use of "psychiatric treatment." Normal, rational, and healthy Falun Gong practitioners have been unlawfully locked up in psychiatric facilities and injected with unknown drugs capable of destroying a person's central nervous system. As a result, some practitioners have suffered partial or complete paralysis. Some have lost the sight in both eyes or lost hearing in both ears. Some have experienced the destruction of muscles or internal organs. Some have lost part or all of their memory and become mentally retarded. The internal organs of some practitioners have been severely injured. Some have suffered complete mental collapse. Some even died shortly after being injected with the drugs.

Statistics indicate that cases of Falun Gong practitioners being persecuted with "psychiatric treatment" have spread to 23 out of 33 provinces, autonomous regions, and municipalities under the direct leadership of the central government in China. At least 100 psychiatric facilities at the provincial, city, county or district level have engaged in the persecution. Based on the number and distribution of these cases, it is clear that the abuse of psychiatric drugs on Falun Gong practitioners has been a well-planned, systematically carried out, top-down policy. At least 1,000 mentally healthy Falun Gong practitioners were sent to psychiatric facilities or drug rehabilitation centers against their will. Many of them were forcibly injected or force-fed numerous drugs capable of destroying the nervous system. These Falun Gong practitioners were also tied with ropes and tortured with electric shocks. At least 15 of them died from abuse.

THE 610 OFFICE EXTENDS ITS TENTACLES BEYOND THE FRAMEWORK OF THE LAW

On June 7, 1999, Jiang Zemin slandered Falun Gong without any basis at a Politburo meeting of the CCP. He classified the issue of Falun Gong as a "class struggle," labeled Falun Gong practitioners as the CCP's political enemy, provoked the CCP's reflex for struggle, and passed orders to set up the "Office for Dealing with the Falun Gong Issue" in the Central Committee. Since it was established on June 10, it was called the "610 Office." After that, 610 offices were set up across the country at all levels of government, from the highest to the lowest, to be specifically in charge of all affairs relating to the suppression of Falun Gong. The Political and Judiciary Committee, the media, public security organizations, the procuratorate, people's courts, and national security organizations subordinate to the leadership of the CCP Committee serve as the thugs and hitmen for the 610 Office. The 610 Office technically reports to the State Council, but in fact, is a Party organization that is allowed to exist outside of the established framework of the state and the Chinese government, free from any legal restriction, regulation or national policies. It is an all-powerful organization very similar to Nazi Germany's Gestapo, with powers far above and beyond the legal and judiciary systems, employing the resources of the country as it sees fit. On July 22, 1999, after Jiang Zemin issued the order to suppress Falun Gong, the Xinhua News Agency released the speeches by people in charge of the CCP Central Organizational Ministry and the CCP Central Propaganda Ministry, giving open support to the persecution of Falun Gong launched by Jiang Zemin. All of these entities cooperated under the CCP's strict organization to carry out Jiang Zemin's vicious scheme.

So many cases have proven that neither the public security departments, nor the procuratorate, nor the people's courts have the power to make their own decisions on cases related to Falun Gong. They have to take orders from the 610 Office. When the family members of many Falun Gong practitioners who were arrested, detained and tortured to death inquired and complained to public security, procuratorial bodies and people's courts, they were told that all decisions would be made by the 610 Office.

However, the existence of the 610 Office has no legal basis. When it issued orders to all organizations under the system of the CCP, there were usually no written commands or notifications, only oral communication. Moreover, it stipulated that all those who receive the orders were forbidden from making sound or video recordings or even written notes.

Using this type of temporary arm of the dictatorship is a tactic the Party has often repeated, totally ignorant of the law. During all previous political purge movements, the Party always utilized irregular tactics and set up irregular temporary organizations, such as the Central Cultural Revolution Team, to lead and spread the Chinese Communist Party's tyranny to the whole country.

During its long-term reign of tyranny and heavy-handed ruling, the Party has created the strongest and most evil system of state terror with violence, lies and information blockage. Its inhumanity and level of deceit are at a highly professional level. Its scale and extent are unprecedented. In all previous political movements, the Party was accumulating systematic and effective methods and experience to punish, harm and kill people in the cruelest, craftiest and most duplicitous ways imaginable. In one case mentioned earlier, the husband could not stand the threats and harassment by the police and killed his kind-hearted wife. This is the evil fruit of the CCP's state terror, including deceit by the media, political pressure, guilt by association, and intimidation, in order to warp human nature and instigate hatred.

USING THE MILITARY AND NATIONAL FINANCIAL RESOURCES TO CARRY OUT THE PERSECUTION

The Party controls all state military forces, which allows it to do as it wants, without fear, when it suppresses people. In the suppression of Falun Gong, Jiang Zemin not only employed police and para-military police, but also directly employed armed military forces during July and August of 1999, when hundreds of thousands and even millions of common people from all over the country intended to go to Beijing empty-handed to appeal for Falun Gong. Soldiers were assigned to places inside the city of Beijing. All main thoroughfares to Beijing were lined with soldiers carrying loaded guns. They cooperated with police to intercept and arrest the Falun Gong practitioners who went to appeal. Jiang Zemin's direct allocation of the CCP's armed forces paved the way for the bloody persecution.

The Party controls the state finances, which provides financial backing for Jiang Zemin to persecute Falun Gong. A high-ranking officer of the Justice Department of Liaoning Province once said in a conference at the Masanjia Forced Labor Camp of Liaoning Province, "The financial resources used to deal with Falun Gong have exceeded the outlay for a war."

It is not clear yet how much of the state's economic resources and the earnings from people's sweat and toil the CCP has employed to persecute Falun Gong. However, it is not hard to see that it would be an enormous figure. In 2001, information from inside the Party's Public Security Department showed that, at just the one place of Tiananmen Square, the expense of arresting Falun Gong practitioners was 1.7 to 2.5 million yuan per day, which amounts to 620 to 910 million yuan per year. In the whole country, from cities to remote rural areas, from the police in police stations and public security departments to the personnel at all branches of the 610 Office, Jiang Zemin employed at least a few million people to persecute Falun Gong. The cost in wages alone may exceed 100 billion yuan per year. Moreover, Jiang Zemin spent huge amounts to expand forced labor camps to detain Falun Gong practitioners and build brainwashing centers and bases. For example, in December 2001, Jiang Zemin expended 4.2 billion yuan to build brainwashing centers and bases to "transform" Falun Gong practitioners. Jiang Zemin also used monetary incentives to stimulate and encourage greater numbers of people to participate in persecuting Falun Gong. In many areas, the prize for arresting a Falun Gong practitioner was several thousand or even ten thousand yuan. The Masanjia Forced Labor Camp in Liaoning Province is one of the most evil places in the persecution of Falun Gong. The Party once awarded Camp Director Su 50,000 yuan and Deputy Director Shao 30,000 yuan.

Jiang Zemin, the former general secretary of the CCP, is the person who launched the persecution of Falun Gong and the person who plotted and commanded it. He utilized the mechanisms of the CCP to launch the persecution of Falun Gong. He bears inescapable responsibility for this historic crime. However, if there were no CCP with its mechanism of violence formed through many political movements, Jiang Zemin would have had no way to launch and carry out the evil persecution.

Jiang Zemin and the Party make use of each other. They risk everyone's condemnation to oppose Truthfulness, Compassion, and Tolerance for the interest of a person and a party. Their collusion is the real reason why such a tragic and absurd crime was able to occur.

V. JIANG ZEMIN BRINGS DOWN THE CHINESE COMMUNITY PARTY FROM THE INSIDE

Motivated by his personal interests, Jiang Zemin utilized the inherent evil of the CCP to launch the immense persecution aimed at innocent people who followed Truthfulness, Compassion, and Tolerance. He launched a punitive movement against a social force most beneficial and least harmful to the country and society. This persecution not only drags the country and people down into crime and disaster, but also defeats the Party at its very foundation.

Jiang Zemin utilized the Party to relentlessly employ all manner of evil means all over the world to deal with Falun Gong. Law, morality and humanity all suffered great harm, which destroys at the root all credibility for the regime's maintenance of power.

Jiang's regime employed all available financial, material and human resources to suppress Falun Gong, which caused an enormous burden for the country and society and huge pressure on the financial system. The Party has no way to sustain the doomed persecution for an extended period of time. It could only use ordinary people's savings, issue national bonds, and entice foreign investment to keep it going.

During the persecution, the Party and Jiang Zemin have devised all kinds of devious, brutal and deceitful tactics, employing its entire repertoire of treachery and evildoing in order to persecute Falun Gong.

The Party and Jiang Zemin employed every known propaganda tool to fabricate rumors, denigrate Falun Gong, and make excuses for the suppression and persecution. However, no lie can last forever. Once the lies are finally exposed, and when all the evil is revealed by the failure of the persecution and becomes known to all, their propaganda methods will no longer be able to deceive. The Party will lose its credibility and people's hearts completely.

At the beginning of the suppression of Falun Gong in 1999, Jiang Zemin intended to solve the issue of Falun Gong in three months. However, the Party underestimated the power of Falun Gong and the power of tradition and belief.

Since ancient times, the evil has never been able to eliminate the righteous. It cannot eradicate kindness from people's hearts. Five years have passed. Falun Gong is still Falun Gong. Moreover, Falun Gong has spread widely all over the world. Jiang Zemin and the Party have suffered a severe defeat in this combat between good and evil. And their devious, cruel and evil nature is fully exposed. The notorious Jiang Zemin is now beset with troubles both at home and abroad and is facing many lawsuits and appeals seeking to bring him to justice.

The Party originally intended to make use of the suppression to consolidate its tyranny. However, the result is that it was not able to recharge, but instead exhausted its own energy. Now the Party is too far gone to resuscitate. It is just like a rotten, withered tree. It will collapse by itself in a gust of wind. Any pipe dream of salvaging the CCP is against the trend of history. It will not only be in vain, but also destroy the participants' own future.

CONCLUSION

The former general secretary of the CCP Jiang Zemin is the one who launched, plotted and commanded the evil persecution. Jiang Zemin fully utilized the CCP's power, position, disciplinary methods, and mechanisms for political movements to start this persecution against Falun Gong. He bears unavoidable responsibility for this historic crime. On the other hand, if there were no CCP, Jiang Zemin would have been unable to launch and conduct this evil persecution. From the day it came into being, the CCP has turned against righteousness and goodness. With suppression as its tool of choice and persecution as its expertise, the CCP based its reign on strict mind control that follows a single, central party. By its very nature, the CCP dreads Truthfulness, Compassion, and Tolerance and regards Falun Gong as the enemy. Therefore, its suppression and persecution of Falun Gong was inevitable. While attacking Truthfulness, Compassion, and Tolerance, Jiang Zemin and the CCP gave the opportunity for falsehood, evil, violence, poison, wickedness and corruption to propagate. What followed was a widespread moral decline in the land of China, which affected everyone.

The collusion between the CCP and Jiang Zemin has tied their fates together. Falun Gong is now suing Jiang Zemin. The day Jiang is brought to justice, the fate of the CCP will be self-evident.

Heavenly principles will not tolerate those who conduct inhumane persecution against a group of good people that follow Truthfulness, Compassion, and Tolerance. The evil actions of Jiang Zemin and the CCP will also become a perpetual and profound lesson for humankind.

COMMENTARY SIX

ON HOW
THE CHINESE COMMUNIST PARTY
DESTROYED TRADITIONAL CULTURE

COMMENTARY SIX

ON HOW THE CHINESE COMMUNIST PARTY DESTROYED TRADITIONAL CULTURE

FOREWORD

Culture is the soul of a nation. This spiritual factor is as important to mankind as physical factors such as race and land.

Cultural developments define the history of a nation's civilization. The complete destruction of a national culture leads to the end of the nation. Ancient nations who had created glorious civilizations were considered to have vanished when their cultures disappeared, even though people of their races may have survived. China is the only country in the world whose ancient civilization has been passed down continuously for over 5,000 years. Destruction of its traditional culture is an unforgivable crime.

The Chinese culture, believed to be passed down by God, started with such myths as Pangu's creation of heaven and the earth,[1] Nüwa's creation of humanity,[2] Shennong's identification of hundreds of medicinal herbs,[3] and Cangjie's invention of Chinese characters.[4] "Man follows the earth, the earth follows heaven, heaven follows the Tao, and the Tao follows what is natural."[5] The Taoist wisdom of unity of heaven and humanity has coursed through the veins of Chinese culture. "Great learning promotes the cultivation of virtue."[6] Confucius opened a school to teach students more than 2,000 years ago and imparted to society the Confucian ideals represented by the five cardinal virtues of benevolence, righteousness, propriety, wisdom, and faithfulness. In the first century, Shakyamuni's Buddhism traveled east to China with its emphasis on compassion

155

and salvation for all beings. The Chinese culture became more wide-ranging and profound. Thereafter, Confucianism, Buddhism, and Taoism became complementary beliefs in Chinese society, bringing the Tang Dynasty (618-907 AD) to the peak of its glory and prosperity, as is known to all under heaven.

Although the Chinese nation has experienced invasion and attack many times in history, the Chinese culture has shown great endurance and stamina, and its essence has been continuously passed down. The unity of heaven and humanity represents our ancestors' cosmology. It is common sense that kindness will be rewarded and evil will be punished. It is an elementary virtue that one does not do to others what one does not want done to oneself. Loyalty, filial piety, dignity, and justice have set the social standards, and Confucius' five cardinal virtues of benevolence, righteousness, propriety, wisdom, and faithfulness have laid the foundation for social and personal morality. With these principles, the Chinese culture embodied honesty, kindness, harmony, and tolerance. Common Chinese people's death memorials show reverence to "heaven, earth, monarch, parents and teacher." This is a cultural expression of the deeply-rooted Chinese traditions, which include worship of god (heaven and earth), loyalty to the country (monarch), and respect for family (parents) and teachers. The traditional Chinese culture sought harmony between man and the universe, and emphasized an individual's ethics and morality. It was based on the faiths of the cultivation practices of Confucianism, Buddhism, and Taoism, and provided the Chinese people with tolerance, social progress, a safeguard for human morality, and righteous belief.

Unlike law, which prescribes hard rules, culture works as a soft constraint. The law enforces punishment after a crime has been committed, while culture, by nurturing morality, prevents crimes from happening in the first place. A society's morality is often embodied in its culture.

In Chinese history, traditional culture reached its peak during the prosperous Tang Dynasty, coinciding with the height of the Chinese nation's power. Science was also advanced and enjoyed a unique reputation among all nations. Scholars from Europe, the Middle East, and Japan came to study in Chang'an, the capital of the Tang Dynasty. Countries bordering China took China as their suzerain state. "Tens of thousands of countries came to pay tribute to China, even though they might have to be translated multiple times and clear successive customs."[7]

After the Qin Dynasty (221-207 BC), China was often occupied by minority groups. This happened during the Sui (581-618 AD), Tang (618-907 AD), Yuan (1271-1361 AD) and Qing (1644-1911 AD) dynasties and at other times when ethnic minorities established their own regimes. Nevertheless, almost all these ethnic groups were assimilated to the Chinese ways. This shows the great integrative power of traditional Chinese culture. As Confucius said, "[Thus] if the people from afar are not compliant, bring them around by cultivating [our] culture and virtue."[8]

Since attaining power in 1949, the CCP has devoted the nation's resources to destroying China's traditional culture. This ill intention did not come from the CCP's zeal for industrialization, nor from simple foolishness in worshipping Western civilization. Rather, it came from the CCP's inherent ideological opposition to traditional Chinese culture. Thus, the CCP's destruction of Chinese culture has been planned, well organized, and systematic, supported by the state's use of violence. Since its establishment, the CCP has never stopped "revolutionizing" Chinese culture in the attempt to destroy its spirit completely.

Even more despicable than the CCP's destruction of traditional culture is its intentional misuse and underhanded modification of traditional culture. The CCP has highlighted the vile parts from China's history, things that occurred whenever people diverged from traditional values, such as internal strife for power within the royal family, the use of tactics and conspiracy, and the exercise of dictatorship and despotism. It has used these historical examples to help create the CCP's own set of moral standards, ways of thinking, and system of discourse. In doing so, the CCP has given the false impression that the "Party culture" is actually a continuation of traditional Chinese culture. The CCP has even taken advantage of the aversion some people have for the Party culture to incite further abandonment of the authentic Chinese tradition.

The CCP's destruction of traditional culture has brought disastrous consequences to China. Not only have people lost their moral bearings, they have also been forcibly indoctrinated with the CCP's evil theories.

I. WHY DID THE CCP WANT TO SABOTAGE TRADITIONAL CULTURE?

THE LONG TRADITION OF CHINESE CULTURE—BASED ON FAITH AND VENERATING VIRTUE

The authentic culture of the Chinese nation started about 5,000 years ago with the legendary Emperor Huang, who is deemed to be the earliest ancestor of Chinese civilization. In fact, Emperor Huang was also credited with founding Taoism—which was also called the Huang-Lao (Lao Zi) school of thought. The profound influence of Taoism on Confucianism can be seen in such Confucian sayings as "Aspire to the Tao, align with virtue, abide by benevolence, and immerse yourself in the arts" and "If one hears the Tao in the morning, one can die without regret in the evening."[9] The *Book of Changes (I Ching)*, a record of heaven and earth, yin and yang, cosmic changes, social rise and decline, and the laws of human life, was regarded as "No. 1 among all Chinese classics" by Confucians. The prophetic power of the book has far surpassed what modern science can conceive. In addition to Taoism and Confucianism, Buddhism—especially Zen Buddhism—has had a subtle yet profound influence on Chinese intellectuals.

Confucianism is the part of the traditional Chinese culture that focused on "entering the mundane world." It emphasized family-based ethics, in which filial piety played an extremely important role, teaching that "all kindness starts with filial piety." Confucius advocated benevolence, righteousness, propriety, wisdom and faithfulness, but also said, "Aren't filial piety and brotherly love the roots of benevolence?"

Family-based ethics can be naturally extended to guide social morality. Filial piety can be extended to subordinates' loyalty to the monarch. Confucius said, "It is seldom that a person with filial piety and brotherly love will be inclined to offend those above."[10] Brotherly love is the relationship among brothers, and can be further extended to righteousness and justice among friends. Confucians teach that in a family, a father should be kind, a son filial, an older brother friendly, and a younger brother respectful. Here, fatherly kindness can be further extended to benevolence of the monarch toward his subordinates. As long as the traditions of a family can be maintained, social morality can naturally be sustained. "Cultivate oneself, regulate one's family, rightly govern one's state and make the whole kingdom tranquil and happy."[11]

Buddhism and Taoism are the parts of Chinese culture that focused on "leaving the mundane world." The influence of Buddhism and Taoism can be found to penetrate all aspects of ordinary people's lives. Practices that are deeply rooted in Taoism include Chinese medicine, qigong, geomancy (Feng Shui), and divination. These practices, as well as the Buddhist concepts of a heavenly kingdom and hell, the karmic reward of good and the retribution of evil, have, together with Confucian ethics, formed the core of traditional Chinese culture.

The beliefs of Confucianism, Buddhism, and Taoism offered the Chinese people a very stable moral system, unchangeable "so long as heaven remains."[12] This ethical system offered the basis for sustainability, peace, and harmony in society.

Morality belongs to the spiritual realm; thus, it is often conceptual. Culture expresses an abstract moral system in a language that can be commonly understood.

Take the Four Chinese Classics, the four most-renowned novels in Chinese culture, as examples. *The Journey to the West*[13] is a mythical tale. *A Dream of Red Mansions*[14] starts with a dialog among a spirited stone, the Deity of Infinite Space and the Tao of Boundless Time at the Baseless Cliff of the Great Waste Mountain—this dialog provides clues for the human drama that unfolds in the novel. *Outlaws of the Marsh*[15] opens with a tale of how Premier Hong, in charge of military affairs, accidentally set free 108 demons. This legend explains the origin of the "108 outlaw militants of prowess." *Three Kingdoms*[16] begins with a heavenly warning of a disaster, and ends with the inescapable conclusion of God's will: "The world's affairs rush on like an endless stream; a heaven-told fate, infinite in reach, dooms all." Other well-known stories, such as *The Romance of the Eastern Zhou*[17] and *The Complete Story of Yue Fei*,[18] all begin with similar legends.

These novelists' use of myths was not a coincidence, but a reflection of a basic philosophy of Chinese intellectuals toward nature and humanity. These novels have had a profound influence on the Chinese mind. When speaking of righteousness, people think of Guan Yu (160-219 AD) of the *Three Kingdoms* rather than the concept itself—how his righteousness to his friends transcended the clouds and reached heaven; how his unmovable loyalty to his superior and sworn-brother Liu Bei gained him respect even from his enemies; how his bravery in battle prevailed in the most dire of situations, his final defeat in a battle near the Town of Mai; and finally, his conference as a deity with his son. When speaking of loyalty, Chinese people naturally think of Yue Fei (1103-1141 AD), a Song Dynasty general who served his country with unreserved integrity and loyalty, and Zhuge Liang (181-234 AD), prime minister of the Shu State during the Three Kingdoms period, who "gave his all until his heart stopped beating."

Traditional Chinese culture's eulogy of loyalty and righteousness has been fully elaborated in these authors' colorful stories. The abstract moral principles they espouse have been made specific and embodied in cultural expressions.

Taoism emphasizes truthfulness. Buddhism emphasizes compassion, and Confucianism values loyalty, tolerance, benevolence and righteousness. "While their forms differ, their purposes are the same...they all inspire people to return to kindness."[19] These are the most valuable aspects of traditional Chinese culture based upon the beliefs in Confucianism, Buddhism and Taoism.

Traditional Chinese culture is filled with concepts and principles such as heaven, the Tao, God, Buddha, fate, predestination, benevolence, righteousness, propriety, wisdom, faithfulness, honesty, shame, loyalty, filial piety, dignity, and so on. Many Chinese may be

161

illiterate, but they are still familiar with traditional plays and operas. These cultural forms have been important ways for ordinary people to learn traditional morals. Therefore, the CCP's destruction of traditional Chinese culture is a direct attack against Chinese morality and undermines the basis for peace and harmony in society.

THE EVIL COMMUNIST THEORY OPPOSES TRADITIONAL CULTURE

The "philosophy" of the Communist Party completely contradicts the authentic traditional Chinese culture. Traditional culture respects the mandate of heaven, as Confucius once said, "Life and death are predestined, and wealth and rank are determined by heaven."[20] Both Buddhism and Taoism are forms of theism, and believe in the reincarnation cycle of life and death, and the karmic causality of good and evil. The Communist Party, on the contrary, not only believes in atheism, but also runs wild in defying the Tao and assaulting heavenly principles. Confucianism values family, but the *Communist Manifesto* clearly promulgates abolition of the family. Traditional culture differentiates the Chinese from the foreign, but the *Communist Manifesto* advocates the end of nationality. Confucian culture promotes kindness to others, but the Communist Party encourages class struggle. Confucians encourage loyalty to the monarch and love for the nation. The *Communist Manifesto* promotes the elimination of nations.

To gain and maintain power in China, the Communist Party first had to plant its immoral thoughts on Chinese soil. Mao Zedong claimed, "If we want to overthrow an authority, we must first make propaganda, and do work in the area of ideology."[21] The CCP realized that the violent communist theory, which is sustained with arms, is the refuse of Western thought and could not stand up to China's profound 5,000-year cultural history. "In for a penny, in for a pound." The CCP then completely destroyed traditional Chinese culture, so that Marxism and Leninism could take China's political stage.

TRADITIONAL CULTURE IS AN OBSTACLE TO THE CCP'S DICTATORSHIP

Mao Zedong once said, fittingly, that he follows neither the Tao nor heaven.[22] Traditional Chinese culture undoubtedly served as a huge obstacle for the CCP's defying the Tao and contending with heaven.

Loyalty in traditional Chinese culture does not mean blind devotion. In the eyes of the people, the emperor is a "son of heaven" with heaven above him. The emperor cannot be correct at all times. Therefore there was a need for observers to point out the emperor's mistakes all the time. The Chinese chronicle system had historians record all the words and deeds of the emperor. Scholastic officials could become teachers for their sage kings, and the behavior of the emperor was judged by the Confucian classics. If the emperor was immoral and unenlightened to the Tao, people might rise up to overthrow him, as was the case when Chengtang attacked Jie, or in King Wu's removal of Zhou.[23] These uprisings, judged from traditional culture, were not considered violations of loyalty or the Tao. Instead, they were seen as enforcing the Tao on behalf of heaven. When Wen Tianxiang[24], a well-known military commander in the Song Dynasty, was taken prisoner, he refused to surrender to the Mongolian invaders even when the Emperor tried to persuade him to surrender. This was because, as a Confucian, he believed that "The people are of supreme importance; the nation comes next; last comes the ruler."[25]

The dictatorial CCP could by no means accept traditional beliefs such as these. The CCP wanted to canonize its own leaders and promote a cult of personality, and so would not allow such long-held concepts as heaven, Tao, and God to govern from above. The CCP was aware that what it did was considered the most heinous and enormous crime against heaven and the Tao if measured by the standards of traditional culture. They were aware that as long as the traditional culture existed, people would not praise the CCP as "great, glorious, and correct." Scholars would continue the tradition of "risking their lives to admonish the monarch," and "maintaining justice at the expense of their lives,"[26] and place the people above the rulers. Thus, the people would not become CCP puppets, and the CCP could not force conformity on the thoughts of the masses.

The traditional culture's respect for heaven, the earth and nature became an obstacle for the CCP's battle with nature in an effort to "alter heaven and the earth." Traditional culture treasures human life, teaching that any situation involving human life has to be treated with the utmost care. Such a perception was a hindrance to the CCP's mass genocide and rule by terror. The traditional culture's ultimate moral standard of the "heavenly Tao" interfered with the CCP's manipulation of moral principles. For these reasons, the CCP made traditional culture an enemy in an effort to bolster its own control.

TRADITIONAL CULTURE CHALLENGES THE LEGITIMACY OF THE CCP RULE

Traditional Chinese culture believes in God and the heavenly mandate. Accepting the mandate of heaven means that rulers have to be wise, follow the Tao and be attuned to destiny. Accepting belief in God means accepting that authority over humanity rests in heaven.

The CCP ruling principle is summarized as, "Never more tradition's chains shall bind us, arise ye toilers no more in thrall. The

164

earth shall rise on new foundations; we are but naught; we shall be all."[27]

The CCP promotes historical materialism, claiming that Communism is an earthly paradise, the path to which is led by the pioneer proletarians, or the Communist Party. The belief in God thus directly challenged the legitimacy of the CCP's rule.

II. HOW THE COMMUNIST PARTY SABOTAGES TRADITIONAL CULTURE

Everything the CCP does serves a political purpose. In order to seize, maintain and consolidate its tyranny, the CCP needs to replace human nature with its evil Party nature, and the Chinese traditional culture with its Party culture of "deceit, wickedness and violence." This destruction and substitution includes cultural relics, historical sites and ancient books, which are tangible, and such intangible things as the traditional outlook on morality, life and the world. All aspects of people's lives are involved, including their actions, thoughts and lifestyles. At the same time, the CCP regards insignificant and superficial cultural manifestations as the "essence," retaining them, and then puts this essence up as a façade. The Party keeps the semblance of tradition while replacing the real tradition with Party culture. It then deceives the people and international society behind a façade of carrying on and developing Chinese traditional culture.

SIMULTANEOUSLY EXTINGUISHING THE THREE RELIGIONS

Since traditional culture is rooted in Confucianism, Buddhism and Taoism, the CCP's first step in destroying traditional culture was to extinguish the manifestation of the divine principles in the human world, eradicating the three religions corresponding to them.

All three major religions, Confucianism, Buddhism, and Taoism, encountered destruction in different historical time periods. Take Buddhism for example. It has suffered four major tribulations in history, which are historically known as the "Three Wus and One Zong" persecution of Buddhist devotees by four Chinese emperors. Emperor Taiwu of the Northern Wei Dynasty (386-534 AD) and Emperor Wuzong of the Tang Dynasty (618-907 AD) both tried to extinguish Buddhism in order to have Taoism prevail. Emperor Wu of the Northern Zhou Dynasty (557-581 AD) tried to extinguish Buddhism and Taoism together, but venerated Confucianism. Emperor Shizong of the Later Zhou Dynasty (951-960 AD) tried to extinguish Buddhism merely to use the Buddha statues to mint coins, and did not touch Taoism or Confucianism.

The CCP is the only regime to extinguish the three religions simultaneously. Soon after the CCP established a government, it began to destroy temples, burn scriptures and forced the Buddhist monks and nuns to return to secular life. Neither was it any softer in destroying other religious places. By the 1960s, there were hardly any religious places left in China. The Cultural Revolution brought even greater religious and cultural catastrophe in the campaign to "cast away the four olds"[28]— old ideas, old culture, old customs and old habits.

For example, the first Buddhist temple in China was the White Horse Temple (Bai Ma Temple) built in the early Eastern Han Dynasty (25-220 AD) outside Luoyang city, Henan Province. It is honored as the "cradle of Buddhism in China" and "the founder's home." During the campaign to "cast away the four olds," the White Horse Temple, of course, could not escape looting.

There was a White Horse Temple production brigade near the temple. The Party branch secretary led peasants to smash the temple in the name of "revolution." The over 1,000-year-old clay statues of the Eighteen Arhats built in the Liao Dynasty (916-1125 AD) were destroyed. The Beiye scripture[29] that an eminent Indian monk brought to China 2,000 years ago was burned. A rare treasure, the Jade Horse, was smashed to pieces. Several years later, Cambodian King-in-Exile Norodom Sihanouk made a special request to pay homage to the White Horse Temple. Zhou Enlai, the Chinese premier at the time, hurriedly ordered the transport to Luoyang of the Beiye scripture stored in the Imperial Palace in Beijing and the statues of the Eighteen Arhats built in the Qing Dynasty from the Temple of Azure Clouds (Biyun Temple) located at the Xiangshan Park[30] in suburban Beijing. With this bogus replacement, a diplomatic difficulty was "solved."[31]

The Cultural Revolution began in May of 1966. It was in fact "revolutionizing" Chinese culture in a destructive way. Starting in August 1966, the raging fire of the campaign to "cast away the four olds" burned the entire land of China. Regarded as objects of "feudalism, capitalism, and revisionism," the Buddhist temples, Taoist temples, Buddha statues, historical and scenic sites, calligraphy, paintings, and antiques became the main targets for destruction by the Red Guards. Take the Buddha statues for example. There are 1,000 colored, glazed Buddha statues in relief on the top of Longevity Hill in the Summer Palace[32] in Beijing. After the campaign to "cast away the four olds," they were all damaged. None of them has a complete set of the five sensory organs any more.

The capital of the country was like this, and so was the rest of the country. Even the remote county seats did not escape.

There is a Tiantai Temple in Dai county in Shanxi Province. It was built during the Taiyan time period of the Northern

Wei Dynasty 1,600 years ago and had precious statues and frescos. Although it was situated on a hillside quite a distance away from the county seat, the people who participated in the campaign to "cast away the four olds" ignored the difficulties and made a clean sweep of the statues and frescos there. … The Louguan Temple, where Lao Zi gave his lecture and left his famous *Tao-te Ching* 2,500 years ago, is situated in the Zhouzhi County of Shaanxi Province. Centered around the platform where Lao Zi lectured, within a radius of 10 *li*,[33] there are over 50 historical sites, including the Temple Venerating the Sage (Zongsheng Gong) that Emperor Tang Gaozu Li Yuan[34] built to show respect for Lao Zi over 1,300 years ago. Now the Louguan Temple and the other historical sites have been destroyed, and all Taoist priests have been forced to leave. According to the Taoist canon, once one becomes a Taoist priest, one can never shave one's beard or have one's hair cut. However, now the Taoist priests are forced to have their hair cut, take off their Taoist robes, and become members of the People's communes.[35] Some of them married daughters of the local peasants and became their sons-in-law. … At the sacred Taoist places in Laoshan Mountain in Shandong Province, the Temple of Supreme Peace, the Temple of the Highest Clarity, the Supreme Clarity Temple, the Doumu Temple, the Huayan Nunnery, the Ningzhen Temple, the Temple of Guan Yu, 'the statues of the divine, sacrificial vessels, scrolls of Buddhist sutras, cultural relics, and temple tablets were all smashed and burned down.' … The Temple of Literature in Jilin Province is one of the four famous Temples of Confucius in China. During the campaign to 'cast away the four olds,' it was severely damaged.[36]

A SPECIAL WAY TO DESTROY RELIGION

Lenin once said, "The easiest way to take a fortress is from within." As a group of children and grandchildren of Marxism-Leninism, the CCP naturally and tacitly understands this.

In the *Mahayana Mahaparinirvana Sutra*,[37] Buddha Shakyamuni predicted that after his nirvana, demons would be reincarnated as monks, nuns, and male and female lay Buddhists to subvert the Dharma. Of course, we cannot verify what Buddha Shakyamuni was referring to exactly. However, the CCP's destruction of Buddhism indeed started with forming a united front with some Buddhists. They even sent some underground Communist Party members to infiltrate the religion directly and subvert it from within. In a criticism meeting during the Cultural Revolution, someone questioned Zhao Puchu, vice president of the Chinese Buddhist Association at the time, "You are a Communist Party member, why do you believe in Buddhism?"

Buddha Shakyamuni attained supreme and complete enlightenment through "precept, concentration, wisdom." So before his nirvana he instructed his disciples to "Uphold and observe the Precepts. Do not let them down or violate them." He also warned, "People who violate the Precepts are abhorred by heaven, dragons, ghosts and the divine. Their evil reputation spreads far and wide. … When their lives end, they will suffer in hell for their karma, and meet their inexorable doom. Then they will come out. They will continue to suffer by bearing the body of hungry ghosts and animals. They will suffer in a circle like this endlessly with no relief."[38]

The political Buddhist monks turned deaf ears to Buddha's warnings. In 1952 the CCP sent representatives to attend the inaugural meeting of the Chinese Buddhist Association. At the meeting, many Buddhists in the association proposed to abolish the Buddhist precepts. They claimed that these disciplines had caused the death of many young men and women. Some people even advocated that "people should be free to believe in any religion. There should also be freedom for the monks and nuns to get married, to drink alcohol, and to eat meat. Nobody should interfere with these." At that time, Master Xuyun was at the meeting and saw that Buddhism was facing the danger of extinction in China. He stepped forward opposing the proposals and appealed for the preservation of the Buddhist precepts and dress. Master Xuyun was then slandered, and labeled as "counter-revolutionary." He was detained in the abbot's room, and denied food and drink. He was not allowed out of the room even to use the toilet. He was also ordered to hand over his gold, silver and firearms. When Xuyun answered that he had none, he was beaten so badly that his skull was fractured and bleeding and his ribs broken. Xuyun was 112 years old at the time. The military police pushed him from the bed to the ground. When they came back the next day and found Xuyun still alive, they brutally beat him again.

The Chinese Buddhist Association founded in 1952 and the Chinese Taoist Association founded in 1957 both clearly declared in their founding statements that they would be "under the leadership of the People's government." In reality, they would be under the leadership of the atheistic CCP. Both associations indicated that they would actively participate in production and construction activities, and implement government policies. They were transformed into completely secular organizations. Yet the Buddhists and Taoists who were devoted and abided by the precepts were labeled as counter-revolutionaries or members of superstitious sects and secret societies. Under the revolutionary slogan of "purifying the Buddhists and Taoists," they were imprisoned, forced to "reform through labor," or even executed. Even religions spread from the West, such as Christianity and Catholicism were not spared.

> Based on the statistics given in the book *How the Chinese Communist Party Persecutes the Christians* published in 1958, even the limited number of documents that have been made public reveal that among the clergymen who were charged as "landlord" or "local bully," a staggering 8,840 were killed and 39,200 were sent to labor camps. Among the clergymen charged as "counter-revolutionary," 2,450 were killed, and 24,800 were sent to labor camps.[39]

Religions are a way for people to remove themselves from the secular world and cultivate themselves. They emphasize "the other shore" (the shore of perfect enlightenment) and "heaven." Shakyamuni used to be an Indian prince. In order to seek *mukti*, a state in which one can obtain peace of mind, higher wisdom, full enlightenment, and nirvana,[40] he gave up the throne and went to a wooded mountain to cultivate by experiencing hardships and toil. Before Jesus became enlightened, the devil brought him to the top of a mountain, showed him all the kingdoms of the world in all their splendor. The devil said, "If you will bow down and worship me, I will give you all these things." But Jesus was not enticed. Yet the political monks and pastors who formed united fronts with the CCP made up a series of deceits and lies such as "human world Buddhism," and "religion is the truth, and so is socialism." They claimed that "there is no contradiction between this shore and the other shore." They encouraged Buddhists and Taoists to pursue happiness, glory, splendor, wealth and rank in this life, and changed the religious doctrines and their meaning.

Buddhism forbids killing. The CCP killed people like flies during the suppression of counter-revolutionaries.[41] The political monks thereupon cooked up the justification that "killing the counter-revolutionaries is an even greater compassion." During the War to Resist US Aggression and Aid Korea (1950-1953),[42] monks were even sent directly to the front line to kill.

Take Christianity as another example. In 1950, Wu Yaozong[43] formed the Three-Self Church, which followed the principles of self-administration, self-support and self-propagation. He claimed that they would break away from "imperialism" and actively join the War to Resist US Aggression and Aid Korea. A good friend of his was imprisoned for over 20 years for refusing to join the Three-Self and suffered all kinds of torture and humiliation. When he asked Wu Yaozong, "How do you regard the miracles Jesus performed?" Wu answered, "I have discarded all of them."

Not acknowledging Jesus' miracles equates to not acknowledging Jesus' heaven. How can one be counted a Christian when one does not even recognize the heaven Jesus ascended to? However, as the founder of the Three-Self Church, Wu Yaozong became a member of the Political Consultative Conference standing committee. When he stepped into the Great Hall of the People,[44] he must have completely forgotten Jesus' words. "Thou shalt love the Lord thy God with all thy heart, and with all thy soul, and with all thy mind. This is the first and greatest commandment" (Matthew 22:37-38). "Render therefore unto Caesar the things that are Caesar's; and unto God the things that are God's" (Matthew 22:21).

The CCP confiscated the temple property, forced monks and nuns to study Marxism-Leninism in order to brainwash them, and even forced them to labor. For instance, there was a "Buddhist workshop" in Ningbo city, Zhejiang Province. Over 25,000 monks and nuns were once forced to work there. What is more absurd is that the CCP encouraged monks and nuns to get married so as to disintegrate

Buddhism. For example, just before the March 8 Women's Day in 1951, the Women's Federation in Changsha city, Hunan Province ordered all nuns in the province to make up their minds to get married in a few days. In addition, young and healthy monks were forced to join the army and were sent to the battlefield to serve as cannon fodder![45]

Various religious groups in China have disintegrated under the CCP's violent suppression. The genuine elites of Buddhism and Taoism have been suppressed. Among those remaining, many returned to secular life, and many others were undisclosed Communist Party members who specialized in putting on kesa robes,[46] Taoist robes or pastor's long gowns to distort the Buddhist Scriptures, the Taoist Canon and the Holy Bible and to look for justification for the CCP's movements in these doctrines.

DESTRUCTION OF CULTURAL RELICS

The ruination of cultural relics is an important part of the CCP's destruction of traditional culture. In the campaign to "cast away the four olds" many one-of-a-kind books, calligraphies and paintings that had been collected by intellectuals were committed to flames or shredded into paper pulp. Zhang Bojun had a family collection of over 10,000 books. The Red Guard leaders used them to make a fire to warm themselves. What was left was sent to paper mills and shredded into paper pulp.

The calligraphy and painting mounting specialist, Hong Qiusheng, was an elderly man known as the "miracle doctor" for ancient calligraphy and paintings. He has mounted countless world-class masterpieces, such as Song Emperor Huizong's[47] painting of scenery, Su Dongpo's[48] painting of bamboo, and the paintings of Wen Zhengming[49] and Tang

Bohu[50]. Over several decades, most of the hundreds of ancient calligraphy and paintings that he had rescued had become a first class national collection. The calligraphy and paintings that he had spared no pains in collecting were labeled as "Four Olds" and were committed to flames. Afterwards, Mr. Hong said in tears, "Over 100 *jin*[51] (50 kilograms) of calligraphy and paintings; it took such a long time to burn them!" [52]

While worldly matters come and go,
Ancient, modern, to and fro,
Rivers and mountains are changeless in their glory,
And still to be witnessed from this trail.[53]

If today's Chinese people were still to remember some of their history, they would probably feel differently when they recite this poem by Meng Haoran. The famous mountain and river historical sites have been ruined and have disappeared in the storm of the campaign to "cast away the four olds." Not only was the Orchid Pavilion, where Wang Xizhi[54] wrote the famous "Prologue to the Collection of Poems Composed at the Orchid Pavilion,"[55] destroyed, Wang Xizhi's own grave was ruined as well. Wu Cheng'en's[56] former residence in Jiangsu Province was demolished, Wu Jingzi's[57] former residence in Anhui Province was smashed, the stone tablet that had Su Dongpo's handwritten article "The Roadside Hut of the Old Drunkard"[58] was pushed over by the young revolutionists,[59] and the characters on the stone tablet were scraped off.

The essence of Chinese culture has been inherited and accumulated over several thousand years. Once destroyed, it cannot be restored. Yet the CCP has barbarously destroyed it in the name of "revolution" without sorrow or shame. When we sighed over the Old Summer Palace, which is known as the "palace of palaces," being burned down by the Anglo-French Allied Forces, when we sighed over the monumental work of the Yongle Encyclopedia[60] being destroyed by invader's flames of war, how could we have anticipated that the destruction caused by the CCP would be so much more widespread, long lasting and thorough than that caused by any invaders?

DESTRUCTION OF SPIRITUAL BELIEFS

In addition to destroying the physical forms of religion and culture, the CCP has also used its utmost capacity to destroy people's spiritual identity formed by faith and culture.

Take the CCP's treatment of ethnic beliefs for example. The CCP considered the traditions of the Hui Muslim group to be one of the "four olds"—old thought, culture, tradition, habit. Therefore, it forced the Hui people to eat pork. Muslim peasants and mosques were required to raise pigs, and each household had to furnish two pigs to the country every year. The Red Guards even forced the second highest Tibetan living Buddha, the Panchen Lama, to eat human excrement. They ordered three monks from the Temple of Bliss located in Harbin City, Heilongjiang Province, which is the biggest Buddhist temple built in modern times, to hold a poster board that said, "The hell with sutras—they are full of shit."

In 1971 Lin Biao, the vice chairman of the CCP's central committee, attempted to escape China but was killed when his plane crashed in Undurkhan, Mongolia. Later, some Confucian quotations were found in Lin's Beijing residence at Maojiawan. The CCP then started a frantic movement of "criticizing Confucius." A writer pen-named Liang Xiao[61] published an article in The Red Flag, the CCP's banner magazine, entitled "Who is

Confucius?" The article described Confucius as a "madman who wanted to turn history backward," and a "deceptive and shrewd demagogue." A series of cartoons and songs followed, demonizing Confucius.

In this way, the dignity and sacredness of religion and culture were annihilated.

ENDLESS DESTRUCTION

In ancient China, the central government only extended its rule to the county level, below which patriarchal clans maintained autonomous control. So in Chinese history the destruction, such as the "burning of books and the burying of Confucian scholars" by Emperor Qin Shi Huang[62] in the Qin Dynasty (221-207 BC) and the four campaigns to eliminate Buddhism between the fifth and tenth century by the "Three Wus and One Zong," all were imposed from the top down, and could not possibly eradicate the culture. Confucian and Buddhist classics and ideas continued to survive in the vast spaces of society. In contrast, the campaign to "cast away the four olds" by teenage students incited by the CCP was a nationwide grass-roots movement with "spontaneous enthusiasm." The CCP's extension to every village through village-level Party branches controlled the society so tightly that the CCP's "revolutionary" movement extended without end and affected every person on every inch of land in China.

Never in history had any emperor eradicated from people's minds what they considered to be the most beautiful and the most sacred, using slanderous and insulting propaganda in addition to violence, as the CCP has. Elimination of belief can often be more effective and long-lasting than physical destruction alone.

REFORMING INTELLECTUALS

The Chinese characters embody the essence of 5,000 years of civilization. Each character's form and pronunciation, and the idioms and literary allusions composed of combinations of the characters, express profound cultural meanings. The CCP has not only simplified the Chinese characters, but also tried to replace them with Romanized pinyin, which would remove all cultural tradition from the Chinese characters and language. But the replacement plan has failed, thus sparing further damage to the Chinese language. However, the Chinese intellectuals who inherited the same traditional culture were not so fortunate as to be spared destruction.

Before 1949 China had about two million intellectuals. Although some had studied in Western countries, they still inherited some Confucian ideas. The CCP certainly could not relax its control of them, because as members of the traditional "scholar-aristocracy" class, their ways of thinking played important roles in shaping the thoughts of ordinary people.

In September 1951 the CCP initiated a large-scale "thought reform movement" starting in Peking University among intellectuals. These intellectuals were required to "organize a movement (among teachers in colleges, middle schools and primary schools, and college students) to confess their history faithfully and honestly so as to cleanse any counter-revolutionary elements."[63]

Mao Zedong never liked intellectuals. He said, "They [the intellectuals] ought to be aware of the truth that actually many so-called intellectuals are, relatively speaking, quite ignorant and the workers and farmers sometimes know more than they do."[64] "Compared with the workers and peasants, the unreformed intellectuals were not clean, and in the last analysis, the workers and

177

peasants were the cleanest people, even though their hands were dirty and their feet smeared with cow-dung..."[65]

The CCP's persecution of intellectuals started with various forms of accusations, ranging from the 1951 criticism of Wu Xun[66] for "running schools with begged money" to Mao Zedong's personal attack in 1955 on writer Hu Feng[67] as a counter-revolutionary. In the beginning, the intellectuals were not categorized as a reactionary class, but by 1957, after several major religious groups had surrendered through the "unified front" movement, the CCP could focus its energy on the intellectuals. The Anti-Rightist Movement was thus launched.

In the end of February 1957, claiming to "let a hundred flowers bloom and a hundred schools of thought contend," the CCP called on intellectuals to voice their suggestions and criticisms to the Party, promising no retaliation. Those intellectuals had been dissatisfied with the CCP for a long time for its ruling in every field (even though it was a layman in those fields) and its killing of innocent people during the movement to suppress counter-revolutionaries in 1950-1953, and the movement to eliminate counter-revolutionaries in 1955-1957. They thought the CCP had finally become open-minded. So they began to speak their true feelings, and their criticism grew more and more intense.

Many years later, there are still many people who believe that Mao Zedong only started to attack the intellectuals after becoming impatient with their overly harsh criticisms. The truth, however, turned out to be different.

On May 15, 1957 Mao Zedong wrote an article entitled "Things Are Beginning to Change" and circulated it among senior CCP officials. The article said, "In recent days the Rightists...have shown themselves to be most determined and most rabid. ...The Rightists, who are anti-Communist, are making a desperate attempt to stir up a typhoon above force seven in China...and are so bent on destroying the Communist Party."[68] After that, those officials who had been indifferent to the "let a hundred flowers bloom and a hundred schools of thought contend" campaign suddenly became enthusiastic and earnest. In her memoir, *The Past Doesn't Disappear Like Smoke*, Zhang Bojun's daughter recounted:

> Li Weihan, Minister of the United Front Work Department, called Zhang Bojun in person to invite him to a rectification meeting to offer his opinion about the CCP. Zhang was arranged to sit on a front row sofa. Not knowing this to be a trap, Zhang articulated his criticisms of the CCP. During the whole course, "Li Weihan appeared relaxed. Zhang probably thought Li agreed with what he said. He didn't know Li was pleased to see his prey falling into the trap." After the meeting, Zhang was classified as the No. 1 rightist in China.

We can cite a string of dates in 1957 that marked proposals or speeches delivered by intellectuals offering criticisms and suggestions: Zhang Bojun's "Political Design Institute" on May 21; Long Yun's "Absurd Anti-Soviet Views" on May 22; Luo Longji's "Redressing Committee" on May 22; Lin Xiling's speech on "Criticizing the CCP's Feudalistic Socialism" at Peking University on May 30; Wu Zuguang's "The Party Should Stop Leading the Arts" on May 31; and Chu Anping's "The Party Dominates the World" on June 1. All these proposals and speeches had been invited, and were offered after Mao Zedong had already sharpened his butcher's knife.

All of these intellectuals, predictably, were later labeled rightists. There were more than 550,000 such rightists nationwide.

Chinese tradition has it that "scholars can be killed but cannot be humiliated." The CCP was capable of humiliating intellectuals by depriving their right to make a living and even incriminating their families unless they accepted humiliation. Many intellectuals did surrender. During the course, some of them told on others to save themselves, which broke many people's hearts. Those who did not submit to humiliation were killed—serving as examples to terrorize other intellectuals.

The traditional scholarly class, exemplars of social morality, was thus obliterated. Mao Zedong said,

What can Emperor Qin Shi Huang brag about? He only killed 460 Confucian scholars, but we killed 46,000 intellectuals. In our suppression of counter-revolutionaries, didn't we kill some counter-revolutionary intellectuals as well? I argued with the pro-democratic people who accused us of acting like Emperor Qin Shi Huang. I said they were wrong. We surpassed him by a hundred times.[69]

Indeed, Mao did more than kill the intellectuals. More grievously, he destroyed their minds and hearts.

CREATING THE APPEARANCE OF CULTURE BY KEEPING THE SEMBLANCE OF TRADITION BUT REPLACING THE CONTENTS

After the CCP adopted economic reform and an open-door policy, it renovated many churches as well as Buddhist and Taoist temples. It also organized some temple fairs in China as well as cultural fairs overseas. This was the last effort of the CCP to utilize and destroy the remaining traditional culture. There were two reasons for the CCP to do this. On the one hand, the kindness inherent in human nature, which the CCP could not possibly eradicate, will lead to the destruction of the "Party culture." On the other hand, the CCP intended to use traditional culture to apply cosmetics to their true face in order to cover up their evil nature of "deceit, wickedness and violence."

The essence of culture is its inner moral meaning, while the superficial forms have only entertainment value. The CCP restored the superficial elements of culture, which entertain, to cover up its purpose of destroying morality. No matter how many art and calligraphy exhibits the CCP has organized, how many culture festivals with dragon and lion dances it has staged, how many food festivals it has hosted, or how much classical architecture it has built, the Party is simply restoring the superficial appearance, but not the essence of the culture. In the meantime, the CCP promoted its cultural showpieces both inside and outside China basically for the sole purpose of maintaining political power.

Once again, temples are an example. Temples are meant to be places for people to cultivate, hearing bells in the morning and drums at sunset, worshiping Buddha under burning oil lamps. People in ordinary human society can also confess and worship there. Cultivation requires a pure heart that pursues nothing. Confession and worship also require a serious and solemn environment. However, temples have been turned into tourist resorts for the sake of economic profits. Among the people actually visiting temples in China today, how many of them have come to contemplate their mistakes with a sincere and respectful heart towards Buddha, right after taking a bath and changing their clothes?

Restoring the semblance, but destroying the inner meaning of traditional culture is the tactic that the CCP has taken to confuse people. Be it Buddhism, other religions, or cultural forms derived from them, the CCP deliberately degrades them in this way.

III. THE PARTY CULTURE

While the CCP was destroying the traditional semi-divine culture, it quietly established its own "Party culture" through continuous political movements. The Party culture has transformed the older generation, poisoned the younger generation and also had an impact on children. Its influence has been extremely deep and broad. Even when many people tried to expose the evilness of the CCP, they couldn't help but adopt the ways of judging good and bad, the ways of analyzing, and the vocabulary developed by the CCP, which inevitably carry the imprint of the Party culture.

The Party culture not only inherited the essential wickedness of the foreign-born Marxist-Leninist culture, but also skillfully combined all the negative elements from thousands of years of Chinese culture with the violent revolution and philosophy of struggle from the Party's propaganda. Those negative components include internal strife for power inside the royal family, forming cliques to pursue selfish interests, political trickery to make others suffer, dirty tactics and conspiracy. During the CCP's struggle for survival in the past decades, its characteristic of "deceit, wickedness and violence" has been enriched, nurtured, and carried forward.

Despotism and dictatorship are the nature of the Party culture. This culture serves the Party in its political and class struggles. One may understand how it forms the Party's "humanistic" environment of terror and despotism from four aspects.

THE ASPECT OF DOMINATION AND CONTROL

1. *A Culture of Isolation*

The culture of the communist party is an isolated monopoly with no freedom of thought, speech, association, or belief. The mechanism of the Party's domination is similar to a hydraulic system, relying on high pressure and isolation to maintain its state of control. Even one tiny leak could cause the system to collapse. For example, the Party refused dialogue with the students during the June 4 student movement,[70] fearing that if this leak spouted, the workers, peasants, intellectuals and the military would also request dialogue. Consequently, China would have eventually moved towards democracy and the one-party dictatorship would have been challenged. Therefore, they chose to commit murder rather than grant the students' request. Today the CCP employs tens of thousands of "cyber police" to monitor the internet and directly blocks any overseas websites that the CCP does not like.

2. *A Culture of Terror*

For the past 55 years, the CCP has been using terror to suppress the minds of Chinese people. They have wielded their whips and butcher's knives—people never know when unforeseen disasters will befall them—to force the people to conform. The people, living in fear, became obedient. Advocates of democracy, independent thinkers, skeptics within the CCP's system and members of various spiritual groups have become targets for killing as a way to warn the public. The party wants to nip any opposition in the bud.

3. *A Culture of Network Control*

The CCP's control of society is all encompassing. There is a household registration system, a neighborhood residents' committee system, and various levels of party committee structure. Party branches are established at the level of the company. Each and every single village has its own Party branch. Party and Communist Youth League members have regular activities. The CCP also advocated a series of slogans accordingly. A few examples are: "Guard your own door and watch your own people." "Stop your people from appealing." "Resolutely implement the system to impose duties, guarantee fulfillment of duties, and ascertain where the responsibility lies. Guard and control strictly. Be serious about discipline and regulations and guarantee 24-hour preventive and maintenance control measures." "The 610 Office[71] will form a surveillance committee to inspect and monitor activities in each region and work unit at irregular intervals."

4. *A Culture of Incrimination*

The CCP completely neglected the principles of rule by law in modern society and vigorously promoted the policy of implication. It used its absolute power to punish relatives of those who were labeled landlords, rich, reactionaries, bad elements, and rightists. It proposed the class origin theory.[72]

Today, the CCP will affix the responsibility of the primary leaders and publicly reprimand them, if they fail in their leadership roles to take adequate measures to prevent Falun Gong practitioners from going to Beijing to stir up trouble. For serious cases, disciplinary action will be taken. "If one person practices Falun Gong, every family member will be laid off." "If one employee practices Falun Gong, the bonus of every one in the whole company will be detained." The CCP also issued discriminative policies that classified children into those who can be educated and transformed, and classified the five black classes (landlords, rich farmers, reactionaries, bad elements, and rightists). The Party promoted complying with the Party and placing righteousness above family loyalty. Systems (such as the personnel and organizational archive system and temporary relocation system) were established to ensure implementation of its policies. People were encouraged to accuse and expose others, and rewarded for contributions to the Party.

ASPECTS OF PROPAGANDA

1. *A Culture of One Voice*

During the Cultural Revolution, China was filled with slogans such as, "Supreme instructions," "One sentence [of Mao] carries the weight of ten thousand sentences, each one is the truth." All media were roused to sing the praises and collectively speak in support of the Party. When needed, leaders from every level of the Party, government, military, workers, youth league and women's organizations would be brought out to express their support. Everyone had to go through the ordeal.

2. *A Culture to Promote Violence*

Mao Zedong said, "With 800 million people, how can it work without struggle?" In the persecution of Falun Gong, Jiang Zemin said, "There is no punishment for beating Falun Gong practitioners to death." The CCP advocated total war, and "the atomic bomb is simply a paper tiger… even if half of the population died, the remaining half would still reconstruct our homeland from the ruins."

3. *A Culture to Incite Hatred*

It becomes a fundamental national policy "not to forget the suffering of the poor classes, and to firmly remember the enmity in tears and blood." Cruelty towards class enemies was praised as a virtue. The CCP taught "Bite into your hatred, chew it and swallow it down. Plant the hatred into your heart so that it sprouts."[73]

4. *A Culture of Deception and Lies*

Here are a few examples of the CCP's lies. "The yield per *mu*[74] is over ten thousand *jin*" during the Great Leap Forward (1958). "Not a single person was killed on Tiananmen Square" during the June 4 massacre in 1989. "We have controlled the SARS virus" in 2003. "It is currently the best time for human rights in China," and the "Three Represents."[75]

5. *The Culture of Brainwashing*

These are a few of the slogans that the CCP made up to brainwash people. "There would be no new China without the Communist Party." "The force at the core leading our cause forward is the CCP and the theoretical basis guiding our thinking is Marxism-Leninism."[76] "Maintain maximum alignment with the Party's Central Committee." "Execute the Party's command whether or not you understand it. Even if you do not understand, carry it out anyway and your understanding should deepen in the process of execution."

6. *A Culture of Adulation*

"Heaven and the earth are great but greater still is the kindness of the Party." "We owe all our achievements to the Party." "I take the Party as my mother." "I use my own life to safeguard the Central Committee of the Party." "A great, glorious and correct Party." "An undefeatable Party," and so on.

7. *The Culture of Pretentiousness*

The Party established models, set up examples one after another, and launched the "socialist ideological and ethical progress" and "ideological education" campaigns. In the end, people continued to do whatever they did before each campaign. All of the public lectures, study sessions and experience sharing have become an "earnest showcase," and society's moral standard has continued to take great leaps backward.

THE ASPECT OF INTERPERSONAL RELATIONS

1. *A Culture of Jealousy*

The Party promoted absolute equalitarianism so that anyone who stands out will be the target of attack. People are jealous of those who have greater ability and those who are wealthier—the so-called "red-eye syndrome."[77]

2. *A Culture of People Stepping Over Each Other*

The CCP promoted "struggle face-to-face and report back-to-back". Reporting on one's associates, creating written materials to frame them, fabricating facts and exaggerating their mistakes— these devious behaviors have been used to measure closeness to the party and the desire to advance.

SUBTLE INFLUENCES ON PEOPLE'S INTERNAL PSYCHE AND EXTERNAL BEHAVIOR

1. *A Culture That Transforms Human Beings into Machines*

The Party wants the people to be the "never rusting bolts in the revolution machine," to be the "tamed tool for the Party," or to "attack in whatever directions the Party directs us." "Chairman Mao's soldiers listen to the Party the most; they go wherever they are needed and settle down wherever there are hardships."

2. *A Culture That Confounds Right and Wrong*

During the Cultural Revolution, the CCP would "rather have the socialist weeds than the capitalist crops." The army was ordered to shoot and kill in the June 4 massacre "in exchange for 20 years of stability." The CCP also "does unto others what one does not want to be done unto oneself."

3. *A Culture of Self-Imposed Brainwashing and Unconditional Obedience*

"Lower ranks obey the orders of the higher ranks and the whole Party obeys the Party's Central Committee." "Fight ruthlessly to eradicate any selfish thoughts that flash through your mind." "Erupt a revolution in the depths of your soul." "Maintain maximum alignment with the Party's Central Committee." "Unify the minds, unify the footsteps, unify the orders, and unify the commands."

4. *A Culture of Securing a Servile Position*

"China would be in chaos without the Communist Party." "China is so vast. Who else can lead it but the CCP?" "If China collapses, it will be a worldwide disaster, so we should help the CCP sustain its leadership." Out of fear and self-protection, the groups constantly suppressed by the CCP oftentimes appear even more left-wing than the CCP.

There are many more examples like these. Every reader could probably find various sorts of elements of the Party culture from his personal experiences.

People who experienced the Cultural Revolution might still remember vividly the "model play" of modern operas, the songs with Mao's words as lyrics, and the Loyalty Dance. Many still recall the words from the dialogues in 'The White-Haired Girl,'[78] 'Tunnel Warfare,'[79] and 'War of Mines.'[80] Through these literary works, the CCP has brainwashed people, forcibly filling their minds with messages such as "how brilliant and great" the Party is; how "arduously and valiantly" the party has struggled against the enemy; how "utterly devoted to the Party" the Party's soldiers are; how willing they are to sacrifice themselves for the Party; and how stupid and vicious the enemies are. Day after day, the CCP's propaganda machine forcibly injects into every individual the beliefs needed by the Communist Party. Today, if one went back to watch the epic poem of musical dance, 'The East is Red,' one would realize that the entire theme and style of the show is about killing, killing, and more killing.

At the same time, the CCP has created its own system of speech and discourse, such as the abusive language in mass criticism, the flattering words to sing the praises of the Party, and the banal official formalities similar to the eight-part essay.[81] People are made to speak unconsciously with the thinking patterns that promote the concept of class struggle, and to extol the Party and use domineering language instead of calm and rational reasoning. The CCP also abuses the religious vocabulary and distorts the content of those terms.

One step beyond the truth is fallacy. The CCP Party culture also abuses traditional morality to a certain extent. For instance, traditional culture values faith, so does the Communist Party. However what it promotes is faithfulness and honesty to the Party. Traditional culture emphasizes filial piety. The CCP may put people in jail if they do not provide for their parents, but the real reason is that these parents would otherwise become a burden to the government. When it fits the Party's needs, the children are required to draw clear boundaries separating them from their parents. Traditional culture stresses loyalty. Nevertheless, "the people are of supreme importance; the nation comes next; last comes the ruler." The loyalty preferred by the CCP is blind devotion—so completely blind that people are required to believe in the CCP unconditionally and obey it unquestioningly.

The words commonly used by the CCP are very misleading. For example, it called the civil war between the Kuomintang and the communists the Liberation War, as if the people were being liberated from oppression. The CCP called the post-1949 period "after the founding of the nation," when, in reality, China existed long before that. The CCP simply established a new political regime. The three-year Great Famine[82] was called "three years of natural disaster," when, in fact, it was not at all a natural disaster but, rather, a complete man-made calamity. However, upon hearing these words used in everyday life and being imperceptibly influenced by them, people unconsciously accept the ideologies that the CCP intended to instill in them.

In traditional culture, music is taken as a way to constrain human desires. In the *Book of Music* (*Yue Shu*), volume 24 of the *Records of the Historian* (*Shi Ji*), Sima Qian (145-85 BC)[83] said the nature of man is peaceful; the sensation of external matters affects one's emotions and stirs up the sentiment of love or hate based upon one's character and wisdom. If these sentiments are not constrained, one will be seduced by endless external temptations and assimilated by one's internal sentiments to commit many bad deeds. Thus, said Sima Qian, the emperors of the past used rituals and music to constrain people. The songs should be "cheerful but not obscene, sad but not overly distressing." They should express feelings and desires, yet have control over these sentiments. Confucius said in the *Analects*, "The three hundred verses of *The Odes* [one of the six classics compiled and edited by Confucius] may be summed up in a single sentence, 'Think no evil.'"

Such a beautiful thing as music, however, was used by the CCP as a method to brainwash the people. Songs like "Socialism is Good," "There would be no new China without the Communist Party," and many others, have been sung from kindergarten to university. In singing these songs, people have unconsciously accepted the meanings of the lyrics. Further, the CCP stole the tunes of the most melodious folk songs and replaced them with lyrics that praise the Party. This has served both to destroy the traditional culture and to promote the Party.

As one of the CCP's classic documents, Mao's "Speech at the Yan'an Forum on Literature and Arts"[84] placed cultural endeavors and the military as the two battle fronts. It stated that it was not enough to have just the armed military; an army of literary arts was also needed. It stipulated that "the literary arts should serve politics" and "the literary arts of the proletariat class... are the 'gears and screws' of the revolution machine." A complete system of Party culture was developed out of this, with atheism and class struggle at its core. This system goes completely against traditional culture.

The Party culture has indeed rendered distinguished service in helping the CCP to win power and control over society. Like its army, prisons, and police force, the Party culture is also a machine of violence, which provides a different kind of brutality—cultural brutality. This cultural brutality, by destroying 5,000 years of traditional culture, has diminished the will of the people, and undermined the cohesiveness of the Chinese nationality.

Today, many Chinese are absolutely ignorant of the essence of traditional culture. Some even equate the 50 years of Party culture to the 5,000 years of Chinese traditional culture. This is a sorrowful thing for the Chinese people. Many do not realize that in opposing the so-called traditional culture they are in fact against the Party culture of the CCP, not the real traditional culture of China.

Many people hope to replace the current Chinese system with the Western democratic system. In reality, Western democracy has also been established on a cultural basis, notably that of Christianity, which, holding that "everyone is equal in the eyes of God," thus respects human nature and human choices. How could the despotic, inhuman Party culture of the CCP be used as the foundation for a Western-style democratic system?

CONCLUSION

China started to deviate from its traditional culture in the Song Dynasty (960-1279 AD), and that culture has experienced constant depredation ever since. After the May Fourth Movement of 1919,[85] some intellectuals who were eager for quick success and instant benefit attempted to find a path for China by turning away from the traditional culture toward Western civilization. Still, conflicts and changes in the cultural domain remained a focus of academic contention without the involvement of state forces. When the CCP came into existence, however, it elevated cultural conflicts to a matter of life-and-death struggle for the Party. So the CCP began to exercise a direct assault on traditional culture, using destructive means as well as indirect abuse in the form of "adopting the dross and rejecting the essence."

The destruction of the national culture was also the process of establishing the Party culture. The CCP subverted human conscience and moral judgment, thus driving people to turn their backs on traditional culture. If the national culture is completely destroyed, the essence of the nation will disappear with it, leaving only an empty name for the nation. This is not an exaggerated warning.

At the same time, the destruction of the traditional culture has brought us unexpected physical damage.

Traditional culture values the unity of heaven and humans and harmonious co-existence between humans and nature. The CCP has declared endless joy from fighting with heaven and earth. This culture of the CCP has led directly to the serious degradation of the natural environment that plagues China today. Take water resources for example. The Chinese people, having abandoned the traditional value that "a nobleman treasures wealth, but he makes fortune in a decent way," have wantonly ravaged and polluted the natural environment. Currently, more than 75 percent of the 50,000 kilometers (30,000 miles) of China's rivers are unsuitable for fish habitat. Over one third of the groundwater had been polluted even a decade ago, and now the situation continues to worsen. A spectacle of a strange kind occurred at the Huaihe River: A little child playing in the oil-filled river created a spark that, upon striking the surface of the river, lit a flame five meters (16 feet) high. As the fire surged into the air, more than ten willow trees in the vicinity were burnt to a crisp.[86] One can easily see that it is impossible for those who drink such water not to develop cancer or other strange diseases. Other environmental problems, such as desertification and salinization in Northwest China and industrial pollution in developed regions, are all related to society's loss of respect for nature.

Traditional culture respects life. The CCP urges that revolt is justifiable, and struggling against human beings is full of joy. In the name of revolution, the Party could murder and starve to death tens of millions of people. This has led people to devalue life, which then encourages the proliferation of fake and poisonous products in the market. In Fuyang City of Anhui Province, for example, many healthy babies developed short limbs, thin and weak bodies, and enlarged heads during their lactation period. Eight babies died because of this strange disease. After investigation, it was discovered that the disease was caused by poisonous milk powder made by a black-hearted and greedy manufacturer. Some people feed crabs, snakes and turtles with hormones and antibiotics, mix industrial alcohol with drinking wine, polish rice using industrial oil and whiten bread flour with industrial brightening agents. For eight years, a manufacturer in Henan Province produced thousands of tons of cooking oil every month using materials containing carcinogens such as waste oil, oil extracted from left-over meals, or discarded argil[87] that contained residual oils after its use. Producing poisonous foods is not a local or limited phenomenon, but is common all over China. This has everything to do with the single-minded pursuit of material gain that comes in the wake of the destruction of the culture and consequent degeneration of human morality.

Unlike the absolute monopoly and exclusiveness of the Party culture, the traditional culture has a tremendous integrative capacity. During the prosperous Tang Dynasty, Buddhist teachings, Christianity, and other Western religions co-existed harmoniously with Taoist and Confucian thought. Authentic Chinese traditional culture would have kept an open and tolerant attitude toward modern Western civilization. The "four dragons" of Asia (Singapore, Taiwan, South Korea and Hong Kong) have created a "New Confucian" cultural identity. Their soaring economies have proven that traditional culture is not a hindrance to social development.

At the same time, authentic traditional culture measures the quality of human life on the basis of happiness from within rather than material comfort from without. "I would rather have no one blame me behind my back, than have someone praise me to my face; I would rather have peace in mind, than have comfort in body."[88] Tao Yuanming (365-427 AD)[89] lived in poverty, but he kept a joyful spirit and enjoyed as a pastime, "picking asters beneath the eastern fence, gazing upon the Southern Mountain in the distance."

Culture offers no answers for questions such as how to expand industrial production or what social systems to adopt. Rather, it plays an important role in providing moral guidance and restraint. The true restoration of traditional culture shall be the recovery of humility toward heaven, the earth and nature, respect for life, and awe before God. It will allow humanity to live harmoniously with heaven and earth and to enjoy a heaven-given old age.

ON THE CHINESE COMMUNIST PARTY'S
HISTORY OF KILLING

COMMENTARY SEVEN

ON THE CHINESE COMMUNIST PARTY'S HISTORY OF KILLING

FOREWORD

The 55-year history of the CCP is written with blood and lies. The stories behind this bloody history are both extremely tragic and rarely known. Under the rule of the CCP, 60 to 80 million innocent Chinese people have been killed, leaving their broken families behind. Many people wonder why the CCP kills. While the CCP recently suppressed protesting crowds in Hanyuan with gunshots and continues its brutal persecution of Falun Gong practitioners, many people wonder whether they will ever see the day when the CCP will learn to speak with words rather than guns.

Mao Zedong summarized the purpose of the Cultural Revolution, "...after the chaos the world reaches peace, but in 7 or 8 years, the chaos needs to happen again."[1] In other words, there should be a political revolution every 7 or 8 years and a crowd of people needs to be killed every 7 or 8 years.

A supporting ideology and practical requirements lie behind the CCP's slaughters.

Ideologically, the CCP believes in the "dictatorship of the proletariat" and "continuous revolution under the dictatorship of the proletariat." Therefore, after the CCP took over China, it killed the landowners to resolve problems with production relationships in rural areas. It killed the capitalists to reach the goal of commercial and industrial reform and solve the production relationships in the cities. After these two classes were eliminated, the problems related to the economic base were basically solved. Similarly, solving the problems related to the superstructure also called for slaughter. The suppressions of the Hu Feng Anti-Party Group and the Anti-Rightist Movement eliminated the intellectuals. Killing the Christians, Taoists, Buddhists and popular folk groups solved the problem of religions. Mass murders during the Cultural Revolution established, culturally and politically, the CCP's absolute leadership. The Tiananmen Square massacre was used to prevent political crisis and squelch democratic demands. The persecution of Falun Gong is meant to resolve the issues of belief and traditional healing. These actions were all necessary for the CCP to strengthen its power and maintain its rule in the face of continual financial crisis (prices for consumer goods skyrocketed after the CCP took power and China's economy almost collapsed after the Cultural Revolution), political crisis (some people not following the Party's orders or some others wanting to share political rights with the Party) and crisis of belief (the disintegration of the former Soviet Union, political changes in Eastern Europe, and the Falun Gong issue). Except for the Falun Gong issue, almost all the foregoing political movements were utilized to revive the evil specter of the CCP and incite its desire for revolution. The CCP also used these political movements to test CCP members, eliminating those who did not meet the Party's requirements.

Killing is also necessary for practical reasons. The Communist Party began as a group of thugs and scoundrels who killed to obtain power. Once this precedent was set, there was no going back. Constant terror was needed to intimidate people and force them to accept, out of fear, the absolute rule of the CCP.

On the surface, it may appear that the CCP was "forced to kill," and that various incidents just happened to irritate the CCP evil specter and accidentally trigger the CCP's killing mechanism.

In truth, these incidents serve to disguise the Party's need to kill, and periodical killing is required by the CCP. Without these painful lessons, people might begin to think the CCP was improving and start to demand democracy, just as those idealistic students in the 1989 democratic movement did. Recurring slaughter every 7 or 8 years serves to refresh people's memory of terror and can warn the younger generation—whoever works against the CCP, wants to challenge the CCP's absolute leadership, or attempts to tell the truth regarding China's history, will get a taste of the "iron fist of the dictatorship of the proletariat."

Killing has become one of the most essential ways for the CCP to maintain power. With the escalation of its bloody debts, laying down its butcher knife would encourage people to take vengeance for the CCP's criminal acts. Therefore, the CCP not only needed to conduct copious and thorough killing, but the slaughter also had to be done in a most brutal fashion to effectively intimidate the populace, especially early on when the CCP was establishing its rule.

Since the purpose of the killing was to instill the greatest terror, the CCP selected targets for destruction arbitrarily and irrationally. In every political movement, the CCP used the strategy of genocide. Take the Suppression of the Counter-Revolutionary Movement as an example. The CCP did not really suppress the reactionary behaviors but the people whom they called the counter-revolutionaries. If one had been enlisted and served a few days in the KMT Army but did absolutely nothing political after the CCP gained power, this person would still be killed because of his "reactionary history." In the process of land reform, in order to remove the "root of the problem," the CCP often killed a landowner's entire family.

Since 1949, the CCP has persecuted more than half the people in China. An estimated 60 million to 80 million people died from unnatural causes. This number exceeds the total number of deaths in both World Wars combined.

As with other communist countries, the wanton killing done by the CCP also includes brutal slayings of its own members in order to remove dissidents who value a sense of humanity over the Party nature. The CCP's rule of terror falls equally on the populace and its members in an attempt to maintain an "invincible fortress."

In a normal society, people show care and love for one another, hold life in awe and veneration and give thanks to God. In the East, people say, "Do not impose on others what you would not want done to yourself."[2] In the West, people say, "Love thy neighbor as thyself."[3] Conversely, the CCP holds that "The history of all hitherto existing society is the history of class struggles."[4] In order to keep alive the "struggles" within society, hatred must be generated. Not only does the CCP take lives, it encourages people to kill each other. It strives to desensitize people towards others' suffering by surrounding them with constant killing. It wants them to become numb from frequent exposure to inhumane brutality, and develop the mentality that the best you can hope for is to avoid being persecuted. All these lessons taught by brutal suppression enable the CCP to maintain its rule.

In addition to the destruction of countless lives, the CCP also destroyed the soul of the Chinese people. A great many people have become conditioned to react to the CCP's threats by entirely surrendering their reason and their principles. In a sense, these people's souls have died—something more frightening than physical death.

I. HORRENDOUS MASSACRE

Before the CCP was in power, Mao Zedong wrote, "We definitely do not apply a policy of benevolence to the counter-revolutionaries and towards the reactionary activities of the reactionary classes."[5] In other words, even before the CCP took over Beijing, it had already made up its mind to act tyrannically under the euphemism of the People's Democratic Dictatorship. The following are a few examples.

Suppression of the Counter-Revolutionaries and Land Reform

In March 1950, the CCP announced "Orders to Strictly Suppress Reactionary Elements," which is historically known as the movement of Suppression of the Counter-Revolutionaries.

Unlike all the emperors who granted amnesty to the entire country after they were crowned, the CCP started killing the minute it gained power. Mao Zedong said in a document, "There are still many places where people are intimidated and dare not kill the counter-revolutionaries openly on a large scale."[6] In February 1951, the central CCP said that except for Zhejiang Province and southern Anhui Province, "other areas which are not killing enough, especially in the large and mid-sized cities, should continue to arrest and kill a large number and should not stop too soon." Mao even recommended that "in rural areas, to kill the counter-revolutionaries, there should be over one thousandth of the total population killed…in the cities, it should be less than one thousandth."[7] The population of China at that time was approximately 600 million and this "royal order" from Mao would have caused at least 600,000 deaths. Nobody knows where this ratio of one thousandth came from. Perhaps, on a whim, Mao decided these 600,000 lives should be enough to lay the foundation for creating fear among the people, and thus ordered it to happen.

Whether those killed deserved to die was not the CCP's concern. *The People's Republic of China Regulations for Punishing the Counter-Revolutionaries* announced in 1951 that those who "spread rumors" can be "immediately executed."

While the Suppression of Counter-Revolutionaries was being hotly implemented, land reform was also taking place on a large scale. In fact, the CCP had already started land reform within its occupied areas in the late 1920s. On the surface, land reform appeared to advocate an ideal similar to that of the Heavenly Kingdom of Taiping[8], namely, all would have land to farm, but it was really just an excuse to kill. Tao Zhu, who ranked 4th in the CCP afterwards, had a slogan for land reform: "Every village bleeds, every household fights," indicating that in every village the landowners must die.

Land reform could have been achieved without killing. It could have been done in the same way as the Taiwanese government implemented its land reform by purchasing the property from the landowners. However, as the CCP originated from a group of thugs and lumpen proletariat, it only knew how to rob. Fearing it might suffer revenge after robbing, the CCP naturally needed to kill the victims, therefore stamping out the source of potential trouble.

The most common way to kill during the land reform was known as the Struggle Meeting. The CCP fabricated crimes and charged the landowners or rich farmers. The public was asked how they should be punished. Some CCP members or activists were already planted in the crowd to shout, "We should kill them!" and the landowners and rich farmers were then executed on the spot.

At that time, whoever owned land in the villages was classified as a "bully." Those who often took advantage of the peasants were called "mean bullies"; those who often helped with repairing public facilities and donated money to schools and for natural disaster relief were called "kind bullies"; and those who did nothing were called "still or silent bullies." A classification like this was meaningless, because all the "bullies" ended up being executed right away regardless of what "bully" category they belonged to.

By the end of 1952, the CCP-published number of executed "reactionary elements" was about 2.4 million. Actually, the total death toll of former KMT government officials below the county level and landowners was at least 5 million.

The Suppression of the Counter-Revolutionaries and land reform had three direct results. Firstly, former local officials who had been selected through clan-based autonomy were eliminated. The CCP killed all the management personnel in the previous system and realized complete control of rural areas by installing a Party branch in each village. Secondly, a huge amount of wealth was obtained by stealing and robbing. Thirdly, civilians were terrorized by the brutal suppression against the landowners and rich farmers.

THE "THREE ANTI CAMPAIGN" AND "FIVE ANTI CAMPAIGN"

The Suppression of Reactionaries and the land reform mainly targeted the countryside, while the subsequent Three Anti Campaign and Five Anti Campaign could be regarded as the corresponding genocide in the cities.

The Three Anti Campaign began in December 1951 and targeted corruption, waste and bureaucracy among the CCP cadres. Some corrupt CCP officials were executed. Soon afterwards, the

CCP attributed the corruption of its government officials to the temptation by capitalists. Accordingly, the Five Anti Campaign against bribery, tax evasion, theft of state property, jerry-building, and espionage of state economic information was launched in January 1952.

The Five Anti Campaign was essentially stealing capitalists' property or rather murdering the capitalists for their money. Chen Yi, the Mayor of Shanghai at that time, was debriefed on the sofa with a cup of tea in hand every night. He would ask leisurely, "How many paratroopers are there today?" meaning, "How many businessmen jumped out of high buildings to commit suicide?" None of the capitalists could escape the Five Anti Campaign. They were required to pay taxes that had been "evaded" as early as the Guangxu Period (1875-1908) in the Qing Dynasty (1644-1911) when the Shanghai commercial market was initially established. The capitalists could not possibly afford to pay such "taxes" even with all their fortunes. They had no other choice but to end their lives, but they didn't dare to jump into the Huangpu River. If their bodies could not be found, the CCP would accuse them of fleeing to Hong Kong, and their family members would still be held responsible for the taxes. The capitalists instead jumped from tall buildings, leaving a corpse so that the CCP could see proof of their death. It was said that people didn't dare to walk next to tall buildings in Shanghai at that time for fear of being crushed by people jumping from above.

According to *Facts of the Political Campaigns after the Founding of the People's Republic of China* co-edited by four government units including the CCP History Research Center in 1996, during the Three Anti Campaign and Five Anti Campaign, more than 323,100 people were arrested and over 280 committed suicide or disappeared. In the Anti-Hu Feng campaign in 1955, over 5,000 were incriminated, over 500 arrested, over 60 committed suicide, and 12 died from unnatural causes. In the subsequent Suppression of the Reactionaries, over 21,300 people were executed, and over 4,300 committed suicide or disappeared.[9]

THE GREAT FAMINE

The highest death toll was recorded during China's Great Famine shortly after the Great Leap Forward. The article "Great Famine" in the book *Historical Records of the People's Republic of China* states, "The number of unnatural deaths and reduced births from 1959 to 1961 is estimated at about 40 million....China's depopulation by 40 million is likely to be the world's greatest famine in this century."[10]

The Great Famine was falsely labeled a "Three-Year Natural Disaster" by the CCP. In fact, those three years had favorable weather conditions without any massive natural disasters like flooding, drought, hurricane, tsunami, earthquake, frost, freeze, hail or plague of locusts. The disaster was entirely caused by man. The Great Leap Forward campaign required everyone in China to become involved in steel-making, forcing farmers to leave their crops to rot in the field. Despite this, officials in every region escalated their claims on production yields. He Yiran, the First Secretary of the Party Committee of Liuzhou Prefecture, on his own fabricated the shocking yield of "65,000 kilograms of paddy rice per *mu*"[11] in Huanjiang County. This was right after the Lushan Plenum when the CCP's Anti-Rightist Movement spread out to the entire country. In order to demonstrate that the CCP was correct all the time, the crops were expropriated by the government as a form of taxation according to these exaggerated yields. Consequently, the grain rations, seeds and staple foods of the peasants were all confiscated. When the demand still could not be met, the peasants were accused of hiding their crops.

He Yiran once said that they must strive to get first place in the competition for highest yield no matter how many people in Liuzhou would die. Some peasants were deprived of everything, with only some handfuls of rice left hidden in the urine basin. The Party Committee of Xunle District, Huanjiang County even issued an order to forbid cooking, preventing the peasants from eating the crops. Patrols were conducted by militiamen at night. If they saw light from a fire, they would proceed with a search and raid. Many peasants did not even dare to cook edible wild herbs or bark, and died of starvation.

Historically, in times of famine, the government would provide rice porridge, distribute the crops and allow victims to flee from the famine. The CCP, however, regarded fleeing from the famine as a disgrace to the Party's prestige, and ordered militiamen to block roadways to prevent victims from escaping the famine. When the peasants were so hungry as to snatch cereals from the grain depots, the CCP ordered shooting at the crowd to suppress the looting and labeled those killed as counter-revolutionary elements. A great number of peasants were starved to death in many provinces including Gansu, Shandong, Henan, Anhui, Hubei, Hunan, Sichuan and Guangxi provinces. Still, the hungry peasants were forced to take part in irrigation work, dam construction, and steel-making. Many dropped to the ground while working and never got up again. In the end, those who survived had no strength to bury the dead. Many villages died out completely as families starved to death one after another.

In the most serious famines in China's history prior to the CCP, there were cases in which families exchanged one another's children to eat, but nobody ever ate his own children. Under the CCP's reign, however, people were driven to eat those who died, cannibalize those who fled from other regions, and even kill and eat their own children. The writer Sha Qing depicted this scene in his book *Yi Xi Da Di Wan (An Obscure Land of Bayou)*[12]: In a peasant's family, a father was left with only his son and daughter during the Great Famine. One day, the daughter was driven out of the house by her father. When she came back, she could not find her younger brother, but saw white oil floating in the cauldron and a pile of bones next to the stove. Several days later, the father added more water to the pot, and called his daughter to come closer. The girl was frightened, and pleaded with her father from outside the door, "Daddy, please don't eat me. I can collect firewood and cook food for you. If you eat me, nobody else will do this for you."

The final extent and number of tragedies such as this are unknown. Yet the CCP misrepresented them as a noble honor, claimed that the CCP was leading people bravely to fight the "natural disasters" and continued to tout itself as "great, glorious and correct."

After the Lushan Plenum was held in 1959, General Peng Dehuai was stripped of his power because he spoke out for the people. A group of government officials and cadres who dared to speak the truth were dismissed from their posts, detained or investigated. After that, no one dared to speak out the truth. At the time of the Great Famine, instead of reporting the truth, people concealed the facts about the deaths from starvation in order to protect their official positions. Gansu Province even refused food aid from Shaanxi Province, claiming Gansu had too great a food surplus.

This Great Famine was also a qualifying test for the CCP's cadres. According to the CCP's criteria, the cadres who had resisted telling the truth in the face of tens of millions starving to death were certainly "qualified." With this test, the CCP would then believe that nothing such as human emotions or heavenly principles could become a psychological burden that would prevent these cadres from following the Party line. After the Great Famine, the responsible provincial officials merely participated in the formality of self-criticism. Li Jingquan, the CCP Secretary for Sichuan Province where millions of people died from starvation, was promoted to be the first secretary of the southwestern district bureau of the CCP.

From the Cultural Revolution and Tiananmen Square Massacre to Falun Gong

The Cultural Revolution was formally launched on May 16, 1966 and lasted until 1976. This period was called the "Ten-Year Catastrophe" even by the CCP itself. Later in an interview with a Yugoslav reporter, Hu Yaobang, former General Party Secretary said, "At that time nearly 100 million people were implicated, which was one tenth of the Chinese population."

Facts of the Political Campaigns after the Founding of the People's Republic of China reported that, "In May 1984, after 31 months of intensive investigation, verification and recalculation by the Central Committee of the CCP, the figures related to the Cultural Revolution were: over 4.2 million people were detained and investigated; over 1.73 million people died of unnatural causes; over 135,000 people were labeled as counter-revolutionaries and executed; over 237,000 people were killed and over 7.03 million were disabled in armed attacks; and 71,200 families were destroyed." Statistics compiled from county annals show that 7.73 million people died of unnatural causes during the Cultural Revolution.

Besides the beating of people to death, the beginning of the Cultural Revolution also triggered a wave of suicides. Many famous intellectuals, including Lao She, Fu Lei, Jian Bozan, Wu

Han and Chu Anping all ended their own lives at an early stage of the Cultural Revolution.

The Cultural Revolution was the most frenzied leftist period in China. Killing became a competitive way to exhibit one's revolutionary standing, so the slaughter of "class enemies" was extremely cruel and brutal.

The policy of "reform and opening up" greatly advanced the circulation of information, which made it possible for many foreign reporters to witness the Tiananmen Square massacre in 1989 and to air television reports showing tanks chase down and crush college students to death.

Ten years later, on July 20, 1999, Jiang Zemin began his suppression of Falun Gong. By the end of 2002, inside information from government sources in Mainland China confirmed the cover-up of over 7,000 deaths in detention centers, forced labor camps, prisons and mental hospitals, with an average of seven people being killed every day.

Nowadays the CCP tends to kill far less than in the past when millions or tens of millions were murdered. There are two important reasons for this. On the one hand, the Party has warped the minds of the Chinese people with its Party culture so that they are now more submissive and cynical. On the other hand, because of excessive corruption and embezzlement by CCP officials, the Chinese economy has become a "transfusion" type of economy, depending substantially on foreign capital to sustain economic growth and social stability. The CCP vividly remembers the economic sanctions that followed the Tiananmen Square massacre, and knows that open killing would result in a withdrawal of foreign capital that would endanger its totalitarian regime.

Nevertheless, the CCP has never given up slaughtering behind the scenes. The difference is that today's CCP spares no effort to hide the bloody evidence.

II. EXTREMELY CRUEL WAYS OF KILLING

Everything the CCP does serves only one purpose: gaining and maintaining power. Killing is a very important way for the CCP to maintain its power. The more people killed and the crueler the killings, the greater the ability to terrify. Such terror started as early as before the Anti-Japanese War.

MASSACRE IN NORTHERN CHINA DURING THE ANTI-JAPANESE WAR

When recommending the book *Enemy Within* by Father Raymond J. de Jaegher and Irene Corbally Kuhn,[13] former U.S. President Hoover commented that the book exposed the naked terror of communist movements. He would recommend it to anyone who was willing to understand such an evil force in this world.

In this book, de Jaegher told stories about how the CCP used violence to terrify people into submission. For instance, one day the CCP required everyone to go to the square in the village. Teachers led the children to the square from school. The purpose for the gathering was to watch the killing of 13 patriotic young men. After announcing the fabricated charges against the victims, the CCP ordered the horrified teacher to lead the children to sing patriotic songs. Appearing on the stage amid the songs were not dancers, but rather an executioner holding a sharp knife in his hands. The executioner was a fierce, robust young communist soldier with strong arms. The soldier went behind the first victim, quickly raised a big sharp knife and struck downwards, and the first head fell to the ground. Blood sprayed out like a fountain as the head rolled on the ground. The children's hysterical singing turned into chaotic screaming and crying. The teacher kept the beat, trying to keep the songs going; her bell was heard ringing over and over in the chaos.

The executioner chopped 13 times and 13 heads fell to the ground. After that, many communist soldiers came over, cut the victims' chests open and took out their hearts for a feast. All the brutality was done in front of the children. The children went completely pale in terror and some started throwing up. The teacher scolded the children, and lined them up to return to school.

After that, Father de Jaegher often saw children being forced to watch killings. The children became used to the bloody scenes and numb to the killing, some even started to enjoy the excitement.

When the CCP felt that simple killing was not horrifying and exciting enough, they invented all kinds of cruel torture. For example, forcing someone to swallow a large amount of salt without letting him drink any water—the victim would suffer until he died of thirst; stripping someone naked and forcing him to roll on broken glass; creating a hole in a frozen river in the winter, then throwing the victim into the hole—the victim would either freeze to death or drown.

Father de Jaegher wrote that a CCP member in Shanxi Province invented a terrible torture. One day when he was wandering in the city, he stopped in front of a restaurant and stared at a big boiling vat. Later he purchased several giant vats and immediately arrested some people who were against the Communist Party. During the hasty trial, the vats were filled with water and heated to boiling. Three victims were stripped naked and thrown into the vats to boil to death after the trial. At Pingshan, de Jaegher witnessed a father being skinned alive. The CCP members forced the son to watch and participate in the inhumane torture, to see his father die in excruciating pain and listen to his father's screams. The CCP members poured vinegar and acid onto the father's body and then all his skin was quickly peeled off. They started from the back, then up to the shoulders and soon the skin from his whole body was peeled off, leaving only the skin on the head intact. His father died in minutes.

THE RED TERROR DURING "RED AUGUST" AND THE GUANGXI CANNIBALISM

After gaining absolute control over the country, the CCP did not end its violence at all. During the Cultural Revolution, such violence became worse.

On August 18, 1966, Mao Zedong met with the Red Guard representatives on the tower of Tiananmen Square. Song Binbin, daughter of Communist Leader Song Renqiong, put a Red Guard sleeve emblem on Mao. When Mao learned of Song Binbin's name, which means gentle and polite, he said, "We need more violence." Song therefore changed her name to Song Yaowu (literally meaning "want violence").

Violent armed attacks soon spread quickly to the whole country. The younger generation educated in communist atheism had no fears or concerns. Under the direct leadership of the CCP and guided by Mao's instructions, the Red Guards, being fanatic, ignorant, and holding themselves above the law, started beating people and ransacking homes nationwide. In many areas, all of the "five black classes" (landlords, rich farmers, counter-revolutionaries, bad elements, and rightists) and their family members were eradicated according to a policy of genocide. A typical example was Daxing County near Beijing, where from August 27 to September 1 of 1966, a total of 325 people were killed in 48 brigades of 13 People's Communes. The oldest killed was 80 years old, and the youngest only 38 days. Twenty-two entire households were killed with no one left.

> Beating a person to death was a common scene. On Shatan Street, a group of male Red Guards tortured an old woman with metal chains and leather belts until she could not move any more, and still a female Red Guard jumped on her body and stomped on her stomach. The old woman died on the scene. ... Near Chongwenmeng, when the Red Guards searched the home of a landlord's wife (a lonely widow), they forced each neighbor to bring a pot of boiling water to the scene and they poured the boiling water down the old lady's collar until her body was cooked. Several days later, the old lady was found dead in the room, her body covered with maggots. ... There were many different ways of killing, including beating to death with batons, cutting with sickles and strangling to death with ropes. ... The way to kill babies was the most brutal: the killer stepped on one leg of a baby and pulled the other leg, tearing the baby in half.[14]

The Guangxi cannibalism was even more inhumane than the Daxing massacre. Writer Zheng Yi, author of the book *Scarlet Memorial* described the cannibalism as progressing in three stages.[15]

The first was the beginning stage when the terror was covert and gloomy. County annals documented a typical scene: at midnight, the killers tip-toed to find their victim and cut him open to remove his heart and liver. Because they were inexperienced and scared, they took his lung by mistake, then they had to go back again. Once they had cooked the heart and liver, some people brought liquor from home, some brought seasoning, and then all the killers ate the human organs in silence by the light of the oven fire.

The second stage was the peak, when the terror became open and public. During this stage, veteran killers had gained experience in how to remove hearts and livers while the victim was still alive, and they taught others, refining their techniques to perfection. For example when cutting open a living person, the killers only needed to cut a cross on the victim's belly, step on his body (if the victim was tied to a tree, the killers would bump his lower abdomen with the knee) and the heart and other organs would just fall out. The head killer was entitled to the heart, liver and genitals while others would take what was left. These grand, yet dreadful scenes were adorned with flying flags and slogans.

The third stage was crazed. Cannibalism became a massive widespread movement. In Wuxuan County, like wild dogs eating corpses during an epidemic, people were madly eating other people. Often victims were first "publicly criticized," which was always followed by killing, and then cannibalism. As soon as a victim fell to the ground, dead or alive, people took out the knives they had prepared and surrounded the victim, cutting any body part they could get hold of. At this stage, ordinary citizens were all involved in the cannibalism. The hurricane of "class struggle" blew away any sense of sin and human nature from people's minds. Cannibalism spread like an epidemic and people enjoyed cannibalistic feasts. Any part of the human body was edible, including the heart, meat, liver, kidneys, elbows, feet, and tendons. Human bodies were cooked in many different ways including boiling, steaming, stir-frying, baking, frying and barbecuing ... People drank liquor or wine and played games while eating human bodies. During the peak of this movement, even the cafeteria of the highest government organization, Wuxuan County revolutionary committee, offered human dishes.

Readers should not mistakenly think such a festival of cannibalism was purely an unorganized behavior by the people. The CCP was a totalitarian organization controlling every single cell of the society. Without the CCP's encouragement and manipulation, the cannibalism movement could not have happened at all.

A song written by the CCP in praise of itself says, "The old society[16] turned humans into ghosts, the new society turned ghosts into humans." However, these killings and cannibalistic feasts tell us that the CCP could turn a human being into a monster or a devil because the CCP itself is crueler than any monster or devil.

PERSECUTION OF FALUN GONG

As the people in China step into the era of computers and space travel, and can talk privately about human rights, freedom and democracy, many people think that the gruesome and disgusting atrocities are all in the past. The CCP has donned civilian clothing and is ready to connect with the world.

But that is far from the truth. When the CCP discovered that there is a group that does not fear its cruel torture and killing, it became even more manic. The group that has been persecuted in this way is Falun Gong.

The Red Guards' violence and the cannibalism in Guangxi Province aimed at eliminating the victim's body, killing someone in several minutes or several hours. However, Falun Gong practitioners are persecuted to force them to give up their belief in Truthfulness, Compassion and Tolerance. Also, the cruel torture often lasts for several days, several months or even several years. It is estimated that more than 10,000 Falun Gong practitioners have died as a result of torture.

Falun Gong practitioners who suffered all kinds of torture and escaped from the jaws of death have recorded more than 100 cruel torture methods; the following are only several examples.

Cruel beating is the most commonly used torture method to abuse Falun Gong practitioners. The police and head prisoners directly beat practitioners and also instigate other prisoners to beat practitioners. Many practitioners have become deaf from these beatings, their outer ear tissues have been broken off, their eyeballs crushed, their teeth broken, and their skull, spine, ribcage, collarbone, pelvis, arms and legs have been broken; arms and legs have been amputated due to the beatings. Some torturers have ruthlessly pinched and crushed male practitioners' testicles and kicked female practitioners' genital areas. If the practitioners did not give in, torturers would continue the beating until the practitioners' skin was torn and the flesh gaped open.

Electric shock is another method commonly used in Chinese forced labor camps to torture Falun Gong practitioners. The police have used electric batons to shock practitioners' sensitive parts of the body, including the mouth, top of the head, chest, genitalia, hips, thighs, soles of the feet, female practitioners' breasts, and male practitioners' penis. Some police have shocked practitioners with several electric batons simultaneously until burning flesh could be smelled and the injured parts were dark and purple. Sometimes, the head and anus are shocked at the same time. The police have often used ten or even more electric batons simultaneously to beat the practitioners for an extended amount of time. The voltage of an electric baton often reaches tens of thousands. When it discharges, it emits blue light with a static-like sound. When the electric current goes through a person's body, it feels like one is being burned or being bitten by snakes. Every shock is very painful. The victim's skin turns red, is broken and burned and the wounds fester. There are even more powerful batons with higher voltage that make the victim feel like his head is being hit with a hammer. Practitioners' bodies have become completely deformed from torture and covered in blood, yet the guards have still poured salt water on them and continued to shock them with electric batons. The smell of blood and burning flesh and the screams of agony are miserable. Meanwhile, the torturers also use plastic bags to cover practitioners' heads in an attempt to make them yield out of fear of suffocation.

Police also use lit cigarettes to burn practitioners' hands, face, bottoms of the feet, chest, back, nipples, and so on. They use cigarette lighters to burn practitioners' hands and genitals. Specially-made iron bars are heated in electrical stoves until they become red-hot. They are then used to burn practitioners' legs. The police also use red-hot charcoal to burn practitioners' faces. The police burned a practitioner to death who, after having already endured cruel torture, still had a pulse and was breathing. The police then claimed his death was a "self-immolation."

Police beat female practitioners' breasts and genital areas. They have raped and gang raped female practitioners. In addition, police have stripped off female practitioners' clothes and thrown them into prison cells filled with male prisoners who have then raped them. They have used electric batons to shock their breasts and genitals. They have used cigarette lighters to burn their nipples, and inserted electrical batons into the practitioners' vaginas to shock them. They have bundled four toothbrushes and inserted them into female practitioners' vaginas and rubbed and twisted the toothbrushes. They have hooked female practitioners' private parts with iron hooks. Female practitioners' hands are cuffed behind their backs, and practitioners' nipples are hooked up to wires through which an electric current is run.

They force Falun Gong practitioners to wear "straight jackets,"[17] and then cross and tie their arms behind their backs. They pull their arms up over their shoulders to the front of their chest, tie up the practitioners' legs and hang them outside a window. At the same time, they gag practitioners' mouths with cloth, put earphones in their ears and continuously play messages that slander Falun Gong. According to an eyewitness account, people who suffer this torture quickly sustain broken arms, tendons, shoulders, wrists and elbows. Those who have been tortured this way for a long time have completely broken spines, and die in agonizing pain.

They also throw the practitioners into dungeons filled with sewage. They hammer bamboo sticks under the practitioners' fingernails and force them to live in damp rooms full of red, green, yellow, white and other molds on the ceiling, floors and walls, which cause their injuries to fester. They also have dogs, snakes and scorpions bite practitioners and they inject practitioners with nerve-damaging drugs. These are just some of the ways that practitioners are tortured in labor camps.

III. CRUEL STRUGGLE WITHIN THE PARTY

Because the CCP unifies its members on the basis of Party nature rather than morality and justice, a central question is the loyalty of its members, especially of senior officials, to the supreme leader. The Party needs to create an atmosphere of terror by killing its members. The survivors then see that when the supreme dictator wants someone to die, that person will die miserably.

The internal fights of communist parties are well known. All members of the politburo of the Russian Communist Party in the first two terms, except Lenin, who had died, and Stalin himself, were executed or committed suicide. Three of the five marshals were executed, three of the five commanders-in-chief were executed, all ten secondary army commanders-in-chief were executed, 57 of the 85 army corps commanders were executed, and 110 of the 195 division commanders were executed.

The CCP always advocates "brutal struggles and merciless attacks." Such tactics not only target people outside the Party. As early as the revolutionary period in Jiangxi Province, the CCP had already killed so many people in the Anti-Bolshevik Corps (AB Corps) that only a few survived to fight the ensuing wars. In the city of Yan'an, the Party carried out a Rectification campaign. Later, after becoming politically established, it eliminated Gao Gang, Rao Shushi, Hu Feng, and Peng Dehuai. By the time of the Cultural Revolution, almost all of the senior members within the Party had been eliminated. None of the former CCP's secretary-generals met with a good ending.

Liu Shaoqi[18], a former Chinese president who was once the No. 2 figure in the nation, died miserably. On the day of his 70th birthday, Mao Zedong and Zhou Enlai specifically told Wang Dongxing (Mao's lead guard) to bring Liu Shaoqi a birthday present, a radio, in order to let him hear the official report of the Eighth Plenary Session of the twelfth central committee, which said, "Forever expel the traitor, spy, and renegade Liu Shaoqi from the Party and continue to expose and criticize Liu Shaoqi and his accomplices' crimes of betrayal and treason."

Liu Shaoqi was crushed mentally and his illnesses rapidly deteriorated. Because he was tied to the bed for a long time and could not move, his neck, back, hip, and heels had painful festering bedsores. When he felt great pain he would grab some clothes, articles, or other people's arms, and not let go, so people simply put a hard plastic bottle into each of his hands. When he died, the two hard plastic bottles had become hourglass-shaped from his gripping.

By October 1969, Liu Shaoqi's body had started to rot all over and the infected pus had a strong odor. He was as thin as a rail and on the verge of death, but the special inspector from the central Party committee did not allow him to take a shower or turn over his body to change his clothes. Instead, they stripped off all his clothes, wrapped him in a quilt, sent him by air from Beijing to Kaifeng City, and locked him up in the basement of a solid blockhouse. When he had a high fever, they not only did not give him medication, but also transferred the medical personnel away. When Liu Shaoqi died, his body had completely degenerated, and he had disheveled white hair that was two feet long. Two days later, at midnight, he was cremated as a person with a highly infectious disease. His bedding, pillow and other things left behind were all cremated. Liu's death card reads: Name: Liu Weihuang; Occupation: unemployed; Cause of death: disease. The CCP tortured the president of the nation to death like this without even giving a clear reason.

IV. EXPORTING THE REVOLUTION, KILLING PEOPLE OVERSEAS

In addition to killing people with great delight and using a variety of methods within China and inside the Party, the CCP also participated in killing people abroad including the overseas Chinese by exporting the "revolution." The Khmer Rouge is a typical example.

Pol Pot's Khmer Rouge only existed for four years in Cambodia. Nevertheless, from 1975 to 1978, more than two million people, including over 200,000 Chinese, were killed in this small country that had a population of only eight million people.

The Khmer Rouge's crimes are countless, but we will not discuss them here. We must, however, talk about its relationship with the CCP.

Pol Pot worshipped Mao Zedong. Beginning in 1965, he visited China four times to listen to Mao Zedong's teachings in person. As early as November 1965, Pol Pot stayed in China for three months. Chen Boda and Zhang Chunqiao[19] discussed with him theories such as "political power grows out of the barrel of a gun," "class struggle," "dictatorship of the proletariat," and so on. Later, these became the basis for how he ruled Cambodia. After returning to Cambodia, Pol Pot changed the name of his party to the Cambodian Communist Party and established revolutionary bases according to the CCP's model of encircling cities from the countryside.

In 1968, the Cambodian Communist Party officially established an army. At the end of 1969, it had slightly more than 3,000 people. But in 1975, before attacking and occupying the city of Phnom Penh, it had become a well-equipped and brave fighting force of 80,000 soldiers. This was completely due to the CCP's support. The book *Documentary of Supporting Vietnam and Fighting with America* by Wang Xiangen[20] says that in 1970, China gave Pol Pot armed equipment for 30,000 soldiers. In April 1975, Pol Pot took the capital of Cambodia, and two months later, he went to Beijing to pay a visit to the CCP and listen to instructions. Obviously, if the Khmer Rouge's killing had not been backed by the CCP's theories and material support, it could not have been done.

For example, after Prince Sihanouk's two sons were killed by the Cambodian Communist Party, the Cambodian Communist Party obediently sent Sihanouk to Beijing on Zhou Enlai's orders.

It was well known that when the Cambodian Communist Party killed people, they would "even kill the fetus" to prevent any possible trouble in the future. However, upon Zhou Enlai's request, Pol Pot obeyed without protest.

Zhou Enlai could save Sihanouk with one word, but the CCP did not object to the more than 200,000 Chinese who were killed by the Cambodian Communist Party. At the time, the Chinese Cambodians went to the Chinese Embassy for help, but the embassy ignored them.

In May 1998, when a large-scale killing and raping of ethnic Chinese took place in Indonesia, the CCP did not say a word. It did not offer any help, and even blocked the news inside China. It seems that the Chinese government does not care about the fate of overseas Chinese; it did not even offer any humanitarian assistance.

V. THE DESTRUCTION OF FAMILY

We have no way to count how many people have been killed in the CCP's political campaigns. Among the people, there is no way to do a statistical survey because of information blocks and barriers among different regions, ethnic groups, and local dialects. The CCP government would never conduct this kind of survey, as that would be the same as digging its own grave. The CCP prefers to omit the details when writing its own history.

The number of families damaged by the CCP is even more difficult to know. In some cases, one person died and the family was broken. In other cases, the entire family died. Even when no one died, many were forced to divorce. Father and son, mother and daughter were forced to renounce their relationships. Some were disabled, some went crazy, and some died young because of serious illness caused by torture. The record of all these family tragedies is very incomplete.

The Japan-based *Yomiuri News* once reported that over half of the Chinese population has been persecuted by the CCP. If that is the case, the number of families destroyed by the CCP is estimated to be over 100 million.

Zhang Zhixin has become a household name due to the amount of reporting on her story. Many people know that she suffered physical torture, gang rape and mental torture. Finally, she was driven insane and shot to death after her trachea was cut. But many people may not know that there is another cruel story behind this tragedy—even her family members had to attend a "study session for the families of death row inmates."

Zhang Zhixin's daughter Lin Lin recalled that in the early spring of 1975,

> A person from Shenyang Court said loudly, "Your mother is a real die-hard counter-revolutionary. She refuses to accept reform, and is incorrigibly obstinate. She is against our great leader Chairman Mao, against the invincible Mao Zedong Thought, and against Chairman Mao's proletariat revolutionary direction. With one crime on top of another, our government is considering increasing the punishment. If she is executed, what is your attitude?" I was astonished, and did not know how to answer. My heart was broken. But I pretended to be calm, trying hard to keep my tears from falling. My father had told me that we could not cry in front of others, otherwise we had no way to renounce our

relationship with my mother. Father answered for me, "If this is the case, the government is free to do what it deems necessary."

The person from court asked again, "Will you collect her body if she is executed? Will you collect her belongings in prison?" I lowered my head and said nothing. Father answered for me again, "We don't need anything."... Father held my brother and me by the hands and we walked out of the county motel. Staggering along, we walked home against the howling snow storm. We did not cook; father split the only coarse corn bun we had at home and gave it to my brother and me. He said, "Finish it and go to bed early." I lay on the clay bed quietly. Father sat on a stool and stared at the light in a daze. After a while, he looked at the bed and thought we were all asleep. He stood up, gently opened the suitcase we brought from our old home in Shenyang, and took out mother's photo. He looked at it and could not hold back his tears.

I got up from bed, put my head into father's arms and started crying loudly. Father patted me and said, "Don't do that, we cannot let the neighbors hear it." My brother woke up after hearing me cry. Father held my brother and me tightly in his arms. This night we did not know how many tears we shed, but we could not cry freely.[21]

One university lecturer had a happy family, but his family encountered a disaster during the process of redressing the rightists. At the time of the Anti-Rightist Movement, the woman who would become the university lecturer's wife was dating someone who was labeled a rightist. Her lover was later sent to a remote area and suffered greatly. Because she, as a young girl, could not go along, she gave her lover up and married the lecturer instead. When her beloved one finally came back to their hometown, she, now a mother of several children, had no other way to repent her betrayal in the past. She insisted on divorcing her husband in order to redeem her guilty conscience. By this time, the lecturer was over 50-years old; he could not accept the sudden change and went insane. He stripped off all his clothes and ran all over to look for a place to start a new life. Finally, his wife left him and their children. The painful separation decreed by the Party is a problem that can't be solved and an incurable social disease that could only replace one separation with another separation.

Family is the basic unit of the Chinese society. It is also the traditional culture's last defense against the Party culture. That is why damage to the family is the cruelest in the CCP's history of killing.

Because the CCP monopolizes all social resources, when a person is classified as being on the opposing side of the dictatorship, he or she will immediately face a crisis in livelihood, be accused by everyone in society, and stripped of his or her dignity. Because they are treated unjustly, the family is the only safe haven for these innocent people to be consoled. But the CCP's policy of implication kept family members from comforting each other; otherwise, they too risked being labeled opponents of the dictatorship. Zhang Zhixin, for instance, was forced to divorce. For many people, family members' betrayal— reporting on, fighting, publicly criticizing, or denouncing them— is the last straw that breaks their spirit. Many people have committed suicide as a result.

VI. THE PATTERNS AND CONSEQUENCES OF KILLING

THE CCP'S IDEOLOGY OF KILLING

The CCP has always touted itself as being talented and creative in its development of Marxism-Leninism, but in reality the CCP creatively developed an unprecedented evil in history and around the world. It uses the communist ideology of social unity to deceive the public and intellectuals. It seizes the opportunity of science and technology's undermining belief to promote complete atheism. It uses communism to deny private ownership, and uses Lenin's theory and practice of violent revolution to rule the country. At the same time, it combined and further reinforced the most evil part of Chinese culture that deviates from mainstream Chinese traditions.

The CCP invented a complete theory and framework of "revolution" and "continuous revolution" under the dictatorship of the proletariat; it used this system to change society and ensure the Party dictatorship. Its theory has two parts—economic base and superstructure under the dictatorship of the proletariat, in which the economic base determines the superstructure, while the superstructure in turn acts on the economic base.

In order to strengthen the superstructure, especially the Party's power, it must first start the revolution from the economic base, which includes:

(1) Killing the landowners to solve the relations of production[22] in the countryside, and

(2) Killing the capitalists to solve relations of production in cities.

Within the superstructure, killing is also repeatedly carried out to maintain the Party's absolute control in ideology. This includes:

(1) Solving the problem of intellectuals' political attitude towards the Party

Over a long period of time, the CCP has launched multiple campaigns to reform the thought of the intellectuals. They have accused intellectuals of bourgeois individualism, bourgeois ideology, apolitical viewpoints, classless ideology, liberalism, etc. The CCP stripped intellectuals of their dignity through brainwashing them and eliminating their conscience. The CCP nearly eliminated completely the independent thinking and many other good qualities of the intellectuals, including the tradition of speaking out for justice and devoting one's life to uphold justice. That tradition teaches: "Do not be led into excesses when wealthy and honored or deflected from his purpose when poor and obscure, nor can he be made to bow before superior force";[22] "One should be the first to worry for the state and the last to claim his share of happiness";[24] "Every ordinary man shall hold himself responsible for his nation's success and failure";[25] and "In obscurity a gentleman makes perfect his own person, but in prominence he makes perfect the whole country as well."[26]

(2) Launching a cultural revolution and killing people in order to gain the CCP's absolute cultural and political leadership

The CCP mobilized mass campaigns inside and outside the Party, starting to kill in the areas of literature, art, theatre, history and education. The CCP targeted the first attacks on several famous people such as the "Three-Family Village,"[27] Liu Shaoqi, Wu Han, Lao She, and Jian Bozan[28]. Later, the number of people killed increased to "a small group inside the Party," then "a small group inside the army," and finally, the killing escalated from among all inside the Party and army to all the people around the country. Armed fighting eliminated physical bodies; cultural attacks killed people's spirit. It was an extremely chaotic and violent period under the CCP's control. The evil side of human nature had been amplified to the maximum by the Party's need to revive its power in a crisis. Everyone could arbitrarily kill under the name of "revolution" and "defending Chairman Mao's revolutionary line." It was an unprecedented nationwide exercise of eliminating human nature.

(3) The CCP fired at students in Tiananmen Square on June 4, 1989 in response to the democratic demands following the Cultural Revolution

This was the first time that the CCP army killed civilians publicly in order to suppress the people's protest of embezzlement, corruption and collusion between government officials and businessmen, and their demand for the freedoms of press, speech, and assembly. During the Tiananmen Square massacre, in order to instigate hatred between the army and civilians, the CCP even staged scenes of people burning military vehicles and killing soldiers, stage-managing the tragedy of the People's Army massacring its people.

(4) Killing people of different beliefs

The domain of belief is the lifeline of the CCP. In order to let its heresy deceive people at the time, the CCP started to eliminate all religions and belief systems at the beginning of its rule. When facing a spiritual belief in a new era—Falun Gong—the CCP took out its butcher's knife again. The CCP's strategy is to take advantage of Falun Gong's principles of Truthfulness, Compassion and Tolerance and the fact that practitioners do not lie, do not use violence, and will not cause social instability. After gaining experience in persecuting Falun Gong, the CCP made itself better able to eliminate people of other faiths. This time, Jiang Zemin and the CCP themselves came to the front of the stage to kill instead of utilizing other people or groups.

(5) Killing people in order to cover up the truth

The people's right to know is another weak point of the CCP; the CCP also kills people in order to block information. In the past, "listening to the enemy's radio broadcast" was a felony that was punished with prison terms. Now, in response to multiple incidents of the interception of the state-owned television system to clarify the truth of the persecution of Falun Gong, Jiang Zemin issued the secret order to "kill instantly without mercy."[29] Liu Chengjun, who carried out such an interception, was tortured to death. The CCP has mobilized the "610 Office" (an organization similar to the Gestapo in Nazi Germany that was created to persecute Falun Gong), the police, prosecutors, courts and a massive Internet police system to monitor people's every action.

(6) Depriving people of their survival rights for the sake of its own interests

The CCP's theory of continuous revolution means, in reality, that it will not give up its power. Currently, embezzlement and corruption inside the CCP have developed into conflicts between the Party's absolute leadership and people's right to life. When people organize to protect their rights legally, the CCP uses violence, waving its butcher's knife toward the so-called "ringleaders" of these movements. The CCP has already prepared over one million armed police for this purpose. Today, the CCP is much better prepared for killing than it was at the time of the Tiananmen Square massacre in

1989, when it had to mobilize temporarily its field army. However, while forcing its people on a road to ruin, the CCP has also forced itself into a dead end. The CCP has come to such an extremely vulnerable stage that it even "takes trees and grass as enemies when the wind blows," as the Chinese saying goes.

We can see from above that the CCP is an evil specter in nature. No matter how it changes at a specific time and place in order to maintain absolute control, the CCP will not change its history of killing—it killed people before, is killing people now, and will continue to kill in the future.

DIFFERENT KILLING PATTERNS UNDER DIFFERENT CIRCUMSTANCES

1. *Leading with Propaganda*

The CCP has used various ways to kill people, depending on the period of time. In most situations, the CCP created propaganda before killing. The CCP has often said, "only killing could appease the public's indignation," as if the people had requested the CCP to kill. In reality, this "public indignation" has been incited by the CCP.

For example, the drama "The White-Haired Girl," a total distortion of a folk legend, and the fabricated stories of rent collection and water dungeons told in the drama "Liu Wencai," were both used as tools to "educate" people to hate landlords. The CCP commonly demonizes their enemies, as it did in the case of China's former President, Liu Shaoqi. In particular, the CCP staged a self-immolation incident on Tiananmen Square in January 2001 to incite people's hatred toward Falun Gong, and then redoubled their massive genocidal campaign against Falun Gong. Not only has the CCP not changed its ways of killing people, but instead has perfected them by employing new information technology. In the past, the CCP could only deceive the Chinese people, but now it also deceives people all over the world.

2. *Mobilizing the Masses to Kill People*

The CCP not only kills people through the machine of its dictatorship, but also actively mobilizes people to kill each other. Even if the CCP observed some regulations and laws in the beginning of these mobilizations, by the time it incited people to join in, nothing could stop the slaughter. For example, when the CCP was carrying out its land reform, a land reform committee could decide on the life and death of landlords.

3. *Destroying One's Spirit before Killing the Physical Body*

Another pattern of killing is to crush one's spirit before killing the human body. In China's history, even the most cruel and ferocious Qin Dynasty (221 - 207 BC) did not destroy people's spirits. The CCP has never given people the chance to die a martyr. They promulgated policies such as, "Leniency to those who confess and severe punishment to those who resist," and "Lowering one's head to admit the crime is the only way out." The CCP forces people to give up their own thoughts and beliefs, making them die like dogs without dignity; a dignified death would encourage followers. Only when people die in humiliation and shame can the CCP achieve its purpose of "educating" the people who admired the victim. The reason that the CCP persecutes Falun Gong with extreme cruelty and violence is that Falun Gong practitioners consider their beliefs more important than their lives. When the CCP was unable to destroy their dignity, it did everything it could to torture their physical bodies.

4. *Killing People by Alliances and Alienation*

When killing people, the CCP would use both carrot and stick, befriending some people and alienating others. The CCP has always tried to attack a small portion of the population, using the proportion of 5 percent. The majority of the population are always good, always the objects of "education." Such education consists of terror and care. Education through terror uses fear to show people that those who oppose the CCP will come to no good end, making them stay far away from those previously attacked by the Party. Education through "care" lets people see that if they can earn the CCP's trust and stand together with the CCP, they will not only be safe but also have a good chance to be promoted or gain other benefits. Lin Biao once said, "A small portion [suppressed] today and a small portion tomorrow, soon there will be a large portion in total." Those who rejoiced surviving one movement often became victims of the next.

5. *Nipping Potential Threats in the Bud and Secretive Extra-Judicial Killings*

Recently the CCP has developed the killing pattern of nipping problems in the bud and killing secretly outside the law. For example, as workers' strikes or peasants' protests become more common in various places, the CCP eliminates the movements before they can grow by arresting the so-called "ringleaders" and sentencing them to severe punishment. In another example, as freedom and human rights have ever more become a commonly recognized trend throughout the world, the CCP did not sentence any Falun Gong practitioner to the death penalty, but under Jiang Zemin's instigation of "no one is held responsible for killing Falun Gong practitioners," Falun Gong practitioners have commonly been tortured to tragic deaths all over the country. The Chinese Constitution stipulates the citizens' right of appeal if one has suffered an injustice. Nevertheless, the CCP uses plainclothes policemen or hires local thugs to stop, arrest and send appellants back home, even putting them into labor camps.

6. *Killing One to Warn Others*

The persecutions of Zhang Zhixin, Yu Luoke and Lin Zhao[30] are all such examples.

7. *Using Suppression to Conceal the Truth of Killing*

Famous people with international influence are usually suppressed, but not killed by the CCP. The purpose of this is to conceal the killing of those whose deaths will not draw public attention. For example, during the campaign of Suppression of the Counter-Revolutionaries, the CCP did not kill high-ranking KMT generals such as Long Yun, Fu Zuoyi and Du Yuming, and instead killed lower level KMT officers and soldiers.

The CCP's killing has, over a long period of time, distorted the Chinese people's souls. Now, in China, many people have the tendency to kill. When terrorists attacked the U.S. on September 11, 2001, many Chinese cheered the attacks on Mainland Chinese Internet message boards. Advocates of "total war" were heard everywhere, making people tremble with fear.

CONCLUSION

Due to the CCP's information blockade, we have no way of knowing exactly how many people have died from the various movements of persecution that occurred during its rule. At least 60 million people died in the foregoing movements. In addition, the CCP also killed ethnic minorities in Xinjiang, Tibet, Inner Mongolia,

Yunnan and other places; information on these incidents is difficult to find. The *Washington Post* once estimated that the number of people persecuted to death by the CCP is as high as 80 million.[31]

Besides the number of deaths, we have no way of knowing how many people became disabled, mentally ill, enraged, depressed, or frightened to death through the persecution they suffered. Every single death is a bitter tragedy that leaves everlasting agony to the family members of the victims.

As the Japan-based *Yomiuri News* once reported[32], the Chinese central government conducted a survey on the casualties inflicted during the Cultural Revolution in 29 provinces and municipalities directly under the central government. Results showed that nearly 600 million people were persecuted or incriminated during the Cultural Revolution, which comprises about half of China's population.

Stalin once said that the death of one man is a tragedy, but the death of one million is merely a statistic. When told that many people starved to death in Sichuan Province, Li Jingquan, the former Party Secretary of Sichuan Province, remarked, "Which dynasty didn't have people die?" Mao Zedong said, "Casualties are inevitable for any struggle. Death often occurs." This is the atheist communists' view on life. That's why 20 million people died as a result of persecution during Stalin's regime, which constitutes 10 percent of the population of the former USSR. The CCP has killed at least 80 million people, which is also nearly 10 percent of the nation's population [at the end of the Cultural Revolution]. The Khmer Rouge killed two million people, or one quarter of Cambodia's population at that time. In North Korea, the death toll from famine is estimated to be over one million. These are all bloody debts owed by the communist parties.

Evil cults sacrifice people and use their blood to worship evil specters. Since its beginnings, the Communist Party has continued to kill people—when it couldn't kill those outside the Party, it would even kill its own people—to commemorate its "class struggles," "inter-party struggles," and other fallacies. It even put its own party general secretary, marshals, generals, ministers and others on the sacrificial altar of the evil cult.

Many think the CCP should be given time to improve itself, saying that it is quite restrained in its killings now. First of all, killing one person still makes one a murderer. Moreover, because killing is one of the methods the CCP uses to govern its terror-based regime, the CCP would then ratchet up and down its killings according to its needs. The CCP's killing is, in general, unpredictable. When people lack a strong sense of fear, the CCP could kill more to increase their sense of terror; when people are already fearful, killing a few could maintain the sense of terror; when people can't help but fear the CCP, then announcing the intention to kill, with no need really to kill, would be enough for the CCP to maintain terror. After having experienced countless political and killing movements, people have formed a conditioned reflex response to the CCP's terror. Therefore, there is no need for the CCP to even mention killing, even the propaganda machine's tone of mass criticism is enough to bring back people's memories of terror.

The CCP would adjust the intensity of its killing once people's sense of terror changes. The magnitude of killing itself is not the goal of the CCP; the key is its consistency in killing for the sake of maintaining power. The CCP has not become lenient, nor has it laid down its butcher's knife. Conversely, the people have become more obedient. Once the people stand up to request something that goes beyond the tolerance of the CCP, the CCP will not hesitate to kill.

Out of the need to maintain terror, random killing gives the maximum result to achieve this goal. In the large-scale killings that took place previously, the identity, crime and sentencing standard for its targets were kept intentionally vague by the CCP. To avoid being included as the targets for killing, people would often restrict themselves to a "safe zone" based on their own judgment. Such a "safe zone" was sometimes even narrower than the one that the CCP intended to set. That's why in every single movement, people tend to act like "a leftist rather than a rightist." As a result, a movement is oftentimes "enlarged" beyond its intended scale, because people at different levels voluntarily impose restrictions on themselves to ensure their own safety. The lower the level, the crueler the movement became. Such society-wide, voluntary intensification of terror stems from the CCP's random killings.

In its long history of killing, the CCP has metamorphosed itself into a depraved serial killer. Through killing, it satisfies its perverted sense of the ultimate power of deciding people's life and death. Through killing, it eases its own innermost fear. Through killing, it suppresses social unrest and dissatisfaction caused by its earlier murders. Today, the compounded bloody debts of the CCP have made a benevolent solution impossible. It can only rely on intense pressure and totalitarian rule to maintain its existence until its final moment. Despite occasionally disguising itself through redressing its murder victims, the CCP's bloodthirsty nature has never changed. It will be even less likely to change in the future.

COMMENTARY EIGHT

ON HOW
THE CHINESE COMMUNIST PARTY
IS AN EVIL CULT

COMMENTARY EIGHT

ON HOW THE CHINESE COMMUNIST PARTY IS AN EVIL CULT

FOREWORD

The collapse of the communist bloc headed by the Soviet Union in the early 1990s marked the failure of communism after almost a century. However, the CCP unexpectedly survived and still controls China, a nation with one-fifth of the world's population. An unavoidable question arises: Is the CCP today still truly communist?

No one in today's China, including Party members, believes in communism. After fifty years of socialism, the CCP has now adopted private ownership and even has a stock market. It seeks foreign investment to establish new ventures, while exploiting workers and peasants as much as it can. This is completely opposite to the ideals of communism. Despite compromising with capitalism, the CCP maintains autocratic control of the people of China. The Constitution, as revised in 2004, still rigidly states "Chinese people of various ethnicities will continue adhering to the people's democratic dictatorship and socialist path under the leadership of the Chinese Communist Party and the guidance of Marxism-Leninism, Mao Zedong's ideology, Deng Xiaoping's theory and the important thought of the Three Represents."

"The leopard has died, but its skin is still left."[1] Today's CCP only has "its skin" left. The CCP inherited this skin and uses it to maintain its rule over China.

What is the nature of the skin inherited by the CCP, that is, the very organization of the CCP?

I. THE CULTISH TRAITS OF THE CCP

The Communist Party is essentially an evil cult that harms mankind.

Although the Communist Party has never called itself a religion, it matches every single trait of a religion. See table 1 below. At the beginning of its establishment, it regarded Marxism as the absolute truth in the world. It piously worshipped Marx as its spiritual God, and exhorted people to engage in a life-long struggle for the goal of building a "communist heaven on earth."

The Communist Party is significantly different from any righteous religion. All orthodox religions believe in God and benevolence, and their purpose is to instruct humanity about morality and to save souls. The Communist Party does not believe in God and opposes traditional morality.

What the Communist Party has done proves itself to be an evil cult. The Communist Party's doctrines are based upon class struggle, violent revolution and the dictatorship of the proletariat and have resulted in the so-called "communist revolution" full of blood and violence. The red terror under communism has lasted for about a century, bringing disasters to dozens of countries in the world and costing tens of millions of lives. The communist belief, one that created a hell on earth, is nothing but the vilest cult in the world.

The Communist Party's cultish traits can be summarized under six headings:

Table 1 : Religious Traits of the CCP

	The Basic Forms of a Religion	The Corresponding Forms of the CCP
1	Church or Platform (pulpit)	All levels of the Party committee; the platform ranges from Party meetings to all media controlled by the CCP
2	Doctrines	Marxism-Leninism, Mao Zedong's ideology, Deng Xiaoping's theory, Jiang Zemin's Three Represents, and the Party Constitution
3	Initiation rites	Ceremony in which oaths are taken to be loyal to the CCP forever
4	Commitment to one religion	A member may only believe in the communist party
5	Priests	Party secretaries and staff in charge of Party affairs on all levels
6	Worshipping God	Slandering all gods, and then establishing itself as an unnamed "God"
7	Death is called "ascending to heaven or descending to hell"	Death is called "going to see Marx"
8	Scriptures	The theory and writings of the Communist Party leaders
9	Preaching	All sorts of meetings; leaders' speeches
10	Chanting scriptures; study or cross-examinination of scriptures	Political studies; routine group meetings or activities for the Party members
11	Hymns (religious songs)	Songs to eulogize the Party
12	Donations	Compulsory membership fees; mandatory allocation of governmental budget, which is money from people's sweat and blood for the Party's use
13	Disciplinary punishment	Party disciplines ranging from house arrest, investigation, expulsion from the Party, to deadly torture and even punishments of relatives and friends

CONCOCTION OF DOCTRINES AND ELIMINATION OF DISSIDENTS

The Communist Party holds up Marxism as its religious doctrine and shows it off as the unbreakable truth. The doctrines of the Communist Party lack benevolence and tolerance. Instead, they are full of arrogance. Marxism was a product of the initial period of capitalism when productivity was low and science was under-developed. It didn't have a correct understanding at all of the relationships between humanity and society or humanity and nature. Unfortunately, this heretical ideology developed into the international communist movement, and harmed the human world for over a century before the people discarded it, having found it completely wrong in practice.

Party leaders since Lenin have always amended the cult's doctrines. From Lenin's theory of violent revolution, to Mao Zedong's theory of continuous revolution under the dictatorship of the proletariat, to Jiang Zemin's Three Represents, the Communist Party's history is full of such heretical theory and fallacy. Although these theories have constantly caused disasters in practice and are self-contradictory, the Communist Party still proclaims it is universally correct and forces the people to study its doctrines.

Eliminating dissidents is the most effective means for the evil cult of communism to spread its doctrine. Because the doctrine and behavior of this evil cult are too ridiculous, the Communist Party has to force people to accept them, relying on violence to eliminate dissidents. After the Chinese Communist Party seized the reins of power in China, it initiated land reform to eliminate the landlord class, socialist reform in industry and commerce to eliminate capitalists, the movement of purging reactionaries to eliminate folk religions and officials who held office before the communists took power, the Anti-Rightist Movement to silence intellectuals, and the

Cultural Revolution to eradicate traditional Chinese culture. The CCP was able to unify China under the communist evil cult and achieve a situation where everyone read the *Red Book*, performed the "loyalty dance[2]," and "asked for the Party's instructions in the morning and reported to the Party in the evening." In the period after Mao's and Deng's reigns, the CCP asserted that Falun Gong, a traditional cultivation practice that believes in Truthfulness, Compassion and Tolerance, would compete with it for the masses. It therefore intended to eradicate Falun Gong and initiated a genocidal persecution of Falun Gong, which continues today.

PROMOTION OF LEADER WORSHIP AND SUPREMACIST VIEWS

From Marx to Jiang Zemin, the Communist Party leaders' portraits are prominently displayed for worship. The absolute authority of the Communist Party leaders forbids any challenge. Mao Zedong was set up as the "red sun" and "big liberator." The Party spoke outrageously about his writing, saying "one sentence equals 10,000 ordinary sentences." As an ordinary Party member, Deng Xiaoping once dominated Chinese politics like an overlord. Jiang Zemin's Three Represents theory is merely a little over 40 characters long including punctuation, but the CCP Fourth Plenary Session boosted it as "providing a creative answer to questions such as what socialism is, how to construct socialism, what kind of party we are building and how to build the Party." The Party also spoke outrageously about the thought of the Three Represents, although in this case actually mocking it when saying it is a continuation and development of Marxism-Leninism, Mao Zedong thought and Deng Xiaoping theory.

Stalin's wanton slaughter of innocent people, the catastrophic Cultural Revolution launched by Mao Zedong, Deng Xiaoping's order for the Tiananmen Square massacre and Jiang

Zemin's ongoing persecution of Falun Gong are the dreadful results of the Communist Party's heretical dictatorship.

On one hand, the CCP stipulates in its Constitution, "All power in the People's Republic of China belongs to the people. The organs through which the people exercise state power are the National People's Congress and the local people's congresses at different levels." "No organization or individual may enjoy the privilege of being above the Constitution and the law."[3] On the other hand, the CCP Charter stipulates that the CCP is the core of the leadership for the Chinese-featured socialist cause, overriding both the country and the people. The chairman of the Standing Committee of the National People's Congress made "important speeches" across the country, claiming that the National People's Congress, the highest organ of state power, must adhere to the CCP's leadership. According to the CCP's principle of democratic centralism, the entire Party must obey the Central Committee of the Party. Stripped to its core, what the National People's Congress really insists upon is the dictatorship of the general secretary, which is in turn protected in the form of legislation.

Violent Brainwashing, Mind Control, Tight Organization and No Quitting Once Admitted

The CCP's organization is extremely tight: one needs two Party members' references before admission; a new member must swear to be loyal to the Party forever once admitted; Party members must pay membership dues, attend organizational activities, and take part in group political study. The Party organizations penetrate all levels of the government. There are basic CCP organizations in every single village, town, and neighborhood. The CCP controls not only its Party members and Party affairs, but also those who are not members, because the entire regime must "adhere to the Party's leadership." In those years when class struggle campaigns were carried out, the "priests" of the CCP religion, namely, the Party secretaries at all levels, more often than not, did not know exactly what they did other than disciplining people.

The "criticism and self-criticism" in the Party meetings serves as a common, unending means for controlling the minds of Party members. Throughout its existence, the CCP has launched a multitude of political movements for purifying the Party members, rectifying the Party atmosphere, capturing traitors, purging the Anti-Bolshevik Corps (AB Corps), disciplining the Party, and periodically testing the sense of Party nature—that is, using violence and terror to test the Party members' devotion to the Party, while assuring they keep in step with it forever.

Joining the CCP is like signing an irrevocable contract to sell one's body and soul. With the Party's rules being always above the laws of the nation, the Party can dismiss any Party member at will, while the individual Party member cannot quit the CCP without incurring severe punishment. Quitting the Party is considered disloyal and will bring about dire consequences. During the Cultural Revolution when the CCP cult held absolute rule, it was well known that if the Party wanted you dead, you could not live; if the Party wanted you alive, you could not die. If a person committed suicide, he would be labeled as "dreading the people's punishment for his crime" and his family members would also be implicated and punished.

The decision process within the Party operates like a black box, as the intra-Party struggles must be kept in absolute secrecy. Party documents are all confidential. Dreading exposure of their criminal acts, the CCP frequently tackles dissidents by charging them with "divulging state secrets."

URGING VIOLENCE, CARNAGE AND SACRIFICE FOR THE PARTY

Mao Zedong said, "A revolution is not a dinner party, or writing an essay, or painting a picture, or doing embroidery; it cannot be so refined, so leisurely and gentle, so temperate, kind, courteous, restrained and magnanimous. A revolution is an insurrection, an act of violence by which one class overthrows another."[4]

Deng Xiaoping recommended "Killing 200,000 people in exchange for 20 years' stability."

Jiang Zemin ordered, "Destroy them [Falun Gong practitioners] physically, ruin their reputation, and bankrupt them financially."

The CCP promotes violence, and has killed countless people throughout its previous political movements. It educates people to treat the enemy "as cold as the severe winter." The red flag is understood to be red for having been "dyed red with martyrs' blood." The Party worships red due to its addiction to blood and carnage.

The CCP makes an exhibition of "heroic" examples to encourage people to sacrifice for the Party. When Zhang Side died working in a kiln to produce opium, Mao Zedong praised his death as being "heavy as Mount Tai."[5] In those frenzied years, "brave words" such as "Fear neither hardship nor death" and "Bitter sacrifice strengthens bold resolve; we dare to make the sun and moon shine in new skies" gave aspirations substance amidst an extreme shortage of material supplies.

At the end of the 1970s, the Vietnam dispatched troops and overthrew the Khmer Rouge regime, which was fostered by the CCP and committed unspeakable crimes. Although the CCP was furious, it could not dispatch troops to support the Khmer Rouge, since China and Cambodia did not share a common border. Instead, in the name of self-defense, the CCP launched a war against Vietnam along the Chinese-Vietnam border to punish it. Tens of thousands of Chinese soldiers therefore sacrificed blood and life for this struggle between communist parties. Their deaths had in fact nothing to do with territory or sovereignty. Nevertheless, several years later, the CCP disgracefully memorialized the senseless sacrifice of so many naive and bright young lives as "the revolutionary heroic spirit," irreverently borrowing the song "The elegant demeanor dyed by blood." One hundred and fifty-four Chinese martyrs died in 1981 recapturing Mount Faka in Guangxi Province, but the CCP casually returned it to Vietnam after China and Vietnam surveyed the boundary.

When the rampant spread of SARS threatened people's lives at the beginning of 2003, the CCP readily admitted many young female nurses. These women were then quickly confined in hospitals to nurse SARS patients. The CCP push young people to the most dangerous frontline, in order to establish its "glorious image" of "Fear neither hardship nor death." However, the CCP has no explanation as to where the rest of the current 65 million Party members were and what image they brought to the Party.

Denying Belief in God and Smothering Human Nature

The CCP promotes atheism and claims that religion is spiritual opium that can intoxicate the people. It used its power to crush all religions in China, and then it deified itself, giving absolute rule of the country to the CCP cult.

At the same time that the CCP sabotaged religion, it also destroyed traditional culture. It claimed that tradition, morality and ethics were feudalistic, superstitious and reactionary, eradicating them in the name of revolution. During the Cultural Revolution, widespread ugly phenomena violated Chinese traditions, such as married couples accusing each other, students beating their teachers, fathers and sons turning against each other, Red Guards wantonly killing the innocent, and rebels beating, smashing and looting. These were the natural consequences of the CCP's smothering human nature.

After establishing its regime, the CCP forced minority nationalities to pledge allegiance to the communist leadership, compromising the rich and colorful ethnic culture they had established.

On June 4, 1989, the so-called "People's Liberation Army" massacred many students in Beijing. This caused the Chinese to completely lose hope in China's political future. From then on, the entire people turned their focus to making money. From 1999 to this day, the CCP has been brutally persecuting Falun Gong, turning against Truthfulness, Compassion and Tolerance and thereby causing an accelerated decline in moral standards.

Since the beginning of this new century, a new round of illegal land enclosure[6] and seizure of monetary and material resources by the corrupt CCP officials in collusion with profiteers has driven many people to become destitute and homeless. The number of people appealing to the government in an attempt to have an injustice settled has increased sharply, and social conflict has intensified. Large-scale protests are frequent, which the police and armed forces have violently suppressed. The fascist nature of the "Republic" has become prominent, and society has lost its moral conscience.

In the past, a villain didn't harm his next door neighbors, or, as the saying goes, the fox preyed far from home. Nowadays, when people want to con someone, they would rather target their relatives and friends, and call it "killing acquaintances."

In the past, Chinese nationals cherished chastity above all else, whereas people today ridicule the poor but not the prostitutes. The history of the destruction of human nature and morals in China is vividly displayed in a ballad below:

In the 50s people helped one another,
In the 60s people strove with one another,
In the 70s people swindled one another,
In the 80s people cared only for themselves,
In the 90s people took advantage of anyone they ran into.

MILITARY SEIZURE OF POWER, MONOPOLIZATION OF THE ECONOMY AND WILD POLITICAL AND ECONOMIC AMBITIONS

The sole purpose of establishing the CCP was to seize power by armed force and then to generate a system of state ownership in which the state holds monopolies in the planned economy. The CCP's wild ambition far surpasses that of the ordinary evil cults who simply accumulate money.

In a country of socialist public ownership ruled by the Communist Party, Party organizations that hold great power (that is, the Party committees and branches at various levels) are imposed upon or possess the normal state infrastructure. The possessing Party organizations control state machinery and draw funds directly from the budgets of the governments at different levels. Like a vampire, the CCP has sucked a huge amount of wealth from the nation.

II. THE DAMAGE THE CCP CULT HAS WROUGHT

When incidents like Aum Shinri Kyo's (Supreme Truth) killing people with sarin nerve gas, the Solar Temple's ascending to heaven by suicide, or the mass suicide of over 900 followers of Jim Jones' People's Temple are mentioned, everyone trembles with fear and outrage. The CCP is, however, an evil cult that commits crimes a thousand times worse, harming countless lives. This is because the CCP possesses the following unique features that ordinary cults lack.

THE EVIL CULT BECAME A STATE RELIGION

In most countries, if you do not follow a religion, you can still enjoy a happy life without reading the literature or listening to the principles of that religion. In mainland China, however, it is impossible for one to live there without a constant exposure to the doctrines and propaganda of the CCP cult, as the CCP has turned this evil cult into a state religion since its seizure of power.

The CCP begins to instill its political preaching as early as kindergarten and elementary school. One cannot receive higher education or promotion to higher office without passing the Political Examination. None of the questions in the Political Examination allow independent thinking. Those taking the exams are required to memorize the standard answers provided by the CCP in order to pass. The unfortunate Chinese people are forced to repeat the CCP's preaching even when they are young, brainwashing themselves over and over again. When a cadre is promoted to a higher office in the government, whether he is a member of the CCP or not, he has to attend the Party School. He won't be promoted until he has met the requirements for graduation from the Party School.

In China, where the Communist Party is the state religion, groups with different opinions are not allowed to exist. Even the "democratic parties" which are merely set up by the CCP as a political screen, and the reformed Three-Self Church (self-administration, self-support and self-propagation) must formally acknowledge the leadership of the CCP. Loyalty to the CCP is the first priority before entertaining any other beliefs, according to the very cultish logic of the CCP.

SOCIAL CONTROLS GO TO EXTREMES

This evil cult was able to become a state religion, because the CCP had complete social control and deprived individuals of freedom. This kind of control is unprecedented, since the CCP deprived people of private property, which is one foundation of freedom. Before the 1980s, people in urban areas could only earn a living by working in Party-controlled enterprises. Farmers in the rural areas had to live on the farm land belonging to the communes of the Party. Nobody could escape the CCP's control. In a socialist country like China, the Communist Party organizations are ubiquitous—from the central government to the most grass-roots levels of society, including villages and neighborhoods. Through the Party committees and branches at all levels, the CCP maintains an absolute control over society. Such strict control completely crushes individual freedom—the freedom of movement (residence registration system), freedom of speech (500,000 rightists were persecuted by the CCP because they exercised free speech), freedom of thought (Lin Zhao[7] and Zhang Zhixin[8] were executed for having doubts about the CCP), and freedom to obtain information (it is illegal to read forbidden books or listen to "enemies' radio stations"; internet browsing is monitored as well).

One might say that private ownership is allowed now by the CCP, but one should not forget that this policy of reform and openness only came about when socialism reached a point where people did not have enough to eat and the national economy was on the brink of collapse. The CCP had to take a step back in order to save itself from destruction. Nevertheless, even after the reform and opening, the CCP has never relaxed its control over the people. The ongoing brutal persecution of Falun Gong practitioners could have only occurred in a country controlled by the Communist Party. If the CCP were to become an economic giant as it wishes, it is certain that the CCP would intensify its control over the Chinese people.

ADVOCATING VIOLENCE AND DESPISING LIFE

Almost all evil cults control their followers or resist external pressure through violence. However, few have resorted to the extent the CCP has to violent means without compunction. Even the total number of deaths caused by all other evil cults across the world cannot compare to the number of people killed by the CCP. The CCP cult sees humanity as merely a means to realize its goal; killing is just another means. Thus, the CCP has no reservations or scruples about persecuting people. Anyone, including supporters, members and leaders of the CCP, can become a target of its persecution.

The CCP fostered the Cambodian Khmer Rouge, a typical case of the Communist Party's brutality and disregard for life. During its reign of three years and eight months, the Pol Pot-led Cambodian Communist Party, inspired and guided by Mao Zedong's teaching, slaughtered two million people—about one-fourth of this small country's entire population—in order to eliminate the system of private ownership. Out of the total number of deaths, more than 200,000 were of Chinese ethnicity.

To commemorate the crimes committed by the Communist Party and memorialize the victims, Cambodia set up a museum for documenting and exhibiting the atrocities of the Khmer Rouge. The museum is in a former Khmer Rouge prison. Originally a high school, the building was transformed by Pol Pot to the S-21 Prison, which was used specifically for dealing with prisoners of conscience. Many intellectuals were detained there and tortured to death. Displayed along with the prison buildings and various torture instruments are the black and white photos of the victims before they were put to death. There are many horrible tortures documented: throats cut, brains drilled, infants thrown to the ground and killed, etc. All these torture methods were reportedly taught by the "experts and technical professionals" that the CCP dispatched in support of the Khmer Rouge. The CCP even trained the photographers, who specialized in taking pictures, whether for documentation or entertainment, of the prisoners before they were executed.

In this same S-21 Prison a head-drilling machine was devised to extract human brains for making nutritious meals for the leaders of the Cambodian Communist Party. The prisoners of conscience were tied to a chair in front of the head-drilling machine. The victim would be extremely terrified, as a rapidly turning drill bit punctured the head from behind and quickly and effectively extracted the brains before the victim died.

III. THE COMMUNIST PARTY'S CULT NATURE

What makes the Communist Party so tyrannical and so evil? When this specter of the Communist Party came to this world, it came with a chilling mission. *The Communist Manifesto* has a very famous passage towards the end,

> The Communists disdain to conceal their views and aims. They openly declare that their ends can be attained only by the forcible overthrow of all existing social conditions. Let

the ruling classes tremble at a Communistic revolution. The proletarians have nothing to lose but their chains. They have a world to win.

The mission of this specter was to use violence to openly challenge human society, to smash the old world, to eliminate private ownership, to eliminate the character, independence and freedom of the bourgeoisie, to eliminate exploitation, to eliminate families, and to let the proletarians govern the world.

This political party, which openly announced its desire to "beat, smash and rob," not only denies that its point of view is evil, but also declared self-righteously in the *Communist Manifesto*, "The Communist revolution is the most radical rupture with traditional relations; no wonder that its development involved the most radical rupture with traditional ideas."

Where do traditional thoughts come from? According to the atheist's law of nature, traditional thoughts come naturally from the laws of nature and society. They are the results of systematic movements of the universe. According to those who believe in God, however, human traditions and moral values are given by God. Regardless of their origin, the most fundamental human morality, behavioral norms, and standards of judging good and bad are relatively stable; they have been the basis for regulating human behavior and maintaining social order for thousands of years. If mankind lost the moral norms and standards for judging good and bad, wouldn't humans degenerate into animals? When the *Communist Manifesto* declares it will bring about "the most radical rupture with traditional relations," it threatens the basis for the normal existence of human society. The Communist Party was bound to become an evil cult that brings destruction to mankind.

The entire *Communist Manifesto*, which sets forth the guiding principles for the communist party, is permeated with extreme pronouncements, but not a bit of kindness and tolerance. Marx and Engels thought they had found the law of social development through dialectic materialism. Hence, with the "truth" in hand, they questioned everything and denied everything. They stubbornly imposed the illusions of communism on the people and did not hold back in advocating the use of violence to destroy existing social structures and cultural foundations. The *Communist Manifesto* had the effect of injecting into the newborn Communist Party an iniquitous specter that opposes the laws of heaven, exterminates human nature, and appears arrogant, extremely selfish and totally unconstrained.

IV. THE COMMUNIST PARTY'S DOOMSDAY THEORY— THE FEAR OF THE PARTY ENDING

Marx and Engels instilled a wicked spirit into the Communist Party. Lenin established the Communist Party in Russia and, through the violence of villains overthrew the transitional government built after the February Revolution,[9] aborted the bourgeois revolution in Russia, took over the government, and obtained a foothold for the communist cult. However, Lenin's success did not make the proletarians win the world. Quite the contrary, as the first paragraph in the *Communist Manifesto* says, "All the powers of old Europe have entered into a holy alliance to exorcise this specter..." After the Communist Party was born, it immediately faced the crisis of its survival and feared elimination at any time.

After the October Revolution,[10] the Russian Communists, or Bolsheviks, did not bring the people peace or bread, but only wanton killing. The front line was losing the war and the revolution worsened the economy in the society. Hence, the people started to rebel. Civil war quickly spread to the entire nation and the farmers refused to provide food to the cities. A full-scale riot originated among the Cossacks near the River Don; its battle with the Red Army brought brutal bloodshed. The barbaric and brutal nature of the slaughter that took place in this battle can be seen from literature, such as Sholokhov's "Tikhii Don" and his other Don River story collections. The troops, lead by the former White Army Admiral Aleksandr Vailiyevich Kolchak and General Anton Denikin, almost overthrew the Russian Communist Party at one point. Even as a newborn political power, the Communist Party was opposed by almost the entire nation, perhaps because the communist cult was too evil to win the people's hearts.

The experience of the Chinese Communist Party was similar to Russia's. From the Mari Incident and April 12th Massacre,[11] to being suppressed five times in areas controlled by the Chinese communists, and eventually being forced to undertake a 25,000-kilometer (15,600 miles)"Long March," the CCP always faced the crisis of being eliminated.

The Communist Party was born with the determination to destroy the old world by all means. It then found itself having to face a real problem: how to survive without being eliminated. The Communist Party has been living in constant fear of its own demise. To survive has become the communist cult's top concern, its all-consuming focus. With the international communist alliance in disarray, the CCP's crisis of survival has worsened. Since 1989, its fear of its own doomsday has become more real as its demise has come nearer.

V. THE TREASURED WEAPON FOR THE COMMUNIST CULT'S SURVIVAL—BRUTAL STRUGGLE

The Communist Party has constantly emphasized iron discipline, absolute loyalty, and organizational principles. Those who join the CCP must swear,

> I wish to join the Chinese Communist Party, to support the Party's constitution, follow the Party's regulations, fulfill the member's obligations, execute the Party's decisions, strictly follow the Party's disciplines, keep the Party's secrets, be loyal to the Party, work diligently, dedicate my whole life to Communism, stand ready to sacrifice everything for the Party and the people, and never betray the Party. [12]

The CCP calls this spirit of cult-like devotion to the Party the "sense of Party nature." It asks a CCP member to be ready any time to give up all personal beliefs and principles and to obey absolutely the Party's will and the leader's will. If the Party wants you to be kind, then you should be kind; if the Party wants you to do evil, then you should do evil. Otherwise you would not meet the standard of being a Party member, having not shown a strong sense of Party nature.

Mao Zedong said, "Marxist philosophy is a philosophy of struggle." To foster and maintain the sense of Party nature, the CCP relies on the mechanism of periodical struggles within the Party. Through continuously mobilizing brutal struggles inside and outside the Party, the CCP has eliminated dissidents and created the red terror. At the same time, the CCP continuously purges Party members, makes its cult-type rules stricter, and fosters members' aptitude for the "Party nature," all to enhance the Party's fighting capacity. This is a treasured weapon the CCP uses to prolong its survival.

Among CCP leaders, Mao Zedong was the most adept at mastering this treasured weapon of brutal struggle within the Party. The brutality of such a struggle and the malevolence of its methods began as early as the 1930s in areas controlled by the Chinese Communists, the so-called "Soviet area."

In 1930 Mao Zedong initiated a full-scale revolutionary terror in the Soviet area in Jiangxi Province, known as the purging of the Anti-Bolshevik Corps, or the AB Corps. Thousands of Red Army soldiers, Party and League members and civilians in the communist bases were brutally murdered. The incident was caused by Mao's despotic control. After Mao established the Soviet area in Jiangxi, he was soon challenged by the local Red Army and Party organizations in southwest Jiangxi led by Li Wenlin. Mao could not stand any organized opposition force right under his nose and he used the most extreme methods to suppress the Party members he suspected of being dissidents. To create a stern atmosphere for the purge, Mao did not hesitate to start with troops under his direct control. From late November to mid-December, the First Front Red Army went through a "quick military rectification." Organizations for purging counter-revolutionaries were established at every single level in the army, including division, regiment, battalion, company, and platoon, arresting and killing Party members who were from families of landlords or rich peasants and those who had complaints. In less than one month, among more than 40,000 Red Army soldiers, 4,400 were named as AB Corps elements, including more than 10 captains (the AB Corps captains); all of them were executed.

In the following period, Mao began to punish those dissidents in the Soviet area. In December 1930, he ordered Li Shaojiu, secretary general of the General Political Department of the First Front Red Army and chairman of the Purge Committee to represent the General Frontier Committee and go to the town of Futian in Jiangxi Province where the communist government is located. Li Shaojiu arrested members of the Provincial Action Committee and eight chief leaders of the 20th Red Army, including Duan Liangbi and Li Baifang. He used many cruel torture methods such as beating and burning the body—people who were tortured like this had injuries all over their bodies, fingers fractured, burns all over, and could not move. According to the documentary evidence at that time, the victims' cries were so loud as to pierce the sky; the cruel torture methods were extremely inhumane.

On December 8, the wives of Li Baifang, Ma Ming and Zhou Mian went to visit their husbands in detention, but they were also arrested as members of the AB Corps and cruelly tortured. They were severely beaten, their bodies and vulvae burned and breasts cut with knives. Under the cruel torture, Duan Liangbi confessed that Li Wenlin, Jin Wanbang, Liu Di, Zhou Mian, Ma Ming and others were leaders of the AB Corps and that there were many members of AB Corps in the Red Army's schools.

From December 7 to the evening of December 12, in merely five days, Li Shaojiu and others arrested more than 120 alleged AB Corps members and dozens of principal counter-revolutionaries in the severe AB Corps purge in Futian; more than 40 people were executed. Li Shaojiu's cruel acts finally triggered the Futian Incident[13] on December 12, 1930 that highly astounded the Soviet area.

From the Soviet area to Yan'an, Mao relied on his theory and practice of struggle and gradually sought and established his absolute leadership of the Party. After the CCP came to power in 1949, Mao continued to rely on this kind of inner-party struggle. For example, in the eighth plenum of the Eighth CCP Central Committee meeting held in Lushan in 1959, Mao Zedong launched a sudden attack on Peng Dehuai and removed him from his position.[14] All of the central leaders who attended the conference were asked to take a stand; the few who dared to express different opinions were all labeled the Peng Dehuai anti-Party bloc. During the Cultural Revolution, the veteran cadres at the CCP's Central Committee were punished one after another, but all of them gave in without putting up a fight. Who would dare to speak a word against Mao Zedong? The CCP has always emphasized iron discipline, loyalty to the Party, and organizational principles, requiring absolute obedience to the hierarchy's leader. This kind of Party nature has been engrained in the continuous political struggles.

During the Cultural Revolution, Li Lisan, once a CCP leader, was driven to the limit of his endurance. At 68 years of age, he was interrogated on average seven times per month. His wife Li Sha was treated as a "Soviet revisionist" spy, and had already been sent to jail; her whereabouts was unknown. With no other choice and in extreme despair, Li committed suicide by swallowing a large quantity of sleeping pills. Before his death, Li Lisan wrote a letter to Mao Zedong, truly reflecting the sense of Party nature, according to which a CCP member does not dare to give up, even on the verge of death:

> Chairman,
>
> I am now stepping onto the path of betraying the Party by committing suicide, and have no means to defend my crime. Only one thing, that is, my entire family and I have never collaborated with enemy states. Only on this issue, I request the central government to investigate and examine the facts and draw conclusions based on truth...
>
> Li Lisan
> June 22, 1967[15]

While Mao Zedong's philosophy of struggle eventually

dragged China into an unprecedented catastrophe, this kind of political campaign and the inner-party struggle, which is widespread once "every seven or eight years," have ensured the survival of the CCP. Every time there was a campaign, a minority of five percent would be persecuted, and the remaining 95 percent would be brought to an obedient adherence to the Party's basic line, thereby enhancing the Party organization's cohesive force and destructive capacity. These struggles also eliminated those "faltering" members who were not willing to give up their conscience, and attacked any force that dared to resist. Through this mechanism of struggle, those CCP members who have the greatest desire for struggle and are best at using the methods of hoodlums have gained control. The CCP cult leaders are all fearless people rich in the experience of struggle and full of the Party spirit. Such brutal struggle also gives those who have experienced it a "blood lesson" and violent brainwashing. At the same time, it continuously energizes the CCP, further strengthening its desire for struggle, ensuring its survival, and preventing it from becoming a temperate group that gives up the struggle.

This kind of party nature required by the CCP has come precisely from the CCP's cult nature. In order to realize its goal, the CCP is determined to break away from all traditional principles, and use all means to fight unhesitatingly with any force that hinders it. Therefore it needs to train and enslave all its members to become the Party's heartless, unjust and faithless tools. This nature of the CCP originates from its hatred toward human society and traditions, its delusional self-evaluation, and its extreme selfishness and contempt for other people's lives. In order to achieve its so-called ideal, the CCP used violence at all costs to smash the world and eliminate all dissidents. Such an evil cult would meet with opposition from people of conscience, so it must eliminate people's conscience and benevolent thoughts to make people believe in its evil doctrine. Therefore, in order to ensure its survival, the CCP first of all must destroy people's conscience, benevolent thoughts and moral standards, turning people into tame slaves and tools. According to the CCP's logic, the Party's life and interest override everything else; they even override the collective interest of all Party members, thus any individual Party member must be prepared to sacrifice for the Party.

Looking at the CCP's history, individuals who retained the mindset of traditional intellectuals like Chen Duxiu and Qu Qiubai, or who still cared about people's interests like Hu Yaobang and Zhao Ziyang, or who are determined to be clean officials and bring real service to the people such as Zhu Rongji—no matter how much they contributed to the Party, and no matter how devoid of personal ambitions they were, they were inevitably purged, cast aside, or restricted by the Party's interests and discipline.

The sense of Party nature or the aptitude for the Party that was fostered in their bones over many years of struggle often made them compromise and surrender in critical moments, because in their subconscious, the Party's survival is the highest interest. They would rather sacrifice themselves and watch the evil force within the Party commit murder, than challenge the Party's survival with their conscientious and compassionate thoughts. This is precisely the result of the CCP's mechanism of struggle: it turns good people into tools that it uses, and uses the Party nature to limit and even eliminate human conscience to the greatest extent. Dozens of the CCP's "line struggles" brought down more than ten top-level Party leaders or designated successors; none of the top Party leaders came to a good end. Although Mao Zedong had been the king for 43 years, shortly after he died, his wife and nephew were put in jail, which was cheered by the entire Party as a great victory of Maoism. Is this a comedy or a farce?

After the CCP seized political power, there were unceasing political campaigns, from inner-party fights to struggles outside the Party. This was the case during the Mao Zedong era, and is still the case in the post-Mao era of "reform and openness." In the 1980s, when people just began to have a slight bit of freedom in their thinking, the CCP launched the campaign of Opposition to Bourgeois Liberalization, and proposed the Four Fundamental Principles[16] in order to maintain its absolute leadership. In 1989, the students who peacefully asked for democracy were bloodily suppressed because the CCP does not allow democratic aspirations. The 1990s witnessed a rapid increase in Falun Gong practitioners who believe in Truthfulness, Compassion and Tolerance, but they were met with genocidal persecution beginning in 1999, because the CCP cannot tolerate human nature and benevolent thoughts. It must use violence to destroy people's conscience and ensure its own power. Since entering the 21st century, the internet has connected the world together, but the CCP has spent great sums of money in setting up network blockades to trap online liberals, because the CCP greatly fears people's freely obtaining information.

VI. THE DEGENERATION OF THE EVIL CULT OF THE CCP

The CCP evil cult essentially rules in opposition to human nature and the principles of heaven. The CCP is known for its arrogance, self-importance, selfishness, and brutal, unrestrained acts. It consistently brings disasters to the country and the people, yet it never admits its mistakes, and would never reveal its true nature to the people. The CCP has never hesitated to change its slogans and labels, which are regarded by the CCP as the means to maintain its control. It will do anything to keep in power with total disregard for morality, justice and human life.

The institutionalization and socialization of this evil cult are bound to lead to its collapse. As a result of the centralization of power, public opinion has been silenced and all possible monitoring mechanisms have been destroyed, leaving no force to stop the CCP from sliding into corruption and disintegration.

Today's CCP has become the largest ruling party of embezzlement and corruption in the world. According to official statistics in China, among the 20 million officials, officers or cadres in the Party or government over the past 20 years, eight million have been found guilty of corruption and disciplined or punished based on Party or government regulations. If the unidentified corrupt officials are also taken into account, the corrupt Party and government officials are estimated to be at over two thirds, of whom only a small portion have been investigated and exposed.

Securing material benefits by means of corruption and extortion has become the strongest coherent force for the unity of the CCP today. The corrupt officials know that without the CCP, they would have no opportunity to connive for personal gain, and if the CCP falls, they would not only lose their power and position, but also face investigation. In *Heaven's Wrath*, a novel that exposes behind-the-scenes dealings of the CCP officials, the author Chen Fang spelled out the CCP's top secret using the mouth of Hao Xiangshou, a deputy director of a municipal CCP office, "corruption has stabilized our political power."

The Chinese people see it clearly, "if we fight corruption, the Party will fall; if we do not fight corruption, the nation will perish." The CCP, however, will not risk its own doom to fight corruption. What it will do is to kill a few corrupt individuals as a token sacrifice for the sake of its image. This prolongs its life for a few more years at the expense of a small number of corrupt elements. Today, the only goals of the CCP evil cult are to keep its power and steer clear of its demise.

In today's China, ethics and morality have degenerated beyond recognition. Shoddy products, prostitutes, drugs, conspiracies between officials and gangs, organized crime syndicates, gambling, bribery; corruption of every kind is prevalent. The CCP has largely ignored such moral decay, while many high ranking officials are the bosses in the back room who are extorting protection fees from people who are afraid. Cai Shaoqing, an expert studying mafia and crime organizations at Nanjing University, estimates that the number of organized crime members in China totals at least one million. Each syndicate figure captured always exposes some behind-the-scenes corrupt communists who are government officials, judges, or police.

The CCP is afraid the Chinese people might gain a sense of conscience and morality, so it does not dare to allow the people to have faith in religion or freedom of thought. It uses all its resources to persecute the good people who have faith, such as the underground Christians who believe in Jesus and God and the Falun Gong practitioners who seek to be truthful, compassionate and tolerant. The CCP is afraid that democracy would end its one-party rule, so it does not dare to give people political freedom. It acts swiftly to imprison independent liberals and civil rights activists. It does, however, give people a deviated freedom. As long as you do not care about politics and do not oppose the CCP's leadership, you may let your desires go in any way you want, even if it means you do wicked, unethical things. As a result, the CCP is deteriorating dramatically and social morality in China is experiencing an alarmingly sharp decline.

"Blocking the road to heaven and opening the gate to hell" best describes how the evil cult of the CCP has devastated Chinese society today.

VII. REFLECTIONS ON THE EVIL RULE OF THE CCP

WHAT IS THE COMMUNIST PARTY?

This seemingly simple question has no simple answers. Under the pretense of being "for the people" and in the guise of a political party, the Communist Party has indeed deceived millions of people. And yet it is not a political party in the ordinary sense, but a harmful and evil cult possessed by an evil specter. The Communist Party is a living being who manifests in this world through the Party organizations. What truly controls the Communist Party is the evil specter that first entered it, and it is that evil specter that determines the evil nature of the Communist Party.

The leaders of the Communist Party, while acting as the gurus of the cult, serve only as the mouthpiece of the evil specter and the Party. When their will and purpose are in line with the Party and can be used by it, they will be chosen as leaders. But when they can no longer meet the needs of the Party, they will be ruthlessly overthrown. The mechanism of struggle of the Party makes sure that only the craftiest, the most evil, and the toughest will hold steadily to the position of guru of the Communist Party. A dozen or so ranking Party leaders have fallen from grace, which proves the truth of this argument. In fact, the top leaders of the Party are walking on a very narrow tight rope. They can either break away from the Party line and leave a good name in history, as Gorbachev did, or be victimized by the Party like many general secretaries of the Party.

The people are the targets of the Party's enslavement and oppression. Under the Party's rule, the people have no rights to reject the Party. Instead, they are forced to accept the Party's leadership and fulfill the obligation to sustain the Party. They are also subjected to regular cult-type brainwashing under the threat of coercion from the Party. The CCP forces the whole nation to believe in and sustain this evil cult. This is rarely seen in the world today, and we have to recognize the CCP's unmatchable skill in such oppression.

The Party members are a physical mass that has been used to fill up the body of the Party. Many among them are honest and kind, and may even be quite accomplished in their public life. These are the people the CCP likes to recruit, since their reputation and competence may be used to serve the Party. Many others, out of their desire to become an official and enjoy a higher social status, would work hard to join the Party and aid the evil being. There are also those who chose to join the Party because they want to accomplish something in their lives and realized that under the Communist rule they could not do so unless they joined the Party. Some joined the Party because they wanted the allocation of an apartment or simply wanted a better image. Thus among the tens of millions of Party members, there are both good and bad people. Regardless of motives, once you swear your allegiance in front of the Party's flag, willingly or otherwise, that means you have voluntarily devoted yourself to the Party. You will then go through the brainwashing process by participating in the weekly political studies. A significant number of Party members will have little, if any, of their own thoughts left and will be easily controlled by the evil specter of the CCP host body as a result of the indoctrination by the Party. These people will function within the Party like the cells of a human body, and work non-stop for the Party's existence, even though they themselves are also part of the population enslaved by the Party.

Sadder still, after the bondage of the "Party nature" is imposed on you, it becomes very hard to take it off. Once you show your human side, you will be purged or persecuted. You cannot withdraw from the Party on your own even if you want to, for the Party, with its entrance-yes and exit-no policy, would regard you as a traitor. That is why people often reveal a dual-nature: in their political life the nature of the Communist Party; in their daily life human nature.

The Party cadres are a group that retains power among Party members. Though they may have choices between good and bad and make their own decisions on specific occasions, at specific times, and specific events, they, as a whole, have to follow the will of the Party. The mandate dictates "the whole Party obeys the Central Committee." The Party cadres are the leaders at different levels; they are the Party's backbones. They too are merely tools for the Party. They too have been deceived, used and victimized during the past political movements. The CCP's underlying criterion is to test whether you are following the right guru and are sincere in your devotion.

WHY DO PEOPLE REMAIN UNAWARE?

The CCP has acted viciously and wickedly throughout its more than 50-year rule over China. But why do the Chinese people lack a realistic understanding of the CCP's evil nature? Is it because the Chinese are dumb? No. The Chinese constitute one of the wisest nations in the world and boast a rich traditional culture and heritage of 5,000 years. Yet the Chinese people are still living under the CCP's rule, completely afraid of expressing their discontent. The key lies in the mind-control practiced by the CCP.

If the Chinese people enjoyed freedom of expression and could debate openly the merits and demerits of the CCP, we could imagine the Chinese would have long ago seen through the evil nature of the CCP and freed themselves from the influence of this evil cult. Unfortunately, the Chinese people lost their freedom of expression and thought over half a century ago with the advent of the CCP's rule. The purpose behind persecution of the rightists among the intellectuals in 1957 was to restrain free expression and to control people's minds. In a society so lacking fundamental freedoms, most of the youth who had wholeheartedly studied the works of Marx and Engels during the Cultural Revolution have ironically been labeled an "anti-Party clique" and are subsequently persecuted. Discussing the CCP's rights and wrongs was simply out of the question.

Not many Chinese would even dare to think of calling the CCP an evil cult. However, were that assertion made, those who have lived in China would not find it hard to discover strong evidence supporting the argument, from both their own experience and those of their family and friends.

The Chinese people have not only been deprived of freedom of thought, they have also been indoctrinated with the teachings and culture of the Party. Thus all that people could hear have been the praises of the Party, and their minds have been impoverished of any thought other than ideas that reinforce the CCP. Take the Tiananmen massacre for example. When shots were fired on June 4, 1989, many people instinctively ran to hide in the bushes. Moments later, despite the risks, they came bravely out of hiding and sang "The Internationale" together. These Chinese were indeed courageous, innocent and respectable, yet why did they sing "The Internationale," the communist anthem, when confronted with the communist killing? The reason is simple. Educated in the Party's culture, all the pitiable people know is communism. Those in Tiananmen Square did not know any songs other than "The Internationale" and a few others that praise the Communist Party.

WHAT IS THE WAY OUT?

The CCP has been moving towards its complete doom. Sadly, it is still trying to tie its fate to the Chinese nation before its demise.

The dying CCP is apparently weakening and its control over people's minds is loosening. With the advance of telecommunications and the Internet, the CCP is finding it difficult to control information and suppress expression. As the corrupt officials increasingly plunder and oppress the people, the public is beginning to wake up from their illusions about the CCP, and many of them have started to exercise civil disobedience. The CCP has not only failed to achieve its goal of increased ideological control in its persecution of Falun Gong, but also further weakened itself while revealing its absolute ruthlessness. This opportune moment has made people reconsider the CCP, paving the way for the Chinese nation to free itself from the ideological bondage and completely break away from the control of the communist evil specter.

Having lived under the evil rule of the CCP for over 50 years, the Chinese people do not need a violent revolution; rather, they need redemption of their souls. This can be achieved through self-help, and the first step towards that goal is to become aware of the evil nature of the CCP.

The day will come when people cast aside the Party's organizations that are attached to the state apparatus, allowing the social systems to function independently, backed up by the core forces of the society. With the passing of a dictatorial Party organization, the efficiency of the government will be improved and enhanced. And that day is right around the corner. In fact, as early as the 1980s, the reformers inside the Party advocated the idea of "separating the Party from the government," in an attempt to exclude the Party from the government. The reform efforts from within the CCP have proven to be inadequate and unsuccessful, because the ideology of "the absolute leadership of the Party" has not been totally rejected.

The Party culture is the environment necessary for the survival of the communist evil cult. Removing the CCP's possession of people's minds may prove to be more difficult than clearing out the CCP's possession of state administrations, but such a removal is the only way truly to uproot the evil of communism. This can be achieved only through the efforts of the Chinese people themselves. With their minds set right and human nature returned to its original state, the public would regain its morality and succeed in a transition to a decent non-communist society. The cure for this evil possession lies in the recognition of the evil specter's nature and harmfulness, eradicating it from people's minds, and clearing it out, so that it has no place to hide. The Communist Party stresses ideological control, since it is nothing but an ideology itself. That ideology will dissipate when all Chinese reject the communist falsehood in their minds, actively wipe out the Party culture, and rid their own mentalities and lives of the influences from the communist evil cult. As people save themselves, the CCP will disintegrate.

Nations ruled by communists are associated with poverty, totalitarianism, and persecution. There are very few such nations left, including China, North Korea, Vietnam, and Cuba. Their days are numbered.

With the wisdom of the Chinese people, inspired by the historical glory of the Chinese nation, a China freed from the evil possession of communism will be a promising nation.

275

CONCLUSION

The CCP no longer believes in communism. Its soul has died, but its shadow remains. It has inherited only the "skin" of communism, but still manifests the nature of an evil cult: arrogance, conceit and selfishness, and indulgence in wanton destructiveness. The CCP has inherited the communist denial of the law of heaven, and its rejection of human nature has remained unchanged.

Today, the CCP continues to rule China with the methods of struggle mastered over the years, using its close-knit organizational system coupled with the ruling form of "Party possession," as well as evil propaganda that functions as a state-religion. The six features of the Communist Party outlined previously place today's CCP firmly within the definition of an evil cult; it does no good, only evil.

As it nears death, this communist evil cult is accelerating the pace of its corruption and degeneration. What is most troublesome is that it is stubbornly doing what it can to take the Chinese nation with it into an abyss of corruption and degeneration.

The Chinese need to help themselves; they need to reflect, and they need to shake off the CCP.

COMMENTARY NINE

ON THE UNSCRUPULOUS NATURE
OF THE CHINESE COMMUNIST PARTY

COMMENTARY NINE

ON THE UNSCRUPULOUS NATURE OF
THE CHINESE COMMUNIST PARTY

FOREWORD

The communist movement, which has made a big fanfare for over a century, has brought mankind only war, poverty, brutality, and dictatorship. With the collapse of the Soviet Union and the Eastern European communist parties, this disastrous and outrageous drama finally entered its last stage by the end of the last century. No one, from the ordinary citizens to the general secretary of the CCP, believes in the myth of communism anymore.

The communist regime came into being due to neither "divine mandate"[1] nor democratic election. Today, with its ideology destroyed, the legitimacy of its reign is facing an unprecedented challenge.

The Chinese Communist Party (CCP) is unwilling to leave the historical stage in accordance with the current of history. Instead, it is using the ruthless methods developed during decades of political campaigns to renew its crazed struggle for legitimacy and to revive its dead mandate.

The CCP's policies of reform and opening up disguise a desperate intention to maintain its group interest and totalitarian rule. Despite tight restrictions, the economic achievements earned by the hard work of the Chinese people in the past 20 years did not persuade the CCP to put down its butcher knife. Instead, the CCP stole these achievements and used them to validate its rule, making its consistently unprincipled behavior more deceptive and misleading.

What is most alarming is that the CCP is going all out to destroy the moral foundation of the entire nation, attempting to turn every Chinese citizen, to various degrees, into a schemer in order to create an environment favorable for the CCP to "advance over time."

In this historical moment today, it is especially important for us to understand clearly why the CCP acts like a band of scoundrels and to expose its villainous nature, so that the Chinese nation can achieve lasting stability and peace, enter an era free of the CCP as soon as possible, and construct a future of renewed national splendor.

I. THE UNSCRUPULOUS NATURE OF THE CCP HAS NEVER CHANGED

WHO IS THE CCP's REFORM FOR?

Throughout history, whenever the CCP encountered crises, it would demonstrate some traces of improvement, enticing people to develop illusions about the CCP. Without exception, the illusions were shattered time and again. Today, the CCP has pursued short-term benefits and in doing so has produced a show of economic prosperity that has once again persuaded the people to believe in fantasies about the CCP. However, the fundamental conflicts between the interest of the CCP and that of the nation and the people determine that this false prosperity will not last. The "reform" the CCP has promised has one purpose – to maintain its rule. It is a lame reform, a change in surface but not in substance. Underneath the lopsided development lies a great social crisis. Once the crisis breaks out, the nation and the people will suffer once again.

With the change of leadership, the new generation of CCP leaders had no part in the communist revolution, and therefore have less and less prestige and credibility in managing the nation. Amidst the crisis of its legitimacy, the CCP's protection of the Party's interests has increasingly become the basic guarantee for maintaining the interests of individuals within the CCP. The CCP's nature is selfish. It knows no restraint. To hope such a Party might devote itself to developing the country peacefully is wishful thinking.

Consider what *People's Daily*, the mouthpiece of the CCP, said in a front page story on July 12th, 2004: "The historical dialectics have taught the CCP members the following: Those things that should be changed must change, otherwise deterioration will follow; those that should not be changed must remain unchanged, otherwise it will lead to self-destruction."

What is it that should remain unchanged? The *People's Daily* explains: "The Party's basic line of "one center, two basic points" must last solidly for one hundred years without any vacillation."[2]

People don't necessarily understand what the "center" and "basic points" stand for, but everyone knows that the communist specter's determination to maintain its collective interest and dictatorship never changes. Communism has been defeated globally, and is doomed to become more and more moribund. Nevertheless, the more corrupt a thing becomes the more destructive it becomes during its dying struggle. To discuss democratic improvements with the Communist Party is like asking a tiger to change its skin.

WHAT WOULD CHINA DO WITHOUT THE COMMUNIST PARTY?

As the CCP is waning, people have come to discover unexpectedly that for decades the evil specter of the CCP, with its ever-changing villainous means, has instilled its vile elements into every aspect of ordinary people's lives.

At the time of Mao Zedong's death, so many Chinese cried bitterly before Mao's portrait, wondering, "How can China continue without Chairman Mao?" Ironically, 20 years later, when the Communist Party has lost its legitimacy to rule the country, the CCP has spread a new round of propaganda, making people again wonder anxiously, "What would China do without the Communist Party?"

In reality, the CCP's all-pervasive political control has so deeply branded the current Chinese culture and the Chinese mindsets that even the criteria with which the Chinese people judge the CCP have the mark of the CCP, or have even come from the CCP. If in the past, the CCP controlled people by instilling its elements into them, then the CCP has now come to harvest what it sowed, since those things instilled in people's minds have been digested and absorbed into their very cells. People think according to the CCP's logic and put themselves in the CCP's shoes in judging right and wrong. Regarding the CCP's killing of student protesters on June 4, 1989, some people said, "If I were Deng Xiaoping, I too would quell the protest with tanks." In the persecution of Falun Gong, some people are saying, "If I were Jiang Zemin, I too would eliminate Falun Gong." About the ban on free speech, some people are saying, "If I were the CCP, I would do the same." Truth and conscience have vanished, leaving only the CCP's logic. This has been one of the vilest and most ruthless methods used by the CCP due to its unscrupulous nature. As long as the moral toxins instilled by the CCP remain in the people's minds, the CCP can continue to gain energy to sustain its iniquitous life.

"What would China do without the CCP?" This mode of thinking fits precisely the CCP's aim of having people reason by its own logic.

China came through her 5,000-year history of civilization without the CCP. Indeed, no country in the world would stop social advancement because of the fall of a particular regime. After decades of the CCP's rule, however, people no longer recognize this fact. The CCP's prolonged propaganda has trained people to think of the Party as their mother. The omnipresent CCP politics have rendered people unable to conceive of living without the CCP.

Without Mao Zedong, China did not fall. Will China collapse without the CCP?

WHAT IS THE REAL SOURCE OF TURMOIL?

Many people know and dislike the CCP's Machiavellian behavior, and loathe its struggles and deceptions. But, at the same time, they fear the CCP's political movements and the resulting turmoil, and fear chaos will visit China again. Thus, once the CCP threatens people with "turmoil," people fall into silent acceptance of the CCP's rule and feel helpless in the face of the CCP's despotic power.

In reality, with its several million troops and armed police, the CCP is the real source of turmoil. Ordinary citizens have neither the cause nor the capability to initiate turmoil. Only the regressive CCP would be so reckless as to bring the country into turmoil at any hint of change. "Stability overrides everything else" and "Nipping the buds of all unstable elements"—these slogans have become the theoretical basis for the CCP to suppress people. Who is the biggest cause of instability in China? Is it not the CCP, who specializes in tyranny? The CCP instigates turmoil, and then in turn uses the chaos it created to coerce the people. This is a common action of all villains.

II. THE CCP SACRIFICES ECONOMIC DEVELOPMENT

TAKING CREDIT FOR THE ACHIEVEMENTS OF PEOPLE'S HARD WORK

The CCP's claim to legitimacy lies in the economic development over the past 20 some years. In reality, however, such development was gradually achieved by the Chinese people after the fetters of the CCP were slightly relaxed and, therefore, has nothing to do with the CCP's own merit. The CCP has, however, claimed this economic development as its own achievement, asking people to be grateful for it, as if none of these developments would have taken place without the CCP. We all know, in reality, that many non-communist countries achieved faster economic growth a long time ago.

The winners of Olympic gold medals are required to thank the Party. The Party did not hesitate to use the contrived image of a "great nation of sports" to eulogize itself. China suffered a great deal in the SARS epidemic, but *People's Daily* reported that China defeated the virus "relying on the Party's basic theory, basic line, basic principle, and basic experience." The launching of China's spaceship Shenzhou-V was accomplished by the professionals of astronautic science and technology, but the CCP used it as evidence to prove that only the CCP could lead the Chinese people to enter the rank of powerful countries in the world. As for China's hosting of the 2008 Olympic Games, what was in reality an "olive branch" given by Western countries to encourage China to improve its human rights, the CCP uses to enhance its claims to legitimacy and to provide a pretext for suppressing the Chinese people. China's "great market potential," which is sought after by foreign investors, stems from the capacity for consumption of China's population of 1.3 billion. The CCP usurps credit for this potential, and turns it into a keen weapon used to coerce Western societies into cooperating with the CCP's rule.

The CCP attributes anything bad to reactionary forces and the ulterior motives of individuals, while crediting everything good to the Party leadership. The CCP will make use of every single achievement to make its claim to legitimacy more attractive. Even the wrongdoing that the CCP commits can be turned into something "good" to serve its purposes. For example, when the truth about the rampant spread of AIDS could no longer be covered up, the CCP suddenly created a new identity. It carefully mobilized its propaganda machine, utilizing everyone from well-known actors to the Party's general secretary, in order to portray the prime culprit, the CCP, as a blessing for patients, a destroyer of AIDS, and a challenger to disease. In dealing with such a serious life-and-death issue, all the CCP could think of was how to use the issue to glorify itself. Only a schemer as vicious as the CCP is capable of such ruthless behavior as brazenly or underhandedly taking credit and utterly disregarding human life.

ECONOMIC DISADVANTAGE CAUSED BY SHORTSIGHTED BEHAVIORS

Facing a serious "crisis of legitimacy," the CCP carried out the policies of reform and opening up in the 1980s in order to maintain its rule. Its eagerness for quick success has placed China at a disadvantage, termed by economists as the "curse of the latecomer."

The concept of "curse of the latecomer", or "latecomer advantage" as some other scholars call it, refers to the fact that underdeveloped countries, which set out late for development, can imitate the developed countries in many aspects. The imitation can take two forms: imitating the social system, or imitating the technological and industrial models. Imitating a social system is usually difficult, since system reform would endanger the vested interests of some social or political groups. Thus, underdeveloped countries are inclined to imitate developed countries' technologies.

Although technological imitation can generate short-term economic growth, it may result in many hidden risks or even failure in long-term development.

It is precisely the "curse of the latecomer," a path to failure, that the CCP has followed. Over the past two decades, China's "technological imitation" has led to some achievements, which have been taken by the CCP for its own advantage in order to prove its legitimacy and continue to resist political reform that would undermine the CCP's own interests. Thus, the long-term interests of the nation have been sacrificed.

A PAINFUL COST FOR THE CCP'S ECONOMIC DEVELOPMENT

While the CCP constantly brags about its economic advancement, in reality, China's economy today ranks lower in the world than during the Qianlong's reign (1711-1799) in the Qing Dynasty. During the Qianlong period, China's GDP accounted for 51 percent of the world's total. When Dr. Sun Yat-sen founded the Republic of China (KMT period) in 1911, China's GDP accounted for 27 percent of the world's total. By 1923, the percentage dropped, but still was as high as 12 percent. In 1949, when the CCP took control, the percentage was 5.7, but in 2003, China's GDP was less than 4 percent of the world's total. In contrast to the economic decline during the KMT period that was caused by several decades of war, the continuing economic decline during the CCP's reign occurred during peaceful times.

Today, in order to legitimize its power, the CCP is eager for quick successes and instant benefits. The crippled economic reform that the CCP launched to safeguard its interests has cost the country dearly. The rapid economic growth in the past 20 years is, to a large extent, built on the excessive use or even waste of resources, and has been gained at the cost of environmental destruction. A considerable portion of China's GDP is achieved by sacrificing the opportunities of future generations. In 2003, China contributed less than four percent to the world economy, but its consumption of steel, cement and other materials amounted to one third of the total global consumption.[3]

From the 1980s to the end of the 1990s, desertification in China increased from a little over 1,000 to 2,460 square kilometers (386 to 950 square miles). The per capita arable land also decreased from about two *mu* in 1980 to 1.43 *mu* in 2003. The widespread upsurge of land enclosure for development has led China to lose 100 million *mu* of arable land in just a few years time. However, only 43 percent of the confiscated land is actually used. Currently, the total amount of wastewater discharge is 43.95 billion tons, exceeding the environmental capacity by 82 percent. In the seven major river systems, 40.9 percent of the water is not suitable for drinking by humans or livestock. Seventy-five percent of the lakes are so polluted as to produce various degrees of eutrophication.[4] The conflicts between man and nature in China have never been as intense as they are today. Neither China nor the world can withstand such unhealthy growth. Deluded by the superficial splendor of high-rises and mansions, people are unaware of the impending ecological crisis. Once the time comes for nature to exact its toll on human beings, however, it will bring disastrous consequences to the Chinese nation.

In comparison, since abandoning communism, Russia has carried out economic and political reforms at the same time. After experiencing a short period of agony, it has embarked on a rapid development. From 1999 to 2003, Russia's GDP increased by a total of 29.9 percent. The living standard of its residents has significantly improved. The Western business circles have begun not only to discuss the "Russian economic phenomenon," but have also begun to invest in Russia, the new hotspot, on a large scale. Russia's ranking among the most attractive nations for investment has jumped from 17th in 2002 to 8th in 2003, becoming one of the world's top ten most popular nations for investment for the first time.

Even India, a country that, to most Chinese, is poverty-stricken and full of ethnic conflicts, has enjoyed a significantly expedited development and has achieved an economic growth rate of seven to eight percent per year since its economic reforms in 1991. India has a relatively complete legal system in a market economy, a healthy financial system, a well-developed democratic system, and a stable public mentality. The international community has recognized India as a country of great development potential.

On the other hand, the CCP only engages in economic reform without political reform. The false appearance of an economy that flourishes in the short run has hindered the natural "evolution of social systems." It is this incomplete reform that has caused an increasing imbalance in the Chinese society and sharpened social conflicts. The financial gains achieved by the people are not protected by stable social systems. Furthermore, in the process of privatizing the state-owned properties, the CCP's power-holders have utilized their positions to fill their own pockets.

THE CCP CHEATS THE PEASANTS ONCE AND AGAIN

The CCP relied on peasants to gain power. The rural residents in the CCP-controlled areas in the early stage of its buildup devoted all they had to the CCP. But since the CCP obtained control of the country, peasants have experienced severe discrimination.

After the CCP established the government, it set up a very unfair system - the residential registration system. The system forcefully classifies people into rural and non-rural populations, creating an unreasonable separation and opposition within the country. Peasants have no medical insurance, no unemployment welfare, no retirement pensions, and cannot take loans from banks. Peasants are not only the most impoverished class in China, but also the class carrying the heaviest tax burden. Peasants need to pay a mandatory provident fund, public welfare fund, administrative management fund, extra education fee, birth control fee, militia organization and training fee, country road construction fee and military service compensation fee. Besides all these fees, they also have to sell part of the grains they produce at a flat rate to the state as a mandatory requirement, and pay agriculture tax, land tax, special local produce tax, and butchery tax in addition to numerous other levies. In contrast, the non-rural population does not pay these fees and taxes.

In the beginning of 2004, China's Premier Wen Jiabao issued the "No. 1 Document," stating that rural China was facing the most difficult time since the beginning of the economic reform in 1978. Income for most peasants had stagnated or even declined. They had become poorer, and the income gap between urban and rural residents continued to widen.

In a tree farm in eastern Sichuan Province, upper level authorities distributed 500,000 yuan (approximately US $60,500) for a reforestation project. The leaders of the tree farm first put 200,000 yuan in their own pockets, and then allocated the remaining 300,000 yuan to tree planting. But as the money was taken away when passing through each level of the government, very little was left in the end for local peasants who did the actual tree planting. The government did not need to worry that the peasants would refuse to work on the project because of inadequate funding. The peasants were so impoverished that they would work for very little money. This is one of the reasons that products made in China are so cheap.

USING ECONOMIC INTERESTS TO PRESSURE WESTERN COUNTRIES

Many people believe that trade with China will promote human rights, freedom of speech and democratic reform in China. After more than a decade, it is clear that this assumption is only wishful thinking. A comparison of the principles for doing business in China and the West provides a common example. The fairness and transparency of Western societies are replaced by nepotism, bribery and embezzlement in China. Many Western corporations have become leading culprits by further exacerbating China's corruption. Some companies even help the CCP hide its human rights violations and persecution of its own people.

The CCP behaves like the Mafia by playing the economic card in foreign diplomacy. Whether China's aircraft manufacturing contract is given to France or the United States depends on which country keeps quiet on the CCP's human rights issues. Many Western businessmen and politicians are driven and controlled by economic profits from China. Some information technology companies from North America have supplied specialized products to the CCP for blocking the Internet. In order to gain entry to the Chinese market, some Internet websites have agreed to censor themselves and filter out information disliked by the CCP.

According to data from China's Ministry of Commerce, by the end of April 2004, China has seen a total US$ 990 billion of foreign investment in various contracts. The huge "blood transfusion" to the CCP's economy from foreign capital is apparent. But in the process of investment, foreign capital did not bring the concept of democracy, freedom and human rights as fundamental principles to the Chinese people. The CCP capitalizes in its propaganda on the unconditional cooperation by foreign investors and foreign governments and the flattery of some countries. By making use of China's superficial economic prosperity, CCP officials have become extremely adept at colluding with businesses to divide state wealth and block political reforms.

III. THE CCP'S BRAINWASHING TECHNIQUES CHANGE FROM UNDISGUISED TO "REFINED"

People are often heard to say, "I know the CCP lied too often in the past, but this time it is telling the truth." Ironically, in retrospect, this was what people would say each time the CCP made a grave mistake in the past. This reflects the ability the CCP has acquired over the decades to use lies to fool people.

People have developed some resistance to the CCP's tall tales. In response, the CCP's fabrication and propaganda have become more subtle and "professional." Evolving from the slogan-style propaganda of the past, the CCP's lies have become more refined and subtle. Particularly under the conditions of the information blockade the CCP has erected around China, it makes up stories based on partial facts to mislead the public, which is even more detrimental and deceptive than tall tales.

Chinascope, an English language journal, carried an article in October 2004 that analyzes cases where the CCP uses more subtle means of fabricating lies in order to cover up the truth. When SARS broke out in Mainland China in 2003, the outside world suspected that China had hidden information about the epidemic, and yet the CCP repeatedly refused to acknowledge it. To find out if the CCP had been truthful about its reporting on SARS, the author of the article read all 400-plus reports on SARS that were posted on the Xinhua website from the beginning to April 2003.

These reports told the following story: As soon as SARS appeared, governments at central and local levels mobilized experts to give timely treatment to the patients who later were discharged from hospitals upon recovery. In response to trouble-makers' inciting people to stock-pile goods in order to avoid going out when the disease became widespread, the government wasted no time in stopping rumors and taking steps to prevent their spread, so the social order was effectively ensured. Although a very small number of anti-China forces groundlessly suspected a cover-up by the Chinese government, most countries and people did not believe these rumors. The upcoming Guangzhou Trade Fair would have the largest participation ever from businesses around the world. Tourists from overseas confirmed that it was safe to travel in China. In particular, experts from the World Health Organization [who had been deceived by the CCP], publicly stated that the Chinese government had been forthcoming in cooperating and taking appropriate measures in dealing with SARS, so that there should be no problems. And specialists gave the go-ahead [after over 20 days delay] to Guangdong Province for field inspection.

These 400-plus articles gave the author the impression that the CCP had been transparent during these four months, had acted responsibly to protect the people's health, and had convinced the people that the CCP hadn't hidden anything. However, on April 20, 2003, the Information Office of the State Council announced in its press conference that SARS had indeed broken out in China and thus indirectly admitted that the government had been covering up the epidemic. Only then did this author see the truth and understand the deceptive, villainous methods employed by the CCP, which had also "advanced with time."

On the general election in Taiwan, the CCP, using the same subtle and "refined" approach, suggested that a presidential election would lead to disasters – a surge in the suicide rate, collapsing stock markets, an increase in "weird diseases," mental disorders, out-migration of the island inhabitants, family feuds, a callous attitude towards life, a depressed market, indiscriminate shooting in the streets, protests and demonstrations, a siege on the presidential building, social unrest, political farce, and so on. The CCP filled the heads of the people in Mainland China with these ideas on a daily basis in an attempt to lead the people to believe that all of these calamities are the disastrous results of an election and that China should never hold a democratic election.

On the issue of Falun Gong, the CCP has displayed an even higher level of skill with deceptions designed to frame Falun Gong. The CCP kept its staged shows coming one after another. No wonder so many Chinese have been misled. The CCP's villainous propaganda has been so deceptive that the victims willingly believe in the lies and think that they have the truth in hand.

The CCP's brainwashing propaganda over the past decades has become more refined and subtle in cheating, which is a natural extension of its unscrupulous nature.

IV. THE CCP'S HYPOCRISY IN HUMAN RIGHTS

FROM USURPING DEMOCRACY TO SEIZE POWER TO FEIGNING DEMOCRACY TO MAINTAIN DESPOTIC RULE

"In a democratic nation, sovereignty should lie in the hands of the people, which is in line with the principles of heaven and earth. If a nation claims to be democratic and yet sovereignty does not rest with its people, that is definitely not on the right track and can only be regarded as a deviation, and this nation is not a democratic nation…how could democracy be possible without ending the Party rule and without a popular election? Return people's rights to people!"

Does this quotation sound like something from an article written by "overseas enemies" intent on slamming the CCP? In fact, the statement comes from an article in *Xinhua Daily*, the official CCP newspaper, on September 27, 1945.

The CCP, that had trumpeted "popular election" and demanded "returning people's rights to the people," has been treating "popular suffrage" as taboo since it usurped power. The people who are supposed to be "the masters and owners of the state" have no rights whatsoever to make their own decisions. Words are inadequate to describe the CCP's unscrupulous nature.

If you fancy that what's done is done and the evil CCP cult that has flourished on killing and has ruled the nation with lies will reform itself, become benevolent, and be willing to "return people's rights to the people," you are wrong. Let us hear what the *People's Daily*, the CCP's mouthpiece, has to say on November 23, 2004, 60 years after the public statement quoted above: "A steadfast control of ideology is the essential ideological and political foundation for consolidating the Party's rule."

Recently, the CCP proposed a so-called new "Three Noes Principle,"[5] the first of which is "Development with no debates." "Development" is phony, but "no debates" that emphasizes "one voice, one hall" is the CCP's real purpose.

When Jiang Zemin was asked by the renowned CBS correspondent Mike Wallace in 2000 as to why China had not conducted popular elections, Jiang responded, "The Chinese people are way too low in education."

However, as early as February 25, 1939, the CCP cried out in its *Xinhua Daily*: "They (the KMT) think that democratic politics in China are not to be realized today, but some years later. They hope that democratic politics will wait until the knowledge and education levels of the Chinese people reach those of bourgeois democratic countries in Europe and America… but only under the democratic system will it become easier to educate and train the people."

The hypocritical difference between what *Xinhua* said in 1939 and what Jiang Zemin said in 2000 reflects the true picture of the CCP's iniquitous nature.

After the Tiananmen Square massacre in 1989, the CCP reentered the world stage with a miserable human rights record. History gave the CCP a choice. Either it could respect its people and truly improve human rights or it could continue to commit abuses inside China while pretending to the outside world to respect human rights in order to evade international condemnation.

Unfortunately, consistent with its despotic nature, the CCP chose the second path without hesitation. It gathered together and sustained a large number of unscrupulous but talented people in the scientific and religious fields and specifically directed them to publish deceptive propaganda overseas in order to promote the CCP's feigned progress in human rights. It concocted a range of rights fallacies such as "the survival right," or rights to shelter and food. The argument went like this: When people are hungry, do they not have the right to speak? Even if the hungry cannot speak, would it be allowed for those who have eaten their fill to speak for the hungry? The CCP even tried to deceive the Chinese people and Western democracies by playing games with human rights, even blatantly claiming that "the present is the best period for China's human rights."

Article 35 of China's Constitution stipulates that citizens of the People's Republic of China have the freedoms of expression, publication, assembly, association, protest, and demonstration. The CCP is simply playing word games. Under the CCP's rule, countless people have been deprived of their rights to belief, speech, publication, assembly and legal defense. The CCP even ordered that the appeal of certain groups be considered illegal. On more than one occasion in 2004, some civilian groups applied to demonstrate in Beijing. Instead of granting approval, the government arrested the applicants. The "one country, two systems" policy for Hong Kong affirmed by the CCP's Constitution is also a ruse. The CCP talks about no change in Hong Kong for 50 years, and yet it has tried to change the two systems into one by attempting to pass tyrannical legislation, Basic Law Article 23, within just five years after Hong Kong's return to China.[6]

The sinister new ploy of the CCP is to use the fake "relaxation in speech" to cover up the extent of its massive monitoring and control. The Chinese now appear to speak their minds more freely and, besides, the Internet has allowed news to travel faster. So the CCP claims that it now allows freedom of speech, and quite a number of people have fallen for this. This is a false appearance. It is not that the CCP has become benevolent; rather, the Party cannot stop social development and technological advancement. Let us look at the role the CCP is playing regarding the Internet: it is blocking websites, filtering information, monitoring chat rooms, controlling emails, and incriminating net users. Everything it does is regressive in nature. Today, with the help of some capitalists who disregard human rights and conscience, the CCP's police have been equipped with high-tech devices by which they are able to monitor, from inside a patrol car, every move net users make. When we look at the degeneracy of the CCP—committing evils deeds in broad daylight—in the context of the global movement toward democratic freedom, how can we expect it to make any progress in human rights? The CCP itself said it all: "It loosens up to the outside but tightens up internally." The CCP's unscrupulous nature has never changed.

To create a good image for itself at the United Nations Commission on Human Rights, in 2004 the CCP staged an array of events to punish severely those who abuse human rights. The events, however, were for foreigners' eyes only and had no substance. That is because in China the biggest human rights abuser is the CCP itself, as well as its former General Secretary Jiang Zemin, former secretary of the Political and Judiciary Commission Luo Gan, Minister Zhou Yongkang, and Deputy Minister Liu Jing, of the Ministry of Public Security. Their show of punishing human rights abusers is like a thief shouting, "Catch the thief!"

An analogy could be made to a serial rapist who, when hidden from public view, used to assault ten girls in a day. Then, there are too many people around, so he assaults only one girl in front of the crowd. Can the rapist be said to have changed for the better? His going from assaults behind the scenes to raping in public only proves that the rapist is even more base and shameless than before. The nature of the serial rapist has not changed at all. What has changed is that it is no longer as easy for him to commit the crime.

The CCP is just like this serial rapist. The CCP's dictatorial nature and its instinctive fear of losing power determine that it will not respect people's rights. The human, material, and financial resources used to cover up its human rights record have far exceeded its efforts in the true improvement of human rights. The indulgence of the CCP in wanton massacre or persecution throughout China has been the biggest misfortune of the Chinese people.

DRESSING UP TO COMMIT EVIL DEEDS WHILE HIDING BEHIND THE "LAW"

To protect the gains of special-interest groups, the CCP has, on one hand, eliminated their previous façade and completely abandoned the workers, peasants, and the populace, and, on the other hand, has advanced their deceitful and villainous means as more and more of the CCP's human rights abuses are exposed to the international community. The CCP has used popular vocabulary such as "the rule of law," "market," "for the people," and "reform" to confuse people. The CCP cannot change its wicked nature even if it dresses itself up in a "Western-style suit." Such an image is even more misleading than the CCP "in a Mao suit." In George Orwell's *Animal Farm* (1945), the pigs learned to stand and walk on two legs. The newly acquired skill gave the pigs a new image, but did not change their pig nature.

1.Making Laws and Regulations in Violation of the Chinese Constitution

Laws and regulations in violation of the Constitution are passed on to law enforcement personnel at various levels as the "legal basis" to obstruct the people's efforts to stop persecution, gain freedom, and uphold human rights.

2.Non-Political Problems Are Handled with Political Means

An ordinary social problem would be elevated to the height of "competing with the Party for the masses," "bringing demise to the Party and the country," "turmoil," and "enemy forces." A non-political issue would intentionally be politicized, so that the CCP could use political movements as a propaganda tool to incite people's hatred.

3. Political Issues Are Managed with Underhanded Means

The CCP's latest ploy for attacking pro-democracy citizens and independent-thinking intellectuals is to set up traps in order to imprison them. Such traps include false accusations of civil offenses such as prostitution and tax evasion. The attackers keep a low profile to avoid condemnation by outside groups. These crimes, which are enough to ruin the reputations of the accused, are also used to humiliate the victims in public.

The only change to the CCP's unscrupulous nature, if any, is that it has become even more disgraceful and inhuman.

THE CCP HOLDS OVER ONE BILLION PEOPLE HOSTAGE TO ITS TWISTED LOGIC

Imagine that a licentious criminal broke into a home and raped a girl. At the trial, this criminal defends himself by arguing that he did not kill the victim; he only raped her. Because killing is worse than raping, he argues that he is innocent and should be released immediately. He says that people should also praise him for only raping but not killing.

This logic sounds ridiculous. However, the CCP's logic in defense of its Tiananmen Square massacre on June 4, 1989 is exactly the same as that of the criminal. The CCP has argued that the "suppression of students" avoided a potential "internal disorder" in China. In order to prevent""internal disorder," the suppression of students was thus justified.

"Raping or killing, which one is better?" For a criminal to ask a judge in court such a question indicates how shameless the criminal is. Similarly, in the issue of the Tiananmen Square massacre, the CCP and its cohorts did not reflect on whether it was guilty of killing. Instead, they asked society which one is better—"Suppression of students or internal disorder that may lead to civil war?"

The CCP is in control of the entire state machine and all means of propaganda. In other words, the 1.3 billion Chinese people are held hostage by the CCP. With the 1.3 billion hostages in hand, the CCP can always argue its "hostage theory," that if it does not suppress a certain group of people, the whole nation will be in turmoil or disaster. Using this as an excuse, the CCP could suppress any individual or group at will, and its suppression could always be justified. Given such deceitful arguments and fallacious reasoning, is there any criminal more shameless in the world than the CCP?

THE CARROT AND THE STICK—FROM BESTOWING "FREEDOM" TO ESCALATING SUPPRESSION

Many Chinese people feel that they enjoy more "freedom" now than before, so they hold out hope for the prospect of the CCP's improvement. As a matter of fact, the degree of freedom "bestowed" upon people depends on the CCP's sense of crisis. The CCP would do anything to maintain the collective interests of the Party, including giving so-called democracy, freedom, or human rights to the people.

However, under the CCP's leadership, the so-called "freedom" bestowed by the CCP is not protected by any legislation. Such "freedom" is purely a tool to deceive and control people amidst the international trend toward democracy. In essence, this "freedom" is in irreconcilable conflict with the CCP's dictatorship. Once such a conflict is beyond the CCP's tolerance level, the CCP could take back all the "freedom" instantly. In the history of the CCP, there were several periods during which speech was relatively free, with each one followed by a period of strict control. Such cyclical patterns occur throughout the history of the CCP, demonstrating the CCP's iniquitous nature.

In today's Internet era, if you visit the CCP's official *Xinhua* website or the *People's Daily* online, you will find that indeed quite a few reports there contain negative information about China. Firstly, this is because there is too much bad news circulating rapidly in China these days, and the news agency has to report these stories in order to stay credible. Secondly, the standpoint of such reports conforms with the CCP's interest, i.e., "minor criticism offers great help." The reports would always attribute the cause of bad news to certain individuals, having nothing to do with the Party, while crediting the CCP's leadership for any solution. The CCP skillfully controls what to report, what not to report, how much to report, and whether to have Chinese media or the CCP-controlled overseas media report it.

The CCP is proficient at manipulating bad news into something that can achieve the desired result of winning people's hearts. Many youth in mainland China feel that the CCP now offers a good degree of freedom of speech, and thus have hopes for and are appreciative of the CCP. They are victims of the "refined" strategies of the iniquitous state controlled media. Moreover, by creating a chaotic situation in the Chinese society and then giving it some media exposure, the CCP can convince people that only the CCP can control such a chaotic society and can thus manipulate people into endorsing CCP rule.

Therefore, we should not mistakenly think the CCP has changed by itself, even if we see some signs of its improving human rights. In history, when the CCP struggled to overthrow the KMT government, it pretended to be fighting for democracy for the nation.

The CCP's villainous nature is such that any promise by the CCP is not reliable.

V. ASPECTS OF THE CCP'S UNSCRUPULOUS NATURE

SELLING OUT THE NATION'S LAND OUT OF VANITY AND BETRAYING THE COUNTRY UNDER THE GUISE OF "NATIONAL UNITY"

"Liberate Taiwan" and "Unify Taiwan" have been the CCP's propaganda slogans over the past few decades. By means of this propaganda, the CCP has acted like a nationalist and a patriot. Does the CCP truly care about the integrity of the nation's territory? Not at all. Taiwan is merely an historic problem caused by the struggle between the CCP and the KMT, and it is a means that the CCP uses to strike at its opponents and win people's support.

In the early days when the CCP set up the "Chinese Soviet" during the KMT reign, Article 14 of its Constitution stated that "any ethnic groups or any provinces inside China can claim independence." In order to comply with the Soviet Union, the CCP's slogan back then was "Protect the Soviet." During the Anti-Japanese War, the primary goal of the CCP was to seize the opportunity to increase itself rather than to fight against Japanese intruders. In 1945, the Soviet Red Army entered northeast China and committed robbery, murder, and rape, but the CCP did not utter a word of disapproval. Similarly, when the Soviet Union supported Outer Mongolia to become independent from China, the CCP was once again silent.

At the end of 1999, the CCP and Russia signed the China-Russia Border Survey Agreement, in which the CCP accepted all the unequal agreements between the Qing Dynasty and Russia made more than 100 years ago, and sold out over one million square kilometers of land to Russia, an area as large as several dozen Taiwans. In 2004, the CCP and Russia signed a China-Russia Eastern Border Supplemental Agreement and reportedly lost sovereignty of half of the Heixiazi Island in Heilongjiang Province to Russia again.

Regarding other border issues such as the Nansha Islands and Diaoyu Island, the CCP does not care at all since these issues do not impact the CCP's control of power. The CCP has made a fanfare of "Unifying Taiwan," which is merely a smoke screen and a devious means for inciting blind patriotism and keeping the public attention off domestic conflict.

POLITICAL VILLAINS WITHOUT ANY MORAL RESTRAINTS

A government should always be monitored. In democratic countries, the separation of powers plus the freedoms of speech and press are good mechanisms for surveillance. Religious beliefs provide additional moral self-restraint.

The CCP promotes atheism; hence there is no divine nature to morally restrain its behavior. The CCP is a dictatorship; hence there is no law to restrain it politically. As a result, the CCP is totally reckless and unrestrained when it acts out of its tyrannical and villainous nature. According to the CCP, who monitors it? "The CCP monitors itself!" This is the slogan the CCP has used to deceive the people for decades. In earlier times it was called "self-criticism," then "self-surveillance" and "self-perfecting the Party's leadership," and recently "self-enhancing the Party's governing capacity." The CCP emphasizes the super power it has for so-called "self-improvement." The CCP does not just say it, but actually takes action, like establishing "The Central Disciplinary Inspection Committee" and "The Office for Appeals" and the like. These organizations are merely pretty yet useless "flower vases" that confuse and mislead the people.

Without moral and legal restraint, the CCP's "self-improvement" amounts to the traditional Chinese saying of "demons emerging from one's own heart." It is only the excuse the CCP uses to avoid external surveillance and refuse to lift the ban on free press and free political parties. Political scoundrels use this trick to fool the people and to protect the CCP's power and the interests of the ruling group.

The CCP is expert at political scheming. "The People's Democratic Dictatorship," "Democratic Centralism," "Political Consultation" and so on are all fraudulent schemes. Except for the dictatorship part, they are lies.

PLAYING TRICKS—FROM THE FALSE RESISTANCE TO THE JAPANESE INVASION TO THE FRAUDULENT COUNTER-TERRORISM

The CCP has always claimed to have led the Chinese people in defeating the Japanese invaders. However, abundant historical archives expose that the CCP intentionally avoided battles in the Anti-Japanese War. The CCP only hampered the Anti-Japanese effort by taking the opportunity of the KMT's involvement in the war to increase its own power.

The only major battles the CCP fought were the Pingxing Pass battle and the Hundred Regiment battle. In the Pingxing Pass battle, the CCP was not at all the leader or predominant force that participated and commanded this battle. Instead, the CCP troops merely ambushed the Japanese supply units. As for the Hundred Regiment battle, it is believed inside the CCP that participating in this battle violated the strategic policies of the Central Party. After these two battles, Mao and his CCP armies did not engage in any serious battles, nor did they produce any Anti-Japanese War heroes like Dong Cunrui during the 1948 war with the KMT and Huang Jiguang during the Korean War. Only a small number of high-level military commanders of the CCP died on the Anti-Japanese battleground. Until today, the CCP still cannot even publish a figure for its casualties during the Anti-Japanese War, nor can one find too many monuments in China's vast land for heroes of the CCP in the Anti-Japanese War.

At the time, the CCP established a Border Region government in Shaanxi, Gansu, and Ningxia provinces away from the battlefront. Using today's nomenclature, the CCP was conducting "one country two systems," or "two Chinas" inside China. Although the CCP's commanders did not lack passion in resisting the Japanese, the CCP's high-level officials were not sincere in fighting the Anti-Japanese War. Instead, they took measures to protect their resources and used the war as an opportunity to strengthen themselves. When China and Japan resumed diplomatic relations in 1972, Mao Zedong let slip the truth to the Japanese Prime Minister, Kakuei Tanaka, that the CCP had to thank Japan, since without the Anti-Japanese War, the CCP would not have gained power in China.

The above is the truth concerning the CCP's deceitful claim that it led the Chinese people to persist in the eight-year war against the Japanese and ultimately win.

More than half a century later, with the 911 terrorist attacks on U.S. soil, a counter-terrorist effort has become a global focus. The CCP again used deceptive strategies, similar to what it deployed during the Anti-Japanese War. Using counter-terrorism as the pretext, the CCP has labeled many religious practitioners, dissidents, and groups engaged in ethnic or territorial conflicts as terrorists. Under the guise of the international counter-terrorist effort, the CCP has launched violent repressions.

On September 27, 2004, the Xinhua News Agency quoted the *Xinjing* newspaper as saying that Beijing might establish the first counter-terrorist bureau among all the provinces and cities in China. Some overseas pro-CCP media even reported it in the headline: "The '610 Office' Joins Counter-Terrorism Efforts," claiming that the counter-terrorism bureau would focus on attacking "terrorist organizations," including Falun Gong.

The CCP slaps the label "terrorists" on the people who hold no weapons in their hands, do not fight back when beaten or slandered, and peacefully appeal for the right to their beliefs. Taking advantage of the climate of counter-terrorism, the CCP has mobilized its "special counter-terrorist force," which is armed to the teeth, to conduct swift repression on this defenseless group of peaceful people. Furthermore, the CCP has used the excuse of counter-terrorism to evade international attention and condemnation of its persecution of Falun Gong. The kinds of deception used today are no different from those used by the CCP during the Anti-Japanese War and are a shameful way to treat such a serious matter as the international anti-terrorism efforts.

FEIGNING SINCERITY AND OVERTLY AGREEING WHILE COVERTLY OPPOSING

The CCP does not believe in its own doctrines but forces others to believe in them. This is one of the most insidious methods used by the CCP cult. The CCP knows that its doctrines are false and that the idea of socialism that has already gone bankrupt is untrue. The CCP doesn't believe in these doctrines itself, but forces people to believe in them. It persecutes people who do not believe in them. The CCP has shamelessly written such deceitful ideology into the Constitution as the foundation of the Chinese state.

In real life, there is an interesting phenomenon. Many high-level officials lose their positions in power struggles in China's political arena because of corruption. But these are the very people who promote honesty and selflessness in public meetings, while engaging in bribery, corruption, and other decadent activities behind the scenes. Many so-called "people's servants" have fallen this way, including Li Jiating, the former Governor of Yunnan Province; Liu Fangren, the Party Secretary of Guizhou Province; Cheng Weigao, the Party Secretary of Hebei Province; Tian Fengshan, Minister of Land and Resources; and Wang Huaizhong, the Lieutenant Governor of Anhui Province. However, if you examine their speeches, you will find that, without exception, they have supported anti-corruption campaigns and repeatedly urged their subordinates to conduct themselves honestly, even as they themselves were embezzling funds and taking bribes.

Although the CCP has promoted many exemplary cadres and has often attracted some idealistic and diligent people to join the Party in order to enhance the Party's image, it is obvious to all how terrible a plight China's ever-declining moral standard has been in. Why hasn't the CCP's propaganda of a "spiritual civilization" worked to correct this?

As a matter of fact, the Communist Party leaders transmitted empty words when they promulgated the "communist moral quality" or the slogan, "Serve the people." The inconsistency between communist leaders' actions and words can be traced all the way back to their founding father Karl Marx. Marx bore an illegitimate son. Lenin contracted syphilis from prostitutes. Stalin was sued for forcing a sexual relationship on a singer. Mao Zedong indulged himself in lust. Jiang Zemin is promiscuous. The Romanian communist leader Ceausescu made his entire family extravagantly rich. The Cuban communist leader Castro hoards hundreds of millions of dollars in overseas banks. North Korea's demonic killer Kim Il Song and his children lead a decadent and wasteful life.

In daily life, ordinary people in China loathe the empty political study sessions. Increasingly, they equivocate in political matters, since everyone knows them to be deceptive games. But no one, neither the speakers nor the listeners at these political meetings, would speak openly about such deception. This is an open secret. People call this phenomenon "sincere pretension." The CCP's high sounding notions, either the "Three Represents" of several years ago, "improving governing capacity" later, or today's "three hearts"—"warming, stabilizing, and gaining people's hearts"—are all nonsense. Which ruling party would not represent the people's benefits? Which ruling party would not care about governing capacity? Which ruling party is not about gaining people's hearts? Any parties that do not concern themselves with these issues would soon be removed from the political stage. But the CCP treats such superfluous slogans as intricate, profound theories and requires the whole country to study them.

When pretending has been gradually molded into a billion plus people's thinking and habits and has become the Party's culture, the society itself becomes false, pretentious, and inane. Lacking honesty and trust, the society is in crisis. Why has the CCP created these conditions? In the past, it was for its ideology; now it is for its benefits. The CCP members know they are pretending, but they pretend anyway. If the CCP did not promote such slogans and formalities, it couldn't bully people. It couldn't make people follow and fear it.

ABANDONING CONSCIENCE AND SACRIFICING JUSTICE FOR THE PARTY'S INTERESTS

In *On the Communist Party's Moral Development*, Liu Shaoqi expounded especially on the need "for party members to subsume their individual interests to the Party's interest." Among the CCP members, there has never been a lack of righteous people who are concerned about the country and its people, nor has there been a shortage of honest and upright officials who have truly served the people. But in the CCP's machinery of self-interest, these officials cannot survive. Under constant pressure to "submit humanity to Party nature," they often find it impossible to continue, risk being removed from positions, or worse, become corrupt.

Chinese people have personally experienced and deeply felt the CCP's brutal regime and have developed a profound fear of the CCP's violence. Therefore, people dare not uphold justice and no longer believe in the heavenly laws. First they submit themselves to the CCP's power. Gradually they become unfeeling and unconcerned about matters not affecting themselves. Even the logic of their thinking has been consciously molded to succumb to the CCP. This is the result of the CCP's mafia nature.

THE CCP MANIPULATES PATRIOTIC SENTIMENTS TO INCITE THE POPULACE

The CCP uses slogans of "patriotism" and "nationalism" to incite people. They are not only the CCP's main rallying cries, but also its frequently issued orders and time-tested strategies. Upon reading the nationalistic propaganda in the overseas edition of the *People's Daily* newspaper, some overseas Chinese, who for decades have not dared to return to China to live, may become more nationalistic than the Chinese living inside China. Manipulated by the CCP, Chinese people, who dare not say "no" to any CCP policy, became bold enough to storm the US Embassy and Consulate in China, throwing eggs and rocks and burning cars and U.S. flags, all under the banner of "patriotism."

Whenever the Communist Party encounters an important issue that demands obedience from the populace, it uses "patriotism" and "nationalism" to mobilize people on short notice. In all cases, including matters related to Taiwan, Hong Kong, Falun Gong, the collision between a U.S. spy plane and a Chinese fighter jet, the CCP has used the combined method of high-pressure terror and collective brainwashing, thus bringing people to a war-like state of mind. This method is similar to that used by the German fascists.

By blocking all other information, the CCP's brainwashing has been incredibly successful. Even though the Chinese people do not like the CCP, they think in the twisted mode instilled by the CCP. During the U.S.-led Iraq war, for example, many people were stirred up when watching the daily analysis on CCTV.[7] They felt a strong sense of hatred, vengeance, and desire to fight, while at the same time cursing another war.

SHAMELESSNESS—PUTTING THE PARTY BEFORE THE COUNTRY AND FORCING PEOPLE TO TAKE THE FOE FOR THEIR FATHER

One of the phrases the CCP often uses to intimidate people is, "the extinction of the Party and the country," thus placing the Party before the country. The founding principle of China is: "There would be no new China without the CCP." From childhood, people were educated to "listen to the Party" and "behave like good children of the Party." They sang praises to the Party: "I consider the Party as my mother." "Oh, Party, my dear mother." "The saving grace of the Party is deeper than the ocean." "Love for my father and mother cannot surpass love for the Party."[8] They would "go and fight wherever the Party points." When the government offered disaster relief, people would "thank the Party and the government"—first the Party and then the government. A military slogan reads, "The Party commands the gun." Even when the Chinese experts tried to design the uniform for court judges, they put four golden buttons on the neckband of the uniform. Those buttons are lined up from top to bottom to symbolize the Party, the people, the law and the country. It indicates that even if you are the judge, the Party will forever be positioned above the law, the country, and the people.

The Party has become supreme in China, and the country has conversely become the Party's subordinate. The country exists for the Party, and the Party is said to be the embodiment of the people and the symbol of the country. Love for the Party, Party leaders, and the country have been mixed together, which is the fundamental reason why patriotism in China has become twisted.

Under the subtle but persistent influence of the CCP's education and propaganda, many people, Party members or not, began to confuse the Party with the country, whether they are aware of it or not. They have come to accept that "the Party's interest" is superior to all, and to concur that "the Party's interests equal the interests of the people and the country." This result of the CCP's indoctrination has created the climate for the Party to betray the national interests.

PLAYING THE "REDRESS" GAME AND CALLING CRIMINAL ACTS "GREAT ACCOMPLISHMENTS"

The CCP has made many blunders in history. But, it has always put the blame on certain individuals or groups through "redress and rehabilitation." This has not only made the victims deeply grateful for the CCP, but also allowed the CCP to completely shirk any responsibility for its criminal deeds. The CCP claims itself to be not only "unafraid of making mistakes, but also good at correcting them,"[9] and this has become the CCP's magic potion with which it repeatedly escapes culpability. Thus, the CCP remains forever "great, glorious, and correct."

Perhaps one day, the CCP will decide to redress the Tiananmen Square massacre and restore the reputation of Falun Gong. But these are simply the Machiavellian tactics that the CCP uses in a desperate attempt to prolong its dying life. The CCP will never have the courage to reflect on itself, to expose its own crimes, or to pay for its own sins.

VI. THE CCP MANIFESTS ITS VILLAINOUS NATURE WHEN USING STATE TERROR IN ITS EFFORT TO ELIMINATE TRUTHFULNESS, COMPASSION, AND TOLERANCE

The fraudulent "Tiananmen self-immolation" staged by the CCP cult may be considered the CCP's lie of the century. In order to suppress Falun Gong, the government was so perverse as to seduce five people to pretend to be Falun Gong practitioners and to choreograph their fake self-immolation on Tiananmen Square. By colluding in the scam, the five participants unwittingly signed their own death warrants and were either beaten to death on the scene or killed afterwards. The slow motion playing of the self-immolation video published by the CCTV unmistakably shows that Liu Chunling, one of the self-immolators, died after being forcefully struck down at the scene by a police officer. Other flaws in the footage include the sitting posture of Wang Jingdong, the plastic bottle (allegedly filled with gasoline) that remained intact between his knees after the fire was extinguished, the conversation between a doctor and the youngest victim Liu Siying, and the presence of cameramen ready to videotape the scene. These facts and more are sufficient evidence to prove that the self-immolation incident was a deception maliciously designed by the iniquitous Jiang Zemin regime in order to frame Falun Gong.[10]

The CCP used despicable and cruel methods in its declared campaign to eradicate Falun Gong. It usurped the nation's financial resources accumulated in the past 20 years of reform and opening up. It mobilized the Party, the government, the military, the police, spies, foreign diplomats and various other governmental and nongovernmental organizations. It manipulated the system of global media coverage, implementing a strict information blockade with individual and high-tech monitoring. It did all this to persecute a peaceful group of people who adhere to Falun Gong, a traditional Chinese *qigong* practice for refining the body, mind, and moral character in accordance with the principles of Truthfulness, Compassion, and Tolerance. Such brutal persecution of innocent people for their beliefs reveals the degenerate nature of the CCP.

No evildoers in history have lied so insidiously and pervasively as Jiang Zemin and the CCP. They use a variety of lies, each designed to target and manipulate different notions and ideas that people hold so that people can easily be duped into believing the lies, and the Party can incite hatred toward Falun Gong. Do you believe in science? The CCP says that Falun Gong is superstitious. Do you find politics distasteful? The CCP says that Falun Gong engages in politics. Do you envy people who get rich whether in China or abroad? The CCP says that Falun Gong gathers wealth. Do you object to organizations? The CCP says that Falun Gong has a tight organization. Are you tired of the Cult of Personality that lasted in China for several decades? The CCP says that Falun Gong exercises mental control. Are you passionate for patriotism? The CCP says that Falun Gong is anti-China. Are you afraid of turmoil? The CCP says Falun Gong disrupts stability. Do you wonder if Falun Gong really upholds "Truthfulness, Compassion and Tolerance"? The CCP says Falun Gong is not truthful, compassionate, nor tolerant. It even twisted the logic, claiming that compassion can generate the desire to kill.

Do you trust that the government would not make up such lies? The CCP makes up lies that are bigger and more shocking, from suicides to self-immolation, from murdering relatives to serial killing—so many lies that you find it hard not to believe them. Do you sympathize with Falun Gong? The CCP connects your political evaluation with the persecution of Falun Gong, and demotes you, fires you, or takes away your bonus if Falun Gong practitioners from your area of responsibility appeal in Beijing. Thus, you are forced to become an enemy of Falun Gong.

The CCP has kidnapped countless Falun Gong practitioners and taken them to brainwashing sessions in an effort to force them to give up their righteous beliefs, denounce Falun Gong, and promise to stop their practice. The CCP has used various evil ways to persuade them, including using their relatives, employment, and education to pressure them, inflicting them with various cruel torture and even punishing their family members and colleagues. Falun Gong practitioners who have been successfully brainwashed are in turn used to torment and brainwash others. The vicious CCP insists on turning good people into demons and forcing them to walk on a dark path to the end of their lives.

VII. THE INIQUITOUS SOCIALISM WITH "CHINESE CHARACTERISTICS"

The term "Chinese characteristics" is used to cover up the CCP's crimes. The CCP claimed all along that it owes its success in China's revolution to "the integration of Marxism-Leninism with the concrete reality of Chinese revolution." The CCP has frequently abused the term "characteristic" as an ideological support for its capricious and villainous policies.

CAPRICIOUS AND DECEPTIVE MEANS

Under the deceptive façade of the "Chinese characteristics," what the CCP has accomplished is nothing but absurdity.

The goal of the CCP's revolution was to realize public ownership of the means of production, and it has deceived many young people into joining the Party organization for the ideals of communism and unity. Many of them even betrayed their property-owning families. But 83 years after the beginning of the CCP, capitalism has returned, only now becoming a part of the CCP itself, which was originally upholding the banner of equalitarianism.

Today, among CCP leaders' children and relatives, many are new capitalists with fortunes, and many Party members have endeavored to join this group of nouveau riche. The CCP eliminated the landlords and capitalists in the name of revolution and stole their property. Now, the CCP's new "royalty" has become even richer capitalists through embezzlement and corruption. Those who followed the Party in the early revolutions now sigh, "If I knew the situation today, I would not have followed it then." After several decades of sweat and struggle, they find themselves to have simply devoted their brothers' and fathers' properties as well as their own lives to the CCP cult.

The CCP speaks of the economic base determining the superstructure; in reality, it is the CCP's corrupt officials' bureaucratic economic base that decides the "high-pressure superstructure"—a superstructure that relies on high pressure to be maintained. Suppressing the people has therefore become the CCP's basic policy.

Another iniquitous characteristic of the CCP is manifest in its changing the definition of cultural concepts and then using these revised definitions to criticize and control people. The concept of "party" is one such example. Since the beginning of time, parties have been established both at home and abroad. Only the Communist Party exercises power beyond the domain of a party collective. If you join the Party, it will control all aspects of your life, including your conscience, subsistence, and private life. When given political authority, the CCP controls the society, government, and the state apparatus. It dictates all matters, from ones as important as who should be the chairman of the country or the minister of defense, or what regulations and rules will be made, to as small as where one should live, with whom one can marry, and how many children one can have. The CCP has mustered all imaginable methods of control.

In the name of dialectics, the CCP has completely destroyed the holistic thinking, reasoning faculties, and inquiring spirit of philosophy. While the CCP speaks about "distribution according to contribution," the process of "allowing some people to get rich first" has been accomplished along with "distribution according to power." The CCP uses the disguise of "serving the people whole-heartedly" to deceive those who hold these ideals, then completely brainwashes and controls them, gradually changing them into docile tools who "serve the Party whole-heartedly" and who dare not speak up for the people.

A MACHIAVELLIAN PARTY WITH "CHINESE CHARACTERISTICS"

Using a principle that values the Party's interests beyond all other considerations, the CCP has distorted the Chinese society with the means of an evil cult, creating a really grotesque being for all humanity. This being is different from any other state, government or organization. Its principle is to have no principle; there is no sincerity behind its smiles. However, kindhearted people cannot understand the CCP. Based on the universal moral standards, they cannot imagine that such an evil entity would be representing a country. Using the excuse of the "Chinese characteristics," the CCP established itself among the nations of the world. The "Chinese characteristics" have become the euphemism for the "CCP's villainous characteristics."

With the "Chinese characteristics," China's crippled capitalism was transformed into "socialism;" "unemployment" became "waiting for employment;" "being laid off" from work became "off duty;" "poverty" became the "initial stage of socialism;" and human rights and freedom of speech and belief were reduced to the mere right to survive.

THE CHINESE NATION FACES AN UNPRECEDENTED MORAL CRISIS

In the beginning of the 1990s, there was a popular saying in China, "I'm a ruffian and I am afraid of no one." This is the pitiful consequence of several decades of the CCP's iniquitous rule, of its imposing corruption on the nation. Accompanying the fake prosperity of China's economy is the rapidly declining morality in all areas of society.

The congressional representatives of China oftentimes talk about the issue of "honesty and trust" during the Chinese People's Congress. In college entrance exams, students are required to write about honesty and trust. This signifies that lack of honesty and trust and decline in morality have become an invisible but ubiquitous crisis in the Chinese society. Corruption, embezzlement, fake products, deception, malice and degenerating social norms are commonplace. There is no longer any basic trust among people.

For those who claim to be satisfied with an improved standard of living, isn't stability in their lives their primary concern? What is the most important factor in social stability? It is morality. A society with degraded morality cannot possibly provide security.

To date, the CCP has cracked down on almost all traditional religions and dismantled the traditional value system. The unscrupulous way by which the CCP seizes wealth and deceives people has had a trickle down effect on the entire society, corrupting the entire society and leading its people towards villainy. The CCP, which rules by devious means, also essentially needs a corrupt society as an environment in which to survive. That is why the CCP tries everything it can to drag the people down to its level, attempting to turn the Chinese people into schemers to various degrees. This is how the CCP's deceitful nature is eradicating the moral foundation that has long sustained the Chinese people.

CONCLUSION

"It is easier to alter rivers and mountains than to change one's nature."[11] History has proven that every time the CCP loosens its bondage and chains, it does so without intending to abandon them. After the Great Famine of the early 1960s, the CCP adopted the "Three-Freedom and One-Contract" (San Zi Yi Bao) program[12] aimed at restoring agricultural production, but without the intent to change the "slave" status of Chinese peasants. The "economic reform" and "liberalization" in the 1980s had no constraint on the CCP's raising a butcher's knife to its own people in 1989. In the future, the CCP will continue to alter its façade but will not change its iniquitous nature.

Some people may think that the past belongs to the past, the situation has changed, and the CCP now is not the CCP of an earlier era. Some may be satisfied with false appearances and even mistakenly believe that the CCP has improved, is in the process of reforming, or intends to make amends. They may constantly push away troublesome memories of the past. All these can only give the CCP's band of villains the opportunity to continue to survive and threaten humankind.

All the efforts by the CCP are designed to make people forget the past. All of the people's struggles are a reminder of the injustices they have suffered at the hands of the CCP.

In fact, the history of the CCP is one that has severed people's memories, a history in which children do not know the true experiences of their parents, a history in which hundreds of millions of citizens endure the enormous conflict between despising the CCP's bloody past and holding out hope for the CCP's future.

When the evil specter of communism fell upon the human world, the Communist Party unleashed the scum of society and utilized the rebellion of hoodlums to seize and establish political power. What it has done, by means of carnage and tyranny, is to establish and maintain despotism in the form of a "Party Possession." By using the so-called ideology of "struggle" that opposes nature, heaven's laws, human nature, and the universe, it destroys human conscience and benevolence, and further destroys traditional civilization and morality. It has used bloody slaughters and forced brainwashing to establish an evil communist cult, creating a nation of warped minds in order to rule the country.

Throughout the history of the CCP, there have been violent periods when the "Red Terror" reached its peak, and awkward periods when the CCP narrowly escaped its demise. Each time, the CCP resorted to the full use of its cunning means to extricate itself from crises, but only to head for the next round of violence, continuing to deceive the Chinese people.

When people recognize the CCP's villainous nature and resist being deceived by its false images, the end will arrive for the CCP and its unscrupulous nature.

In comparison with China's 5,000-year history, the 55 years of the CCP's rule are but the blink of an eye. Before the CCP came into existence, China had created the most magnificent civilization in the history of humankind. The CCP seized the opportunity of China's domestic troubles and foreign invasion to wreak havoc on the Chinese nation. It has taken away tens of millions of lives, destroyed countless families, and sacrificed the ecological resources upon which China's survival depends. What is even more devastating is the near destruction of China's moral foundation and rich cultural traditions.

What will China's future be? What direction will China take? Such serious questions are too complicated to discuss in a few words. However, one thing is for certain—if there is no renewal of the nation's morality, no restoration of a harmonious relationship between humans and nature, and between humans, heaven and earth, if there is no faith or culture for a peaceful coexistence among humans, it will be impossible for the Chinese nation to have a bright future.

After several decades of brainwashing and suppression, the CCP has instilled its way of thinking and its standards for good and bad into the Chinese people's lives. This has led people to accept and rationalize the CCP's perversion and fraudulence, to become part of its falsehood, thereby providing the ideological basis for the CCP's existence.

To eliminate from our lives the iniquitous doctrines instilled by the CCP, to discern the CCP's utterly unscrupulous nature, and to restore our human nature and conscience—this is the first and essential step on the path toward a smooth transition to a society free from the Communist Party.

Whether this path can be walked steadily and peacefully will depend on the changes made in the heart of every Chinese citizen. Even though the CCP appears to possess all the resources and violent apparatus in the country, if every citizen believes in the power of the truth and safeguards morality, the evil specter of the CCP will lose the foundation for its existence. All resources may instantly return to the hands of the just. That is when the rebirth of China will take place.

Only without the Chinese Communist Party, will there be a new China.

Only without the Chinese Communist Party, does China have hope.

Without the Chinese Communist Party, the upright and kindhearted Chinese people will rebuild China's historical magnificence.

NOTES

COMMENTARY ONE

1. The Hundred Days' Reform lasted 103 days from June 11 to September 21, 1898. The Emperor of the Qing Dynasty, Guangxu (1875-1908), ordered a series of social and institutional changes despite the intense opposition to the reform from the conservative ruling elite. With the support of the political opportunist Yuan Shikai, Empress Dowager Cixi engineered a *coup d'etat* on September 21, 1898. She forced the young reform-minded Guangxu into seclusion and took over the government as regent. The Hundred Days' Reform ended with the rescinding of the new edicts. In the meantime, six of the reform's chief advocates were beheaded.
2. Xinhai Revolution (or Hsinhai Revolution), named for the Chinese year of Xinhai (1911), was the overthrow (October 10, 1911-February 12, 1912) of China's ruling Qing Dynasty and the establishment of the Republic of China.
3. The May Fourth Movement was the first mass movement in modern Chinese history, beginning on May 4, 1919.
4. From http://eserver.org/marx/1848-communist.manifesto/cm4.txt.
5. Mao Zedong's letter to his wife Jiang Qing (1966).
6. Information from http://www.debates.org/pages/trans2004a.html.
7. Superstructure in the context of Marxist social theory refers to the way of interaction between human subjectivity and the material substance of society.
8. From Chapter 25 of *Tao-te Ching* or *Dao De Jing*, one of the most important Taoist texts, written by Lao Zi or Lao Tze (Lao Tzu).
9. From http://eserver.org/marx/1848-communist.manifesto/cm1.txt.

COMMENTARY TWO

1. By Xu Shen, *Shuowen Jiezi* (Xu Shen d. 147 AD in the Eastern Han Dynasty).
2. Zhu Xi, *Collection of Footnotes of Analects (Lunyu)*.
   See http://www.confucius2000.com/confucius/lunyujzh7.htm (in Chinese).
3. See http://www.epochtimes.com/gb/2/4/5/n181606.htm (in Chinese).

4. From the communist anthem, *The Internationale*.

5. Mao Zedong, *Report on an Investigation of the Peasant Movement in Hunan* (1927).

6. A Chinese folk legend, *The White-Haired Girl*, is the story of a female immortal living in a cave who had supernatural abilities to reward virtue and punish vice, support the righteous and restrain the evil. However, in the Chinese "modern" drama, opera, and ballet, she was described as a girl who was forced to flee to a cave after her father was beaten to death for refusing to marry her to an old landlord. She became white-haired for lack of nutrition. This became one of the most well known""modern" dramas in China and incited class hatred of landlords.

7. Lumpen proletariat, roughly translated as slum workers. This term identifies the class of outcast, degenerate or underground elements that make up a section of the population of industrial centers. It includes beggars, prostitutes, gangsters, racketeers, swindlers, petty criminals, tramps, chronic unemployed or unemployables, persons who have been cast out by industry, and all sorts of declassed, degraded or degenerated elements. The term was coined by Marx in *The Class Struggles in France* (1848-1850).

8. Karl Marx and Frederick Engels, *The Communist Manifesto* (1848).

9. Mao Zedong, (1927)

10. Zhou Enlai (1898-1976) also spelled Chou En-lai, was second in prominence to Mao in the history of the CCP. He was a leading figure in the CCP and Premier of the People's Republic of China from 1949 until his death.

11. Gu Shunzhang was originally one of the heads of the CCP special agent system. In 1931 he was arrested by the KMT and assisted them in uncovering many of the CCP's secret agents. All eight members of Gu's family were later strangled to death and buried in the French concession in Shanghai. See: The Epoch Times (2004, July). *The CCP's History of Assassinations.* http://english.epochtimes.com/news/4-7-14/22421.html

12. June 1946. The war between the CCP and the KMT. The war is marked by three successive campaigns: Liaoxi-Shenyang, Huai-Hai and Beiping-Tianjin, after which the CCP overthrew the rule of the KMT, leading to the founding of the People's Republic of China on October 1, 1949.

13. Chiang Kai-shek (also called Jiang Jieshi) was leader of the KMT, and later exiled to become the ruler of Taiwan.

14. Hu Zongnan (1896-1962), a native of Xiaofeng County (now part of Anji County), Zhejiang province, was successively Deputy Commander, Acting Commander and Chief of Staff of the KMT's southwest military and administrative headquarters.

15. Li Xiannian (1909-1992), one of the senior leaders of the CCP. He was President of China in 1983. He played an important role in helping Deng Xiaoping regain his power at the end of the Cultural Revolution in October 1976.

16. Mao Zedong, (1927)

17. Mao Zedong, (1927)

18. When the CCP began land reform it categorized the people. Among the defined classes of enemies, intellectuals were next to landlords, reactionaries, spies, etc., and ranked as the ninth class.

19. Hu Jintao, *Speech in the Symposium to Commemorate the 100th Anniversary of the Birth of Ren Bishi* (April 30, 2004).

20. From a poem by Sima Qian (about 140-87 BC), a historian and scholar in the West Han Dynasty. His famous poem says, "Everyone has to die; one dies either more solemn than Mount Taishan or lighter than a feather." Mount Taishan is one of the major mountains in China.

21. Mao Zedong, *On the People's Democratic Dictatorship* (1949).

22. Yang Kuisong, *A synopsis of the financial support that Moscow provided to the Chinese Communist Party from the 1920s to 1940s (1)*, (June 30, 2004)., Retrieved from no. 27, web edition of the *21st Century* website: http://www.cuhk.edu.hk/ics/21c/supplem/essay/040313a.htm (in Chinese). The author, Yang Kuisong, was a research fellow of contemporary history in the Chinese Academy of Social Sciences. Currently, he is a professor in the Department of History, Beijing University and adjunct professor at the Eastern China Normal University.

23. The Northern Expedition was a military campaign led by Chiang Kai-shek in 1927 intended to unify China under the rule of the KMT and end the rule of local warlords. It was largely successful in these objectives. During the Northern Expedition, the CCP had an alliance with the KMT.

24. The revolutionary movement during the CCP-KMT alliance, marked by the Northern Expedition.

25. Sun Yat-sen (1866-1925), founder of modern China.

26. The National Revolutionary Army, controlled by the KMT, was the National Army of the People's Republic of China. During the period of the CCP-KMT alliance, it included CCP members who joined the alliance.

27. On April 12, 1927, the KMT led by Chiang Kai-shek initiated a military operation against the CCP in Shanghai and several other cities. Over 5,000 CCP members were captured and many of them were killed between April 12 and the end of 1927 in Shanghai.

28. The Jinggangshan Mountain area is considered the first rural revolutionary base of the CCP, and is called "the cradle for the Red Army."

29. Mao Zedong, 1927

30. Mao Zedong, 1927

31. Liaoxi-Shenyang, Beijing-Tianjin, and Huai-Hai battles were the three major battles the CCP fought with the KMT from September 1948 to January 1949, which annihilated many of the KMT's crack troops. Millions of lives were lost in these three battles.

32. Lin Biao (1907-1971), one of the senior CCP leaders, served under Mao Zedong as a member of China's Politburo, as Vice-Chairman (1958) and Defense Minister (1959). Lin was designated as Mao's successor in 1966 but fell out of favor in 1970. Sensing his downfall, Lin reportedly became involved in a coup attempt and tried to flee to the USSR once the alleged plot became exposed, and his plane crashed in Mongolia, resulting in his death.

33. Qu Qiubai (1899-1935) is one of the CCP's earlier leaders and famous leftist writers. He was captured by the KMT on February 23, 1935 and died on June 18 of the same year.

34. The "Three Represents" was initially mentioned in a speech by Jiang Zemin in February, 2000. According to this doctrine, the Party must always represent the development trend of China's advanced productive forces, the orientation of China's advanced culture and the fundamental interests of the overwhelming majority of the Chinese people.

35. Zhang Bojun (1895-1969) was one of the founders of the China Democratic League, a democratic party in China. He was classified as the No. 1 rightist in 1957 by Mao Zedong, and was one of the few rightists who were not redressed after the Cultural Revolution.

36. Luo Longji (1898-1965) was one of the founders of the China Democratic League. He was classified as a rightist in 1958 by Mao Zedong, and was one of the few "rightists" who were not redressed after the Cultural Revolution.

37. Pu-yi, Aisin Gioro in Manchuriar (1906-1967), was the last emperor of China. After his abdication, the new republican government granted him a large government pension and permitted him to live in the Forbidden City of Beijing until 1924. After 1925, he lived in the Japanese concession in Tianjin. In 1934, he became the emperor of the Japanese puppet state of Manchuria. In 1945, he was captured by the Russian army and became a prisoner until 1950 when he was handed over to the Chinese Communist Party. In 1946, Puyi testified at the Tokyo war crimes trial that he had been the unwilling tool of the Japanese militarists and not, as they claimed, the instrument of Manchurian self-determination. He was imprisoned at Shenyang until 1959, when Mao granted him amnesty.

38. This was an event of CCP's internal struggle in 1930 when Mao ordered the killing of thousands of Party members, Red Army soldiers, and innocent civilians in Jiangxi province in an attempt to consolidate his power in the CCP-controlled areas. More information is available on: http://kanzhongguo.com/news/articles/4/4/27/64064.html (in Chinese).

39. Qu Qiubai, *A Few More Words* (May 23, 1935). Written before his death on June 18, 1935.

40. Zhang Wentian (1900-1976), an important leader of the CCP since the 1930s. He was Deputy Foreign Minister of China from 1954 to 1960. He was persecuted to death in 1976 during the Cultural Revolution. His case was redressed in August 1979.

41. The last of the ten General Secretaries of the CCP that was dismissed due to his disagreement with using force to end the student demonstrations in the Tiananmen Square massacre in 1989.

42. Zhang Guotao (1897-1979), one of the founders of the CCP. He was expelled from the CCP in April 1938. He went to Taiwan in November 1948, then to Hong Kong in 1949. He immigrated to Canada in 1968.

43. The "Gang of Four" was formed by Mao Zedong's wife Jiang Qing (1913-1991), Shanghai Propaganda Department official Zhang Chunqiao, literary critic Yao Wenyuan and Shanghai security guard Wang Hongwen. They rose

to power during the Cultural Revolution and dominated Chinese politics during the early 1970s.

COMMENTARY THREE

1. From the "Annals of Foods and Commodities" in *History of the Former Han Dynasty* (*Han Shu*).
2. Translated from *Oriental Culture* by Qian Bocheng, fourth edition (2000).
3. Gao Gang and Rao Shushi were both members of the Central Committee. After an unsuccessful bid in a power struggle in 1954, they were accused of plotting to split the Party and were subsequently expelled from the Party.
4. Hu Feng, scholar and literary critic, opposed the sterile literature policy of the CCP. He was expelled from the Party in 1955 and sentenced to 14 years in prison. From 1951 to 1952, the CCP initiated the Three Anti Campaign and the Five Anti Campaign, movements with the stated goal of eliminating corruption, waste and bureaucracy within the Party, government, army and mass organizations.
5. *How the Chinese Communist Party Persecuted Christians* (1958) (In Chinese).
6. Lu Xun or Lu Hsün (September 25, 1881 - October 19, 1936) is often considered the founder of modern vernacular (Baihua) Chinese literature. As a left-wing writer, Lu made an important mark in the history of Chinese literature. Having returned to China from medical studies in Sendai, Japan, in 1909, he became a lecturer in Peking University and began writing. His books have influenced many contemporary Chinese youth.
7. Both the Jade Emperor and Dragon King are Chinese mythological figures. The Jade Emperor, known formally as the August Personage of Jade and called informally by children and commoners as Grandpa Heaven, is the ruler of heaven and among the most important gods of the Chinese Daoist pantheon. Dragon King is the divine ruler of the four seas. Each sea, corresponding to one of the cardinal directions, is ruled by one dragon king. The dragon kings live in crystal palaces, guarded by shrimp soldiers and crab generals. Besides ruling over the aquatic life, the dragon kings also manipulate clouds and rain. The dragon king of the Eastern Sea is said to have the largest territory.

8. Peng Dehuai (1898-1974), communist Chinese general and political leader. Peng was the Chief Commander in the Korean War, Vice-Premier of the State Council, Politburo member, and Minister of Defense from 1954-1959. He was removed from his official posts after disagreeing with Mao's leftist approaches at the CCP's Lushan Plenum in 1959.

9. Zhao Gao (birth date unknown, died 210 BC) was the chief Eunuch during the Qin Dynasty. In 210 BC, after Emperor Qin Shi Huang's death, Zhao Gao, Prime Minister Li Si and the emperor's second son Hu Hai forged two wills of the emperor, making Hu Hai the new emperor and ordering Crown Prince Fu Su to commit suicide. Later, conflicts grew between Zhao Gao and Hu Hai. Zhao brought in a deer to the royal court and said it was a horse. Only a handful of the officials dared to disagree and said it was a deer. Zhao Gao believed those officials who called the animal a deer were against him and removed them from their court positions.

10. Translated from http://www.boxun.com/hero/dings/39_1.shtml.

11. Red Guards were civilians who were the frontline implementers of the Cultural Revolution. Most were youngsters in their mid-teens.

12. The Daxing massacre occurred in August 1966 during the change of the Party leadership in Beijing. At that time, Xie Fuzhi, the minister of public security, made a speech at a meeting with the Public Security Bureau of Beijing, encouraging no intervention with the Red Guards' actions against the five black classes. This speech was soon relayed to a Standing Committee meeting of the Daxin Public Security Bureau. After the meeting, the Daxin Public Security Bureau immediately took action and formed a plan to incite the masses in Daxin County to kill the five black classes.

13. As of December 19, 2004.

14. From Kang Youwei, *Collections of Political Writings* (Beijing: Zonghua Shuju, 1981). Kang Youwei (1858-1927) was an important reform thinker of the late Qing period.

COMMENTARY FOUR

1. Lao Zi (also known as Lao Tzu, Li Er or Li Dan), Chinese philosopher, lived in the 6th century BC. He is credited as the author of *Tao-Te Ching (Dao De Jing)*, the seminal book for Taoism.

2. *Tao-Te Ching*, Chapter 25.
3. These expressions come from *Mencius*, Book 2.
4. *Rhymes of Three (San Zi Jing)*, a traditional Chinese text for elementary education.
5. *Mencius*, Book 6.
6. Karl Marx, "A Contribution to the Critique of Hegel's *Philosophy of Right.*"
7. Leon Trotsky (1879-1940), Russian communist theorist, historian, and military leader, founder of the Russian Red Army. He was murdered in Mexico City by agents of Stalin on August 22, 1940.
8. According to Zhu Xi or Chu Hsi (1130-1200), also known as Zhu-zi or Chu-tzu, a neo-Confucian scholar from the Song Dynasty, *Small Learning* deals with proper behavior, while *Great Learning* expounds on the underlying principles behind those behaviors. Source: *Classified Conversations of Master Zhu (Zhu Zi Yu Lei)*, Volume 7 (Learning 1).
9. From Mao's "Talks at the Yan'an Forum on Literature and Art" (1942).
10. Schistosomiasis is a disease caused by parasitic worms. Infection occurs upon contact with contaminated fresh water. Common symptoms include fever, chills, cough, and muscle aches. In more serious cases, the disease can cause liver, intestine, lung, and bladder damage, and, in rare cases, seizures, paralysis, or spinal cord inflammation.
11. From Chapter 3 of the book *Mao Zedong* published by Chinese Archive Publishing House. This book was originally published in English: D. Wilson, *The People's Emperor Mao: A Biography of Mao Tse-Tung* (New York: Doubleday & Company, 1980).
12. *Tao-Te Ching*, Chapter 2.
13. *jin* is a Chinese unit for measuring weight. 1 *jin* = 0.5 kg; *mu* is a Chinese unit for measuring land area. 1 *mu* = 0.165 acres.
14. General Peng Dehuai criticized Mao Zedong's Great Leap Forward movement, which is widely seen both within China and outside as a major economic disaster. As a consequence, he was removed from all posts and placed under constant supervision and house arrest. His humiliation and disgrace at the hands of the Red Guards during the Cultural Revolution continued until he died due to a liver disorder in 1974.
15. From http://www.law007.com/zq/zqls6.htm. Translated by the editors.
16. See part 3, endnote 6.

17. *The Complete I Ching*, translated by Alfred Huang. Rochester, VT: Inner Traditions (1998).
18. Matthew, 22:21.
19. Lumpen proletariat, roughly translated as slum workers. This term identifies the class of outcast, degenerate or underground elements that make up a segment of the population of industrial centers. It includes beggars, prostitutes, gangsters, racketeers, swindlers, petty criminals, tramps, chronic unemployed or unemployables, persons who have been cast out by industry, and all sorts of degraded or degenerated elements and the underclass. The term was coined by Marx in *The Class Struggles in France*, 1848-1850.
20. Three-Self Patriotic Committee (or Three-Self Patriotic Church, TSPC) is a creation of the CCP. "Three-self" refers to "self-governing, self-supporting, and self-propagating." The committee requires Chinese Christians to sever ties with Christians outside of China. The TSPC controls all official churches in China. Churches that did not join the TSPC were forced to close. Leaders and followers of independent house churches are persecuted and often sentenced to prison terms.
21. John Pomfret. "Jiang has caution for U.S. – China's leader says Taiwan arms deal would spur buildup." *Washington Post*, March 24, 2001.

COMMENTARY FIVE

1. More information about this case may be found at:
   http://www.clearwisdom.net/emh/articles/2004/7/23/50560p.html
   http://www.clearwisdom.net/emh/articles/2004/6/7/48981p.html
2. More information about this case may be found at:
   http://www.clearwisdom.net/emh/articles/2004/9/25/52796.html
3. Related information is also available in Chinese from:
   http://search.minghui.org/mh/articles/2004/7/9/79007.html
4. Li Xiannian (1902-1992) was a former president of the PRC and president of the People's Political Consultative Conference. Chen Yun (1905-1995) was one of the most influential leaders of Communist China. Chen was a Politburo Standing Committee member for decades and was chairman of the Central Advisory Committee from 1987 to 1992.

5. Qigong is a generic name in Chinese for energy exercises. There are many schools of qigong, most of which are rooted in traditional spiritual beliefs. Falun Gong is a form of qigong.

6. In 1992, Deng Xiaoping came out of semi-retirement, toured Shenzhen in southern China near Hong Kong, and gave speeches to promote a socialist market economy in China. Deng's tour is largely considered to have rekindled China's economic reform after a lull beginning with the Tiananmen Square massacre in 1989.

7. Hemudu Cultural Ruins is an important village ruin of the Chinese New Stone Age. It was discovered in 1973 and is 7,000 years old.

8. Qiao Shi was a former chairman of the Chinese National People's Congress.

9. Deng once said, "Black cat or white cat, it's a good cat as long as it catches mice," meaning that the goal of the economic reforms was to bring prosperity to the people, regardless of the form being socialist or capitalist.

10. Zhang Zhixin was a female intellectual who was tortured to death by the CCP in the Cultural Revolution for being outspoken in telling the truth.

11. The procuratorate is the Chinese state organization responsible for prosecution and legal supervision. Its functions include deciding on arrest and prosecution in cases involving major crimes, conducting investigations, initiating and supporting public prosecutions, interpreting the law in specific applications, supervising court decisions, monitoring judicial procedures, and supervision over activities of prisons, detention centers, and labor camps.

12. As of December 19, 2004.

COMMENTARY SIX

1. Pangu was the first living being and the creator of all, according to Chinese mythology.

2. Nüwa was the mother goddess who created humankind, according to Chinese mythology.

3. Shennong (literally, "the Heavenly Farmer") is a legendary figure in Chinese mythology who lived about 5,000 years ago. He taught the ancient people the practices of agriculture. He is also credited with risking his life to identify hundreds of medicinal (and poisonous) herbs and various plants of that

nature, which were crucial to the development of traditional Chinese medicine.

4. Cangjie, or Cang Jie, is a legendary figure in ancient China. He is said to have been the Yellow Emperor's official historian, and the inventor of the Chinese characters. The Cangjie method of Chinese character computer input is named after him.

5. From *Tao-Te Ching* or *Dao De Jing*.

6. Opening remarks from *The Great Learning* by Confucius.

7. From *Records of the Historian* (*Shi Ji*, also translated as *The Grand Scribe's Record*) by Sima Qian (145-85 BC) the first major Chinese historian. It served as model for the official standard histories of the imperial dynasties for the next 2,000 years.

8. From Confucius *Analects*.

9. ibid.

10. ibid.

11. This is in reference to a statement made by Confucius in *The Great Learning*, "Their persons being cultivated, their families were regulated. Their families being regulated, their states were rightly governed. Their states being rightly governed, the whole kingdom was made tranquil and happy."

12. This is in reference to a statement made by Dong Zhongshu (c. 179-104 BC) in a treatise *Three Ways to Harmonize Humans with Heaven* (*Tian Ren San Ce*), "if heaven remains, the Tao does not change." Dong Zhongshu was a Confucian thinker during the Han Dynasty.

13. *The Journey to the West* (known to westerners as *Monkey King*), written by Wu Cheng'en (c. 1506-1582), is one of the renowned classical Chinese novels. It is based on a true story of a famous Chinese monk in the Tang Dynasty, Xuan Zang (602-664). Xuan Zang traveled on foot to what is today India, the birthplace of Buddhism, to search for the sutras. In the novel, the Buddha arranged for the Monkey King, Pigsy and Sandy to become disciples of Xuan Zang and escort him to the West to get the sutras. They went through 81 dangers and calamities before they finally arrived at the West and achieved True Fruition.

14. *A Dream of Red Mansions*, (*Hung Lou Meng* also translated as *The Dream of the Red Chamber*), was written by Cao Xueqin (or Tsao Hsueh-Chin) (c. 1715-1763) in the Qing (Ching) Dynasty. It is a tragic love story set against the background of the decline of an aristocratic family. It is universally recognized as the epitome of the art of the classical novel in China.

15. *Outlaws of the Marsh* (also translated as *Heroes of Water Margins*), written in the 14th century by Shi Nai'an, is one of China's great classic novels. It describes how 108 men and women band together to be outlaws of the marsh.

16. *Three Kingdoms*, written by Luo Guanzhong (c. 1330-1400), is one of the most famous Chinese classic novels based on the history of the Three Kingdoms period (220-280). It describes the intricate and tense struggles for the throne among three powerful political forces: Liu Bei, Cao Cao and Sun Quan, and focuses on various great talents and bold strategies during that period.

17. *The Romance of the Eastern Zhou*, was originally written by Yu Shaoyu in the Ming Dynasty, revised and rewritten by Feng Menglong at the end of the Ming Dynasty, and further revised by Cai Yuanfang in the Qing Dynasty. The novel covers a history of more than 500 years during the Spring and Autumn period (770-476 BC) and the Warring States period (475-221 BC).

18. *The Complete Story of Yue Fei* was written by Qian Cai in the Qing Dynasty. It described the life of Yue Fei (1103-1142) from the Southern Song Dynasty, one of the most famous generals and patriotic heroes in Chinese history. General Yue Fei distinguished himself in battles against northern invaders from the Jin nation. He was framed for crimes that he did not commit, sent to prison and executed, as Prime Minister Qin Hui attempted to eliminate the war party. Yue Fei was later cleared of the groundless charges and a temple was built in his memory. Four cast-iron figures were made for his tomb. With chests bare and hands bound behind their backs and kneeling before it, they represent those people who are responsible for Yue Fei's murder. Yue Fei has become a model in Chinese culture of loyalty to the country.

19. Quoted from *Abstract of Collected Taoist Scriptures (Dao Cang Ji Yao)* compiled in the Qing Dynasty.

20. See note 8.

21. From Mao's speech at the Eighth Session of the Tenth CCP Plenary Meeting.

22. Mao's original words in Chinese were a pun: I am like a monk holding an umbrella—no Tao (or Fa, pun for "hair") nor heaven (pun for "sky").

23. Jie is the name of the last ruler of the Xia Dynasty (c. 2100-1600 BC), and Zhou is the name of the last ruler of the Shang Dynasty (c. 1600 -1100 BC). Both are known as tyrants.

24. Wen Tianxiang (1236-1283) was a military commander who fought against the Mongolian troops to protect the integrity of the Southern Song Dynasty. He was killed on January 9, 1283 for refusing to surrender to the Mongolians after being taken prisoner.

25. From *Mencius*.

26. From a famous saying by Mencius, "Life, my desire; justice, my desire too. When I cannot have both of them at the same time, I will maintain justice at the expense of my life."

27. From the *Communist Internationale* anthem. The Chinese translation literally means: "There has never been a savior, and we do not rely on God either; to create human happiness, we rely entirely on ourselves."

28. The campaign to "cast away the four olds" was a campaign in the mid-1960s during the Cultural Revolution in China. In August 1966, the Red Guards declared "a war against the old world" and announced to "smash all old ideas, old culture, old customs and old habits," "including barbershops, tailor's shops, photo shops, used-book stores, and so on, with no exceptions."

29. In the Dai language, the Beiye scripture is pronounced *Tanlan*. Beiye is a subtropical plant belonging to the palm family. It is a tall tree with thick leaves, which are mothproof and very slow to dry out. In ancient times before paper was invented, the Dai's ancestors imprinted letters or articles on the leaf. The letters carved on the leaf are called the Beiye correspondence, and the scripture is called Tanlan (Beiye scripture).

30. Xiangshan Park, also called Fragrant Hills Park, is located 28 kilometers (17 miles) northwest of downtown Beijing. Initially built in 1186 in the Jin Dynasty, it became a summer resort for imperial families during the Yuan, Ming and Qing Dynasties.

31. From *How Many Cultural Relics Were Committed To Flames* by Ding Shu.

32. The Summer Palace, located 15 kilometers (9 miles) from Beijing, is the largest and best-preserved royal garden in China, with a history of over 800 years.

33. *li* is a Chinese unit of length (1 *li* is 0.5 kilometer or 0.3 miles).
34. Emperor Gaozu of the Tang Dynasty, alias Li Yuan, (ruled 618-626), was the first emperor of Tang Dynasty.
35. People's communes (Renmin Gongshe), were formerly the highest of three administrative levels in rural areas in the period from 1958 to around 1982 in China. The communes had governmental, political, and economic functions. They were the largest collective units and were further divided into production brigades and production teams. After 1982, they were replaced by townships.
36. See note 31.
37. The *Mahayana Mahaparinirvana Sutra* purports to be the Buddha's final Mahayana sutra, delivered on the last day of his earthly life. It claims to constitute the quintessence of all Mahayana sutras.
38. From Taisho Tripitaka Vol. T01, No. 7, *Mahayana Mahaparinirvana Sutra*. Provisional translation subject to improvement.
39. Translated from *The Theory and Practice of the Chinese Communist Party's Suppression of Religions* by Bai Zhi. Website: http://www.dajiyuan.com/gb/3/4/15/n300731.htm (in Chinese).
40. *Nirvana*, in Buddhism or Hinduism, is a state of blissful peace and harmony beyond the sufferings and passions of individual existence; a state of oneness with the eternal spirit.
41. The "suppression of counter-revolutionaries" campaign in 1951 dealt violently with "counter-revolutionaries", including bandits, local bullies, spies, former members of KMT and religious associations. According to the CCP's published records, more than two million people were executed by 1952, while the actual number may be even higher.
42. The "War to Resist US Aggression and Aid Korea", as the CCP called it, broke out in 1950. It is commonly known in the Western world as the Korean War.
43. Wu Yaozong (1893-1975) and others published the so-called "Means for Chinese Christianity to Exert Efforts in the Construction of the New China," also called the "Innovation Manifesto of Three Self" in 1950. They formed the Three-Self Church thereafter.

44. The Great Hall of the People, located at the west side of Tiananmen Square, is a meeting place for the National People's Congress of China.

45. See Note 39.

46. A kesa robe is a monk's robe or cassock.

47. Emperor Huizong of the Song Dynasty, alias Zhao Ji (ruled 1100-1126).

48. Su Dongpo (1036-1101) was a famous Chinese poet and writer of the Song Dynasty. He was one of the eight great prose masters of the Tang and Song dynasties.

49. Wen Zhengming (1470-1559) was a Chinese painter of the Ming Dynasty.

50. Tang Bohu (1470-1523) was a renowned Chinese scholar, painter, and poet of the Ming Dynasty.

51. *Jin*, a unit of weight used in China. One *jin* is 0.5 kg, or about 1.1 lb.

52. See Note 31.

53. From a poem by Meng Haoran (689-740), a well-known poet of the Tang Dynasty.

54. Wang Xi Zhi (321-379), from the Tang Dynasty, is the most famous calligrapher in history.

55. The original Lan Ting Prologue, allegedly written by Wang Xi Zhi at the prime of his calligraphy career (51 years old, 353 AD), is universally recognized as the most important piece in the history of Chinese calligraphy.

56. Wu Cheng'en (c. 1506-1582) was a Chinese novelist and poet of the Ming Dynasty and author of *The Journey to the West*, one of the four best-known Chinese novels.

57. Wu Jingzi (1701-1754) was an elegant writer of the Qing Dynasty and author of *The Scholars* (*Rulin Waishi*, also known as *Unofficial History of the Scholars*).

58. Prose written by Ouyang Xiu (1007-1072), one of the eight great prose masters of the Tang and Song dynasties. Ouyang Xiu called himself an "old drunkard."

59. Alternative name for the Red Guards.

60. The *Yongle Encyclopedia* or *Yongle Dadian*, an encyclopedia compiled by scholars in Ming Dynasty in 1403-1408. It consisted of more than 22,000 manuscript volumes with 370 million words, occupying 40 cubic meters (1,400 cubic feet). Currently only about 800 volumes were partially recovered and the rest have been destroyed or lost.

61. "Liang Xiao" represents a group of assigned writers, including Zhou Yiliang, whose involvement in the writing group earned him an anonymous letter from an old friend that referred to "the extreme of shamelessness."

62. Emperor Qin Shi Huang (259-210 BC), alias Ying Zheng, was the first emperor in the history of the unified China. He standardized legal codes, written language, currencies, weights and measures, and ordered the Great Wall be built. All these measures had a profound influence on Chinese history and culture. Qin Shi Huang ordered the books of various schools burned including those of Confucianism and Daoism, and once ordered 460 Confucian scholars be buried alive. These events were later called in history "the burning of books and the burying of Confucian scholars." He built a huge mausoleum for himself and the terracotta army of the tomb of Emperor Qin became known as the eighth wonder of the world.

63. From *The Writings of Mao Zedong* 1949-1976 (Vol. 2)

64. From Mao's "Rectify the Party's Style of Work" (1942).

65. From Mao's "Talks at the Yan'an Forum on Literature and Art" (1942).

66. Wu Xun (1838-1896), originally Wu Qi, was born in Shandong's Tangyi. He lost his father at an early age and his family was impoverished. He had to beg for food to feed his mother and became known as the filial piety beggar. After his mother passed away, begging became his only means of making a living. He ran free schools with the money he received from begging.

67. Hu Feng (1902-1985), scholar and literary critic, opposed the doctrinaire literature policy of the CCP. He was expelled from the Party in 1955 and sentenced to 14 years in prison.

68. From *Selected Works of Mao Zedong* (Vol. 5), "Things Are Beginning to Change" (1957).

69. Qian Bocheng, *Oriental Culture*, fourth edition (2000).

70. The June 4 student movement was initiated by college students advocating democratic reforms in China between April 15 and June 4, 1989. Its later suppression by the People's Liberation Army is generally referred to as the June 4th massacre, or Tiananmen Square massacre.

71. The "610 office" is an agency specifically created to persecute Falun Gong, with absolute power over each level of administration in the Party and all other political and judiciary systems.

72. The class origin (or bloodline or pedigree) theory claims that one's nature is determined by the class of the family in which one is born.

73. From the song of the modern opera "Legend of the Red Lantern," a popular official "model play" developed during the Cultural Revolution (1966-1976).

74. *Mu* is a unit of area used in China. One *mu* is 0.165 acres.

75. Jiang Zemin's "Three Represents" claims that the Party must always represent the development trend of China's advanced productive forces, the orientation of China's advanced culture, and the fundamental interests of the overwhelming majority of the Chinese people.

76. The opening address at the First Session of the First National People's Congress of the People's Republic of China (September 15, 1954).

77. The "Red-eye syndrome" is similar in meaning to the western expression "green-eyed." Here it is used to describe a person who feels unequal and uncomfortable when he sees other people doing better than he is, and thinks that he should be the one who is doing better.

78. "The White-Haired Girl" was a popular official "model play" developed during the Cultural Revolution (1966-1976). In folk legend, the white-haired girl was a female immortal who lived in a cave. She had supernatural abilities to reward virtue and punish vice, support the righteous and restrain the evil. However, in this Chinese modern opera, she was described as a girl who was forced to flee to a cave after her father was beaten to death for refusing to marry her to an old landlord. She became white-haired due to lack of nutrition. This became one of the most well-known modern dramas in China and incited class hatred of landlords.

79. "Tunnel Warfare" (Didao Zhan) is a 1965 black and white film in which the CCP claimed that its guerrillas in Central China fought Japanese invaders through various underground tunnels in the 1940s.

80. "War of Mines" (Dilei Zhan) is a 1962 black and white film in which the CCP claimed that its guerrillas in Hebei Province fought Japanese invaders with homemade mines in the 1940s.

81. The eight-part essay is a literary composition prescribed for the imperial civil service examinations, known for its rigidity of form and poverty of ideas.

82. China's Great Famine of 1959-1961 is the largest famine in human history. The estimated numbers of abnormal deaths in the famine range from 18 to 43 million.

83. See Note 7.

84. By Mao Zedong (1942).

85. The May Fourth Movement was the first mass movement in modern Chinese history, beginning on May 4, 1919.

86. Chen Guili, *Warning of Huaihe River* (1995).

87. Argil is a type of clay used to fade salad oil in the manufacturing process.

88. From *Prologue to See Li Yuan to Return to Pangu* by Han Yu (768-824), one of the eight great prose masters of the Tang and Song dynasties.

89. Tao Yuanming (365-427), also known as Tao Qian, was a great poet in Chinese literature.

COMMENTARY SEVEN

1. Mao Zedong's letter to his wife Jiang Qing (1966).

2. *The Analects of Confucius.*

3. *Leviticus* 19:18.

4. Karl Marx and Frederick Engels, *The Communist Manifesto* (1848).

5. Mao Zedong, *The People's Democratic Dictatorship* (1949).

6. Mao Zedong, *We Must Fully Promote [the Suppression of Counter-Revolutionaries] So Every Family is Informed* (1951).

7. Mao Zedong, *We Must Forcefully and Accurately Strike the Counter-Revolutionaries* (1951).

8. The Heavenly Kingdom of Taiping (1851 - 1864), also known as the Taiping Rebellion, was one of the bloodiest conflicts in Chinese history. It was a clash between the forces of Imperial China and those inspired by a self-proclaimed mystic of the Hakka cultural group named Hong Xiuquan, who was also a Christian convert. At least 30 million people are believed to have died.

9. Excerpt from the book published by the Hong Kong-based *Chengming* magazine (October issue, 1996) www.chengmingmag.com.

10. *Historical Records of the People's Republic of China* (Red Flag Publishing House, 1994).

11. Unit of Chinese land measurement: 1 *mu* = 0.165 acres.

12. Sha Qing, *Yi Xi Da Di Wan* (*An Obscure Land of Bayou*) (1988).

13. Raymond J. de Jaegher and Irene Corbally Kuhn, *Enemy Within*. (Guild Books, Catholic Polls, Incorporated, 1968).

14. Yu Luowen, *Investigation of Daxing Massacre*. The Daxing Massacre occurred in August 1966 during the change of the Party secretary of Beijing. At that time, a speech was made by the Minister of Public Security, Xie Fuzhi, in a meeting with the public security bureau of Beijing regarding no intervention with the Red Guards' actions against the "black five classes." Such a speech was soon relayed to a standing committee meeting of the Daxin public security bureau. After the meeting, the Daxin Public Security Bureau immediately took action and formed a plan to incite the masses in Daxin County to kill the "five black classes."

15. Zheng Yi, *Scarlet Memorial* (Taipei: Chinese Television Publishing House, 1993). This book is also available in English: Yi Zheng, *Scarlet Memorial: Tales of Cannibalism in Modern China*, translated and edited by T. P. Sym (Boulder, Colorado: Westview Press, 1998).

16. The "old society," as the CCP calls it, refers to the period prior to 1949 and the "new society" refers to the period after 1949 when the CCP took control over the country.

17. The strait jacket is a jacket-shaped torture implement. The victim's arms are twisted and tied with a rope on the back and then pulled to the front from over the head; this torture can instantly cripple one's arms. After that, the victim is forcefully put into the strait jacket and hung up by the arms. The most direct consequence of this cruel torture is the fracture of the bones in the shoulder, elbow, wrist, and back, causing the victim to die in excruciating pain. Several Falun Gong practitioners have died from this torture. For more information see: Chinese: http://search.minghui.org/mh/articles/2004/9/30/85430.html and English: http://www.clearwisdom.net/emh/articles/2004/9/10/52274.html.

18. Liu Shaoqi, Chairman of the PRC between 1959 and 1968, was considered to be the successor to Mao Zedong. During the Cultural Revolution (1966-1976), he was persecuted as a traitor, spy, and renegade by the CCP itself. He died in 1969 after being severely abused under the CCP's imprisonment.

19. Chen Boda (1904-1989) served as Mao Zedong's political secretary and editor-in-chief of the CCP journal *Hongqi* (*Red Flag*). He was a leader of the

Cultural Revolution Group and wrote the *People's Daily* editorial "Sweep Away All Monsters and Demons" in 1966, which marked the beginning of one of the biggest purges during the Cultural Revolution. Zhang Chunqiao (1917) served as second deputy premier in 1975. He was a member of the Gang of Four, a group of leaders during the Cultural Revolution. His most widely known article is "On Exercising All-Round Dictatorship over the Bourgeoisie."

20. Wang Xiangen, *Documentary of Supporting Vietnam and Fighting with America.* (Beijing: International Cultural Publishing Company, 1990).

21. Laogai Research Foundation (October 12, 2004) *Report: Children among victims of Falun Gong persecution.*
http://www.laogai.org/news2/newsdetail.php?id=391 (in Chinese).

22. One of the three tools (means of production, modes of production and relations of production) that Marx used to analyze social class. Relations of production refers to the relationship between the people who own productive tools and those who do not, e.g., the relationship between landlord and tiller or the relationship between capitalist and worker.

23. *Mencius*, Book 3. Penguin Classics series, translated by D.C. Lau.

24. By Fan Zhongyan (989-1052), prominent Chinese educator, writer and government official from the Northern Song Dynasty. This quote was from his well-known prose, "Climbing the Yueyang Tower."

25. By Gu Yanwu (1613-1682), an eminent scholar of the early Qing Dynasty.

26. *Mencius*, Book 7. Penguin Classics series, translated by D.C. Lau.

27. Three-Family Village was the pen name of three writers in the 1960s, Deng Kuo, Wu Han and Liao Mosha. Wu was the author of a play, "Hai Rui Resigning from His Post," which Mao considered a political satire about his relationship with General Peng Dehuai.

28. Lao She (1899-1966) was a Chinese writer known for depicting the life of the Chinese during the war years. Many of his books have been turned into TV shows and movies. He was cruelly treated during the Cultural Revolution and drowned himself in a lake in 1966. Jian Bozan (1898-1968) was vice president of Peking University and a history professor. Mao had specially instructed that he be used as a negative example of a counter-revolutionary intellectual. He and his wife committed suicide together by taking an overdose of sleeping pills in December 1968.

29. According to Clearwisdom.net, Falun Gong's official website, Jiang Zemin had ordered that Falun Gong practitioners be killed without mercy, and that any death be counted as suicide. See "Sweden: Letter from Falun Dafa Association to Foreign Minister Regarding the Geneva UN Human Rights Conference." http://www.clearwisdom.net/emh/articles/2003/3/18/33461.html.

30. Yu Luoke was a human rights thinker and fighter who was killed by the CCP during the Cultural Revolution. His monumental essay, *On Family Background*, written on January 18, 1967, was one that enjoyed the widest circulation and the most enduring influence of all the essays reflecting the non-CCP thoughts during the years of the Cultural Revolution. Lin Zhao, a Beijing University student majoring in journalism, was classified as a rightist in 1957 for her independent thinking and outspoken criticism of the communist movement. She was charged with conspiracy to overthrow the people's democratic dictatorship and arrested in 1960. In 1962, she was sentenced to 20 years of imprisonment. She was killed by the CCP on April 29, 1968 as a counter-revolutionary.

31. Data based on a Laogai Research Foundation report on http://www.laojiao.org/64/article0211.html (in Chinese).

32. Data directly quoted from "An open letter from Song Meiling to Liao Chengzhi" (August 17, 1982). See http://www.blog.edu.cn/more.asp?name=fainter&id=16445 (in Chinese).

COMMENTARY EIGHT

1. "The leopard has died, but its skin is still left" is from the ancient Chinese book of prophecy, the *Plum Blossom Poem* by Shao Yong (1011-1077). The leopard here refers to the geographic territory of the former Soviet Union, which indeed resembles a running leopard in shape. With the collapse of the former Soviet Union, the essence of the communist system has disintegrated, leaving only the "skin" (the form), which the Chinese Communist Party inherited.

2. A kind of group dance popular during the Cultural Revolution to show loyalty to Mao and the Party. See a picture of the dance on http://www.shm.com.cn/yantai/2004-05/13/content_3717.htm, or http://www.chinaphotocenter.com/pop-photo/2004-2/2004-2p40-4.jpg.

3. Constitution of the People's Republic of China (official translation, 1999).

4. From Mao's "Report on an Investigation of the Peasant Movement in Hunan" (1927).

5. From a poem by Sima Qian (about 140-87BC), a historian and scholar in the West Han Dynasty. His famous poem says, "Everyone has to die; one dies either more solemn than Mount Taishan or lighter than a feather." Mount Taishan is one of the major mountains in China.

6. The Land Enclosure Movement relates to a dark side of the economic reforms of China. Similar to the industrial revolution in England (1760-1850), agricultural lands in today's China have been demarcated to build various economic zones at all levels (county, city, provincial and state). As a result of the land enclosure, Chinese farmers have been losing their land. In the cities, residents in older city and town districts were frequently forced to relocate to vacate the land for commercial development, with minimal compensation for the residents. More information is available at: http://www.uglychinese.org/enclosure.htm

7. Lin Zhao, a Beijing University student majoring in journalism, was classified as a "rightist" in 1957 for her independent thinking and outspoken criticism of the communist movement. She was charged with conspiracy to overthrow the people's democratic dictatorship and arrested in 1960. In 1962, she was sentenced to 20 years of imprisonment. She was killed by the CCP on April 29, 1968 as a counter-revolutionary.

8. Zhang Zhixin was an intellectual who was tortured to death by the CCP during the Cultural Revolution for criticizing Mao's failure in the Great Leap Forward, and for being outspoken in telling the truth. Prison guards stripped off her clothes many times, handcuffed her hands to her back and threw her into male prison cells to let male prisoners gang rape her until she became insane. The prison feared she would shout slogans to protest when she was being executed, so they cut her trachea before her execution.

9. The February Revolution refers to the Russian Bourgeois Revolution in February 1917, which resulted in the abdication of Tsar Nicholas II.

10. The October Revolution, also known as the Bolshevik Revolution, was led by Lenin and occurred in October 1917. During the revolution, the revolutionaries of the capitalist class who had overthrown the Tsar were murdered, thus strangling the Russian Bourgeois Revolution.

11. Both the Mari Incident and the April 12th Massacre refer to the Kuomintang's attacks on the CCP. The Mari Incident happened on May 21, 1927, in Changsha City of Hunan province. The April 12th Massacre occurred on April 12, 1927 in Shanghai. In both cases, some CCP members and pro-CCP activists were attacked, arrested or killed.

12. See the CCP Constitution, Chapter One, Article Six.

13. Liu Di, a political officer of the 20th Red Army who was accused of being a member of "AB Corps," led a revolt in Futian, charging Li Shaojiu as a counter-revolutionary. They took control of Futian city and released more than 100 people arrested for being members of the "AB Corps," and shouted the "Down with Mao Zedong" slogan. For information about the AB Corps purge, see Gao Hua,"*Historical Investigation of Mao Zedong's Purge of "AB Corps" in Soviet Area, Jiangxi Province.*

14. Peng Dehuai (1898-1974) was a Chinese communist general and political leader. Peng was the chief commander in the Korean War, vice-premier of the State Council, Politburo member, and minister of defense from 1954-1959. He was removed from his official posts after disagreeing with Mao's leftist approaches at the CCP's Lushan Plenum in 1959.

15. From "Li Lisan: The Person for Whom Four Memorial Services Have Been Held."

16. The four principles are: socialist path, dictatorship of the proletariat, the CCP's leadership, and Marxism-Leninism and Mao Zedong thought.

COMMENTARY NINE

1. According to traditional Confucian thought, emperors or kings rule according to a mandate from heaven, and to be given such an authority, their moral achievements have to match that supreme responsibility. From the *Mencius*, a similar thought can also be found. In the verse "Who Grants the Monarchical Power?" when asked who granted the land and the governing authority to Emperor Shun, Mencius said, "It was from heaven." The idea of the divine origin of power can also be found in western Christian tradition. In Romans 13:1 (King James version), for example, one finds: "Let every soul be subject unto the higher powers. For there is no power but of God: the powers that be are ordained of God."

2. The one center refers to economic development, while the two basic points are: Maintain the four basic principles (socialist path, dictatorship of the proletariat, the CCP's leadership, Marxism-Leninism and Mao's Thought), and continue with the policies of reform and openness.

3. Xinhua News Agency report (March 4, 2004).

4. Xinhua News Agency report (February 29, 2004).

5. The "Three Noes Principle" has occurred in the past. In 1979, Deng Xiaoping proposed a "Three Noes Principle" to encourage people to speak their minds: No labeling, no attacking, and no picking on mistakes. This should remind people of Mao similarly encouraging intellectuals in the 1950s, which was followed by brutal persecution of those who did speak up. Now, the newly proposed "Three Noes" refers to "Development with no debates, advancement with no struggles, and progress with no contentment in lagging behind."

6. Hong Kong Basic Law Article 23 was proposed in 2002 by the Hong Kong government under pressure from Beijing. The article represented a serious erosion of freedom and human rights in Hong Kong, undermining the "one country, two systems" policy promised by the CCP. Article 23 was opposed globally, and was finally withdrawn in 2003.

7. CCTV (China Central Television) is owned and directly operated by the central government. It is the major broadcast network in Mainland China.

8. These quoted phrases are all titles of songs written and sung during the Mao era in the 1960s and early 1970s.

9. Mao once said that we are afraid of making mistakes, but we are concerned about correcting them.

10. For detailed analysis of the self-immolation video, see: http://www.faluninfo.net/tiananmen/immolation.asp.

11. This is a Chinese proverb that confirms the permanence of one's nature. The proverb has also been translated as "The fox may change his skin but not his habits."

12. The economic reform policies, known as the "Three-Freedom and One-Contract" program (San Zi Yi Bao) proposed by Liu Shaoqi, then President of China. The program stipulated plots of land for private use, free markets, enterprises having sole responsibility for their own profits and losses, and the fixing of output quotas on a household basis.

INDEX

349